Working and Caring over the Twentieth Century

The Future of Work Series

Series Editor: Peter Nolan, Director of the ESRC Future of Work Programme and the Montague Burton Professor of Industrial Relations at Leeds University Business School in the UK.

Few subjects could be judged more vital to current policy and academic debates than the prospects for work and employment. *The Future of Work* series provides the much needed evidence and theoretical advances to enhance our understanding of the critical developments most likely to impact on people's working lives.

Titles include:

Julia Brannen, Peter Moss and Ann Mooney
WORKING AND CARING OVER THE TWENTIETH CENTURY
Change and Continuity in Four-Generation Families

Michael White, Stephen Hill, Colin Mills and Deborah Smeaton
MANAGING TO CHANGE?
British Workplaces and the Future of Work

The Future of Work Series
Series Standing Order ISBN 1–4039–1477–X

You can receive future titles in this series as they are published by placing a standing order. Please contact your bookseller or, in case of difficulty, write to us at the address below with your name and address, the title of the series and one of the ISBNs quoted above.

Customer Services Department, Macmillan Distribution Ltd, Houndmills, Basingstoke, Hampshire RG21 6XS, England

Working and Caring over the Twentieth Century

Change and Continuity in Four-Generation Families

Julia Brannen, Peter Moss and Ann Mooney

E·S·R·C
ECONOMIC
& SOCIAL
RESEARCH
COUNCIL

First published 2004 by
PALGRAVE MACMILLAN
Houndmills, Basingstoke, Hampshire RG21 6XS and
175 Fifth Avenue, New York, N.Y. 10010
Companies and representatives throughout the world

PALGRAVE MACMILLAN is the global academic imprint of the Palgrave Macmillan division of St. Martin's Press, LLC and of Palgrave Macmillan Ltd. Macmillan® is a registered trademark in the United States, United Kingdom and other countries. Palgrave is a registered trademark in the European Union and other countries.

ISBN 1–4039–2059–1 hardback

This book is printed on paper suitable for recycling and made from fully managed and sustained forest sources.

A catalogue record for this book is available from the British Library.

Library of Congress Cataloging-in-Publication Data
Brannen, Julia.
    Working and caring over the twentieth century : change and continuity in four generation families / Julia Brannen, Peter Moss, Ann Mooney.
        p.   cm. — (The future of work)
    Includes bibliographical references and index.
    ISBN 1–4039–2059–1 (cloth)
    1. Family—Great Britain.   2. Intergenerational relations—Great Britain.   3. Work and family—Great Britain.   I. Moss, Peter, 1945–   II. Mooney, Ann, 1950–   III. Title.   IV. Future of work (Series)
    HQ613.B7 2004
    306.874—dc22

                                                                2004050433

10   9   8   7   6   5   4   3   2   1
13   12   11   10   09   08   07   06   05   04

Printed and bound in Great Britain by
Antony Rowe Ltd, Chippenham and Eastbourne

For our parents whose lives spanned most of the 20th century,
two of whom were also grandparents and great-grandparents

Contents

List of Tables and Figures

Tables

Figures

Acknowledgements

We wish to acknowledge the work and support of a number of people. First, we were very fortunate in having Emily Gilbert as a member of our research team. We are only sorry that she had to leave us before the writing began in earnest. She contributed so much to the project and would have contributed a great deal more had this been possible. Second, we want to recognise the inspirational teaching and generous support which Tom Wengraf and Prue Chamberlayne provided when we attended their course in biographical methods. We are additionally indebted to Tom for his detailed and insightful comments on our manuscript and hope we have sufficiently addressed them. We wish also to thank Ann Nilsen for the many ideas which she has shared with one of us (Julia) and for her collaboration in writing part of Chapter 5 (originally written as a conference paper for the British Sociological Association Conference, April 2003). Thanks are due also to Peter Nolan, Director of the ESRC Future of Work Programme, who was always encouraging about our project and to ESRC who provided the funding (project award L212252027). We want as well to acknowledge the support of the many people in Thomas Coram Research Unit who have helped us in this research, especially Tamara Boake with the references, those who did the transcribing of the interviews, and those who provided computer support. Last and most important, suffice it to say that this book could not have been written without the research participants. That this has been a most rewarding project for us to work on is due to them. We hope we have begun to do justice to their stories although there is still a great deal left to write about.

All the names of research participants and their families have been changed.

1
Setting the Scene

This book focuses on family life across four generations and explores in depth twelve families. It examines how members of the three adult generations engage as over the life course of parents, grandparents and great-grandparents (over the life course). It thereby covers a vast panorama of social change that has occurred over the 20th century. Most of the surviving great-grandparents in our study families were born in the second decade of the 20th century, overshadowed by the First World War, and had witnessed much of the 20th century. The grandparents mostly were born in the 1940s, another decade dominated by war, and had lived through the second half of the century; while the current parent generation were born, on average, around 1970 on the cusp of enormous economic, social and political changes, which have dominated the last quarter of the century.

The book is the story of these generations both as historical cohorts and as family generations. It is therefore also the story of intergenerational relations: the processes of transmission between family members of different generations and the negotiations and reciprocities these imply. It focuses on two important facets of people's lives: the care they give and receive from family members and their employment practices over the life course phases of parenthood. Our story has a number of central and competing themes: continuity and change over generations, both for individuals and families; the transmission of parenthood identities and other resources from one generation to another; and the structural influences that shape relations between generations. We shall return to our families later in this chapter, introducing them and placing their lives in their historical contexts, but first we turn to some broader considerations.

1

Multi-generation families

Over the 1980s and 90s households have received rather more consideration than relations between households linked by kinship. And in the beginning of this millennium the dynamics of family lives are coming to the fore with a renewed interest in the concept generation. Particular attention has been drawn to the multi-generation family, sometimes termed the 'beanpole family' – long and thin in form. While more family generations are alive simultaneously with greater life expectancy, the size of each successive generation shrinks as the number of children born declines and partnerships are no longer lifelong. In Britain, one-third of those aged 80 and above are members of four-generation families, as are one-fifth of those aged 20 to 29 and 50 to 59, and a quarter of those in their 30s (Grundy *et al.*, 1999). Viewed from another perspective, by the age of 50, three-fifths of the British population still has a living parent and just over a third are grandparents (ibid.).

While change in the structure and shape of families can be defined and documented, the implications of this and other parallel changes for family dynamics – the relationships between different generations and between family members – are less clear. One reading suggests *vertical* relationships within families have become more important especially in recent years in Britain, due both to increased possibilities and to greater necessity. Thus, with many people now enjoying longer, more prosperous and healthier old age, multi-generation families may constitute an enhanced source of support, for example through older generations passing on assets and other support to younger generations. At the same time, with increased longevity, the need for support for frail elderly family members may be increasing, placing greater demands upon intergenerational family ties. Intergenerational support may also become more important in a situation where other sources of support may be declining: those transmitted via a diminishing welfare state, bringing increased societal expectation that the individual assume responsibility for managing risk; and weakened support from nuclear families who are increasingly affected by separation and divorce.

Against the case for the increasing importance of intergenerational family ties, there is the counter argument. Intergenerational support is likely to be curtailed because of major changes in the world of work, not least more women working when they have young children and working full time, which have not been matched by changes in the provision of formal 'childcare' services. Moreover, some social theorists argue that, as the long arm of tradition has lifted, so the onus is on individuals to construct their own lives (Beck and Beck-Gernsheim, 1996) and to create 'families of choice' (Giddens, 1991). In short the growth of individualism and the detraditionalisation of society are said to fracture family ties and turn us into atomised individuals. Thus if people choose which persons to support and exchange resources with, there is the risk that some family members will be left out. Similarly, if some groups decide not to have, or are unable to have, children, there is likely to be a polarisation between those with intergenerational ties and those without such ties. The processes of change are likely to be uneven, complex and ambivalent. For instance, it may be that the availability of some resources for transfer between generations increases, while in other cases it reduces or, at least, proves unable to keep up with rising demand. To take one example, due to growing employment among women in their 50s and the fact that they are increasingly working long hours, the pool of grandmothers available to provide childcare for their grandchildren may be less than hitherto, especially in respect of full-time care. Indeed, as the new generation of young people defer parenthood, women will enter grandmotherhood at older ages, with implications for grandmothers' willingness to take on the care of grandchildren. As studies are currently showing, grandmothers would prefer to give part-time or occasional care to grandchildren (Dench and Ogg, 2002). A study of people aged 50 to 65 found 17 per cent providing childcare for at least one grandchild although few did more than 20 hours per week (Mooney and Statham, 2002). The availability of the 'pivot generation' to provide care for older generations may also be affected. On the other hand, increased income available to women may enable them to help other generations in financial and material ways.

So the narrative we will be telling is by no means clear from the outset. Some degree of change can be guaranteed. But while broad trends may be described, they will not be uniform, and in many cases there will be strong continuities. Making generalisations is likely to be more risky than usual.

Studying change and time

In focusing on changes in work and care across generations, this book must address issues of *time* – time passing and time as it is perceived and experienced. In interpreting the lives and accounts of families and their members we have had to engage also with time both in terms of life course time and historical time, a topic to which we return in Chapter 8.

Much of the family lives which we have elicited and studied lie in the past, some in the dim, distant past. It is, for example, very different for a great-grandmother, possibly in her 80s, to speak about her experience of early motherhood compared, say, to a mother currently caring for a young child. The former is in a different life course stage, her memory may be less clear and she is interpreting memories of one historical time from the vantage point of another historical time and through the lens of intervening time: the experience of an event at the time, and 50 years later how you think you experienced that event may well not coincide. These different types of time frame the research and writing of this book. So too do our own histories. Some of the stories told to us resonate with our own earlier research careers in which, 20 years ago, we studied work and care among new parents (Brannen and Moss, 1991). We cannot avoid thinking of today's parents in relation to this earlier work, which was undertaken at a time when it was very unusual for women to resume full-time employment after childbirth. Some stories reflect our personal life course trajectories: growing up in post-war Britain; becoming parents in the 1970s; returning to education post-childrearing and building research careers during motherhood in the 1970s. Two of us became grandparents and members of four-generation families in the 1990s; then returned to being a three-generation family again. As interpreters of other people's stories, we cannot stand outside our own life course and historical time.

Writing this book has forced us to engage with the past and what has now become 'history', both in personal terms as we have just indicated, and also professionally. While two of the four of us who worked on the study have backgrounds as historians, we are mindful that social science is governed by present concerns and assumptions and has grown up with its 'face set towards the present and its back on the past' (Fielding, 2004) especially through the influence of Modernity and its preoccupation with Progress. For example, the social survey, currently a powerful method in social science, is used as a litmus test of change, in its identification of patterns and regularities as the basis for predicting trends (Krausz and Miller, 1974). Moreover, too often we plunder the past to serve our current purposes (Hammersley, 2004).

The case for studying twelve families

The reader may ask: what can we learn from studying the past in only twelve four-generation families? Why look at the particular? What, if anything, can we say about the general from the particular? How can such a few cases validate or refute the generalised trends proposed by historians and sociologists? We would answer these questions thus.

We recognise that ours is but one approach to the study of multi-generation families, and that there is a trade-off to be made between depth and breadth: between understanding and developing theory in particular conditions and on the basis of specific cases and making inferences to the wider population. Our argument is that for our purposes – understanding a complex social phenomenon, a strategy based upon 'thick description' of a small number of case studies (Geertz, 1973), is preferable to the 'thin description' which is generated by studying a large number of cases, even if selected on statistical grounds. A qualitative sample of multi-generation families, such as ours, where it is selected to produce contrasting cases, provides a strong foundation on which both to generate and to examine theoretical questions. Thus, by selecting the particular and understanding the particular conditions of the 'case' (the families and their members), we may build in-depth analyses of work–family lives. Furthermore, in comparing the cases, we may identify patterns of change and continuity and create typologies of family relations and cultures which we can situate in specific times and spaces. We would add that, as Wengraf (2001) suggests, in understanding such complex social phenomena as multi-generation families, the raw materials which the researcher brings are crucial.

In short, in our view an analysis of twelve families is a powerful research strategy when combined with a strategic choice of cases, an historical contextualisation of the material – and the particular biographical method we have chosen, to which we now turn.

A biographical approach to family change

Family and social change is a product of individuals' habits, actions and conscious decisions carried out in particular contexts and life course phases. As Paul Thompson (1977) wrote in his study *The Edwardians*, it is imperative to look closely at the actions and meanings of individuals that underpin the grander picture, which historians and sociologists create from statistical sources and the documentation of 'facts'. This is not to suggest that people's recollections of the past represent the past as it was lived and experienced at the time. Indeed, in employing a biographical approach which we have done here, we have sought to give emphasis to three issues: the shaping and scheduling of life course time; the location of individuals and families in historical time; and subjective experience and interpretation (Wengraf, 2001).

How then did we approach these several aims, in particular the conceptual and analytical distinction between what Wengraf (2001) refers to as 'the lived life' and 'the told story'? The contextualisation of stories in relation to the life course was an organising framework for the interviews both because a life course frame shaped our approach to interviewing family members and because many of the research participants themselves chose to organise their stories (in the first unstructured part of the interview) around a life course frame. The research participants less commonly referred to external events and circumstances, that is beyond their own lives and those of their families. In producing their accounts of the 'facts' of the lived life, research participants punctuated their narratives about the past with argumentation and evaluation. In justifying past actions, they did so often in relation to the normative climates of the present or current life course phase. Thus we have tried to interpret subjective interpretations of actions and events in relation to life course and historical/contemporary time.

Making the link between biography and historical time proved as demanding. To recreate the historical context, we often had to draw upon our own knowledge of the particular historical periods in question. A study of families covering four generations requires a wealth of knowledge, encompassing as it does the lives of three birth cohorts as well as extending into a variety of fields of research – family life, work and care. (We return to our strategy for eliciting both context and meaning later.)

Connecting biography and the wider context is currently rather unfashionable in biographical research; a structuralist perspective is often seen as incompatible with a biographical approach (Miller, 2000). Some biographical researchers are critical of realist epistemological standpoints and positivist research practice (see, for a discussion, Hammersley, 1989; Giele and Elder, 1998) and have preferred to draw upon the tradition of ethnographic interpretative writing (Denzin, 1997), through an emphasis on the subjective aspects of experience (Plummer, 2001).

Despite such current epistemological tensions between the two research traditions of realism and interpretivism, we believe that there is nevertheless a strong case for combining them in research practice. It is worth remembering that such tensions have been successfully accommodated in the past. Znaniecki, writing in the early part of the 20th century (see Thomas and Znaniecki, 1996) and an original exponent of analytic induction in biographical research, drew his inspiration from the natural sciences. For Mills (1980), the study of the intersection between biography and history was central and an approach we consider well suited to providing insights into the complexities of family lives as they unfold in specific historical circumstances.

Research design and methods

In studying the past, it is necessary and inevitable to be selective. Four-generation families by definition only include those with a long-lived oldest generation; and only those who are in the main healthy are likely to want to participate in research. Moreover, they are less likely to include male members among the oldest generation since men on average die younger than women. Also, over time, it has remained the case that death rates vary enormously between occupational groups. This means that working-class great-grandfathers are likely to be absent in a study such as ours which sought to reflect the social class spectrum.

In designing the study, we considered that a focus upon a small number of case studies, purposively selected, was appropriate, enabling us to examine in detail how employment and care play out over the life course and across the generations. Our aim was to provide a thorough description of the families, to identify patterns and typologies, and to develop and further theoretical interpretation. In the analysis we have undertaken a difficult juggling act: between looking across all the members of each historical cohort, thereby doing justice to all our material and exploring commonalities across generations; exploring intergenerational relations and patterns within particular families; and drawing out the narratives of individual family members.

Twelve case-study kin groups were theoretically chosen where the third (i.e. youngest adult) generation had at least one young child (or, in one case, where a child was shortly expected). The three adult generations are accordingly referred to in the book from the vantage point of the youngest generation as: the parent, grandparent and great-grandparent generations. We did not aim to interview the whole family but to cover the following: one set of grandparents; one child of the grandparents (with at least one child under 10 years) and his or her partner; and both sets of the grandparents' parents (i.e. both the grandfather's and grand-mother's parents). We did not interview the youngest generation of children. The maximum number of family members that could be interviewed was eight (i.e. where all four great-grandparents were alive and willing to take part), and the minimum five (i.e. where only one great-grandparent could be interviewed). It is important therefore to stress that while we sought to cover the generations, we also had to put tight parameters around those included within each generation.

In the event, we interviewed 71 family members: 8 in two families, 7 in one, 6 in three and 5 in six (Table 1.1). We saw all 24 parents (one couple were expectant parents, their first child due a few weeks after the interviews); 24 grandparents (of whom one was a step grandfather); and 23 great-grandparents. Of the 25 'missing' great-grandparents, 21 were dead (7 women and 14 men) and 4 refused, including one couple where the husband was very ill and two couples where the husband refused but the wife agreed.

The families were sampled to 'represent' the grandparent generation. We sought to stratify them by occupational status, to include an equal proportion of grandparents employed (currently or in the past) in a professional or managerial occupation, and in lower status occupations. We also sought to ensure that the grandparent generation would be split between those couples where currently both were in employment and those where one or both were retired or not working, in order to create variation in employment and care roles.

A final sampling criterion related to marital status. We decided to rule out further complexity in the analysis by including only those grandparents who were still in the same relationship as when they were bringing up their own children and, similarly, to include only those in the current parent generation who were living with the parent of their children. This study has therefore little to say about the impact of divorce on intergenerational relations.

We screened and recruited families through a variety of strategies: postal questionnaire surveys of current and recent employees of two public-sector employers in London; advertisements in local newspapers; and our own social networks. Discussions took place with 59 families who initially appeared eligible. Some turned out on closer inspection not to meet our criteria; in other cases, one generation refused to take part or could not be interviewed because they lived abroad. We chose families who were all living in England since we had limited time and money available for travel: because our recruitment efforts were focused on London and the Home Counties, most of the people we interviewed (46) were living in these areas, with a further 20 in the south of England and five in the Midlands or the North.

Despite great efforts to make contact with minority ethnic families, we found none that matched our criteria in terms of numbers of generations and geographical location. This is not surprising given the history of migration to Britain. However, the great-grandparents in one of our 12 families were German Jews who had come to Britain in the 1930s as refugees.

Table 1.1 Summary of key characteristics for each family at the time of interview

Family	Who we interviewed	Employment and occupational status when interviewed[a]	Geographical proximity[b]
Ashton	7		Close
Great-grandparents	Bill and Mildred $\rightarrow$ Edna		
Grandparents	Joseph and Shirley $\rightarrow$	Joseph a window fitter and Shirley a sales administrator, both full time	
Parents	Luke and Claire	Luke a window estimator and Claire an administrator, both full time	
Brand	8		Close
Great-grandparents	Jimmy and Mary $\rightarrow$ Arthur and Gwen		
Grandparents	Gordon and Janice $\rightarrow$	Gordon a self-employed builder, full time, and Janice retired	
Parents	Sean and Janet	Sean a self-employed builder, full time, and Janet a clerk, part time	

Table 1.1 (Continued)

Family	Who we interviewed	Employment and occupational status when interviewed[a]	Geographical proximity[b]
Hillyard	6		
Great-grandparents	Nat and Margot		Close
Grandparents	Thelma and Stan →	Thelma a chief secretary and Stan a draughtsman, both full time	
Parents	Sarah and Ben	Sarah a nanny and Ben a labourer, both full time	
Horton	6		
Great-grandparents	Maureen → Grace →		Dispersed
Grandparents	Bernard and Diana →	Both teachers, full time	
Parents	Patrick and Geraldine	Patrick a TV production manager, full time and Geraldine a TV floor manager, part time	
Hurd	5		
Great-grandparents	Doreen →		Dispersed
Grandparents	Celia and Michael →	Both retired	
Parents	Graeme and Rachael	Graeme a student and Rachael a teacher, full time	

Kent 5   Close

Great-grandparents Margaret

Grandparents Miriam and Robert   Miriam an administrator in family
                                        business and Robert a company chair,
                                        both part time
              ↓
              Juliet and James

Parents Juliet and James   Both senior managers, James full time and
                                        Juliet part time

Miller 5   Dispersed

Great-grandparents Jessie
                    ↓
Grandparents Kate and John   Kate retired and John a driver, full time
              ↓
Parents Alison and Thomas   Alison a student, Thomas a senior
                                        manager, full time

Masters 5   Dispersed

Great-grandparents Ida
                    ↓
Grandparents Carol and George   Carol retired and George a chemical
                                        engineer, part time
              ↓
Parents Douglas and Sonia   Douglas an accountant, full time and
                                        Sonia a teacher, part time

Table 1.1 (Continued)

Family	Who we interviewed	Employment and occupational status when interviewed[a]	Geographical proximity[b]
Prentice	6		
Great-grandparents	Jack and Josephine		Dispersed
Grandparents	Fiona and Paul $\rightarrow$	Fiona not working and Paul a postman, full time	
Parents	Andrew and Sheila	Andrew a customer relations clerk, full time and Sheila a shop assistant, part time	
Peters	8		
Great-grandparents	Donald and Eileen Wilfred and Dora $\rightarrow$		Dispersed
Grandparents	George and Pricilla $\rightarrow$	Gordon a technical designer, full time and Pricilla retired	
Parents	Annabelle and Mark	Annabelle a baby gym worker, part time and Mark an electrical engineer, full time	

Smith   5   Close

Great-grandparents	Brenda	
	↓	
Grandparents	Pauline and Peter	Pauline a finance officer and Peter a bus driver, both full time
	↓	
Parents	Neil and Jane	Neil a scaffolder, full time and Jane not working

Samuels   5   Dispersed

Great-grandparents	Ruth	
	↓	
Grandparents	Richard and Marjorie	Richard a senior lecturer and Marjorie a senior manager, both full time
	↓	
Parents	Stephen and Naomi	Stephen managing own business, full time, Naomi a teacher, part time

a All great-grandparents were retired.
b All interviewees living within 45 minutes travelling distance of one another.

Our completed sample included five families where *both* grandparents were employed full time; five families in which the grandfather still worked full time and the grandmother was not employed; and one family where both grandparents were retired and another where both worked part time. In the case of five couples, both grandparents were in or had held professional or managerial jobs. In the remaining cases, the grandfather was in a lower level non-manual occupation (2), a skilled manual occupation (2) or a low skilled manual job (3).

Table 1.1 summarises information about each of the families: the members we interviewed; the names we have given them; the occupational and employment statuses of the grandparents and parents at the time of the interview; and the geographic proximity of the family members to one another.

There are two important points to make about our sampling strategy. First, self-selection in studies of multi-generational families operates at more than the individual level. Our sample is inevitably biased towards families where contact between members was maintained and relations were reasonably good, though it would be wrong to assume that relations were all close, as we shall see in the following chapters. But a study such as ours will not include families where there is estrangement or little contact.

Second, the role played by the person negotiating consent from other family members on our behalf was crucial and one that is not easy for us to assess. Six of the twelve families were recruited via grandmothers, reflecting perhaps the fact that grandmothers are typically pivotal 'kin keepers' (Firth *et al.*, 1969). Of the remainder, one family was via the grandfather, two families via great-grandparents (one great-grandfather and one great-grandmother) and three via parents, all mothers. We anticipated that our first link person to the family would act as gatekeeper and secure (or not) the agreement of those whom we wished to interview, but in some families responsibility was handed over to another who was blood related. Thus, for example, a great-grandfather who asked his son-in-law to contact his own parents or a grandmother who asked her partner to contact her parents-in-law. It is to be expected that the time taken to negotiate access will vary: in some families the process was relatively quick, while in others it took longer. But access tended to be quicker in families where there was frequent contact and close intergenerational relationships.

The interview approach and the analysis

The method adopted in this study is based on the Biographic-Interpretive Narrative Interviewing and Analysis approach (Wengraf, 2001). The narrative aspects of interviews, particularly where biographical interviews are concerned, are very important in understanding informants' meaning (Ricoeur, 1980, 1992; Nilsen, 1996; Wengraf, 2001). However, lives are lived in and through time and cannot be divorced from the historical settings in which they occur (see Erben, 1998). Our perspective, therefore, is sensitive to both the 'told story' (biography) and the chronology and historical context of the 'lived life' (life course) (Wengraf, 2001).

Having trained in the particular type of biographical approach as set out in Wengraf (2001), we adapted it for our own study. Our interviews were in three parts. In the first part, interviewees were invited to give an account of their lives, with a minimum of guidance and intervention from the interviewer. The invitation, at the start of the interview, took this form: 'I am interested in the story of your life bearing in mind that the focus of the study is work and care. Take your time. Start where you want. I will not interrupt you.' Encouraged in this way to begin their story where they chose their own words, the interviewee was provided with an opportunity to present his or her own *gestalt*. Some spoke for some considerable time without interruption while others' narratives lasted only minutes. In the second part of the interview, the interviewer invited the respondent to elaborate the initial narrative in relation to salient events or experiences that had figured in it. (These were chosen by the interviewer drawing upon her/his notes and they were covered in the order of their original telling.) Finally, using a more traditional semi-structured style of interview, the interviewer asked additional questions relating to the specific foci of the study. Depending upon interviewees' responses in the first two parts, this could be a lengthy or short part of the interview.

Confidentiality was of particular importance in this study. Before starting interviews, we emphasised that what we were told would be treated in confidence and not repeated to other family members. Having four researchers on the study meant than none of us interviewed more than two members of the same family, thus helping to reinforce confidentiality. Most couples, for example, were interviewed at the same time though separately by a different researcher. All interviews were recorded and transcribed and respondents signed consent forms indicating their copyright wishes in the future use of these recordings and transcripts.

The interviews were conducted between September 1999 and August 2000. They lasted on average three hours. Although shorter and less extensive than the full Biographic-Interpretive Narrative Interviewing approach (two sessions of interviewing were carried out only in a few cases), we found this three-phase interview method very productive both for eliciting biographical 'facts', and for enabling respondents to reflect through different time lenses. The mix of types of data generated by this approach, while providing challenges to us in reporting on their use in the analysis, constitutes, we believe, a methodological strength of the work.

In the analysis, we followed to some extent the analytic procedure of separating the biographical and historical 'facts' of the interview from the interviewee's subjective experience and interpretation of them (Wengraf, 2001), in particular in our first phase of analytic writing. We also sought to map the historical time lines and life histories of each family member.

The analysis proceeded through three stages, working from the individual level, to the level of the 'whole' family, and culminating in comparisons of the 12 families. In the first stage, immediately following the interview, each researcher wrote up their recollection and impressions of the interview. Next, when the transcript became available, each of us was responsible for writing a full summary of each interview that she or he had conducted. This detailed preliminary analysis (around 10 pages with page references to the transcript) organised the material under a number of pre-specified sections or themes:

- the interview encounter, including the response to the invitation to give a biographical account;
- the 'life history chronology' with dates and information on biographical events and their timings;
- perceptions and experience of childhood and growing up;
- perceptions and experience of education, work and working life; and the intersections between work and care;
- perceptions and experience of settling down, marriage, becoming a mother/father, being a mother/father with particular reference to the period of having a young child;
- reports of help with children and housework;
- reports and perceptions of the use of childcare facilities when parents had young children;
- reports and perceptions on withdrawal from the labour market and the empty nest syndrome;
- perceptions and experience of becoming and being grandparents including the care provided to grandchildren;
- reports of contributions to eldercare and care of other family members including material resources and other support;

- the experience of great-grandparenthood;
- reports of receipt and experience of care by great-grandparents;
- attitudes to own (future) care in old age;
- attitudes to formal support including from the state;
- thinking about and planning for the future;
- responses to vignettes concerning decisions by a mother and father with a young child in relation to work (not to work, to work part time or to work full time) and in relation to choice of childcare (informal and formal) (for text of vignette, see Chapter 3, footnote 1).

Sections were also included in which we set out the main themes which emerged from the interview and a section noting key turning points in the life course.

In the second stage, we sought to make cross-generational comparisons within a particular family. Each of the four team members was responsible for carrying out several analyses at the kin-group level for three of the 12 families (around 20 pages for each analysis). In two analyses we sought to focus upon lineages of men and women within the same family according to a number of themes, for example a separate analysis of motherhood and one of fatherhood over the generations. A third analysis examined care transactions and material support between family generations (and within couples), and covered the justifications interviewees gave for care and employment decisions and for giving or not giving support.

This second analysis stage brought together what Wengraf (2001) refers to as different 'systems of relevancy': the contextual information of historical time, the lived life (the biographical 'facts'), and the told story. This, together with the first stage, provided a sound basis upon which to build the final analysis. At the third stage, we compared the multi-generation families in relation to the analyses generated in stage two. We worked with particular themes such as fatherhood and motherhood and with subgroups such as men and women; this extended writing formed the basis for the chapters.

Introducing the families and their historical times

In further introducing the families, we will first identify some key life course characteristics that define each cohort, summarised in Tables 1.2 (women) and 1.3 (men). Employment histories are described and considered later, in Chapters 3 and 5. We then place each cohort within a very broad historical context.

Table 1.2   Key life course characteristics of women in 12 case families

	Great-grandmothers ($n = 16$)	Grandmothers ($n = 12$)	Mothers ($n = 12$)
Date of birth			
Range	1906–35	1940–55	1962–80
Median	1919	1945/46	1968/69
Siblings			
Range	1–12	1–4	1–4
Median	3	2	2
Left full-time education			
16 or under	13	5	4
17	2	4	2
18 or over	1	3	6
Qualification			
None	14	2	1
Others	1	6	6
Professional/degree	1	4	4 (+1 studying)
Age cohabited with present partner	1 couple cohabited	None cohabited	11 cohabited
Range	–	–	17–30
Median	–	–	21
Age at marriage	All married	All married	9 married
Range	18–27	19–21	21–27
Median	22/23	20	23
Age at first child			
Range	19–30	18–24	19–31
Median	23	22	25/26
Number of children			
One	0	1	1 pregnant with first child
Two	5	4	10
Three or more	11	7	1
Age of grandparenthood			
Range	38–59	35–54	Not applicable
Median	49/50	49	

Great-grandparents

The 16 great-grandmothers and 7 great-grandfathers represent at least one maternal or paternal great-grandparent in each of the 12 families. Born mainly between 1911 and 1921, 15 of the 23 great-grandparents were in their 80s at the time of the interview, with a median age of

Table 1.3 Key life course characteristics of men in 12 case families

	Great-grandfathers (*n* = 7)	Grandfathers (*n* = 12)	Fathers (*n* = 12)
Date of birth			
Range	1911–31	1937–53	1962–80
Median	1918	1943	1968/69
Siblings			
Range	1–5	1–5	1–4
Median	2	2/3	2
Left full-time education			
16 or under	6	6	5
17	0	1	0
18 or over	1	5	7
Qualification			
None	4	3	1
Others	3	5	5
Professional/degree	0	4	5 (+1 studying)
Age cohabited with present partner	1 couple cohabited	None cohabited	11 cohabited
Range	–	–	17–26
Median	–	–	23
Age at marriage	All married	All married	9 married
Range	22–31	17–27	21–29
Median	27	20/21	24
Age at first child			
Range	23–32	19–29	18–31
Median	27	24	26
Age of grandparenthood			
Range	41–60	35–54	Not applicable
Median	50/51	49	

81 years. Many came from large families and most left school at 14 or 15; only two stayed on in full-time education to 18 or beyond. No great-grandfathers and only two great-grandmothers gained any qualifications while at school, though three great-grandfathers subsequently took apprenticeships and other job-related training. Only one couple cohabited before marriage (in unusual wartime circumstances) and all got married. Eight of the great-grandmothers' lives were marked by widowhood (one at the age of 22), two were widowed twice and two went through a divorce. Great-grandparents had their first children rather later than the next generation but earlier, at least in the case of

great-grandmothers than the current parent generation. The median age for becoming a grandparent was 50.

Grandparents

The 12 grandparent couples, most of whom were born between 1940 and 1948, were in all cases but one 'original couples' (a criterion of the selection of the grandparent sample): in this case, both grandparents were remarried and the parent generation was the child of the grandmother's first marriage. Their median age at interview was 53–54. They grew up in slightly smaller families, with a range of 1 to 5 siblings, in contrast to their parents whose siblings ranged from 1 to 12. This is a better qualified generation than their parents. Although most left school at 16 or younger, 8 had stayed in full-time education to 18 or beyond. Two grandmothers had a nursing training and two gained university degrees. Five grandfathers had been through higher education either immediately after schooling or later in life and only three had no qualifications. Marriage was commonplace as in the older generation while none cohabited beforehand. Marriage took place earlier than for their parents (at a median age of 20 for grandmothers and 20–21 for grandfathers, compared to 22–23 and 27 respectively for women and men in the older generation) and they also started families earlier. But, like their parents' generation, the median number of children among grandparents was three. Grandparenthood came at a slightly earlier age than the older generation (49 median).

Current parents

Again, all twelve couples were interviewed and were selected on the basis that they were still living with partners of their children. Most were born between 1965 and 1975; the median age at interview was 31 years for mothers and fathers. This was the only generation in which some participants grew up as only children; thus they have a lower median number of siblings. Their educational achievement again surpassed that of their parents; 13 (six mothers and seven fathers) left school at 18 or older while only one father and one mother had no qualifications. Four men and five women had degrees and two more were studying at university level when interviewed. In contrast to the older generations, all but one couple had cohabited and three were still not married. They started families at an older age than their parents and grandmothers (a median age for mothers and fathers of 25/26). It is likely that some have yet to complete their families (seven had at least one child under 5, with a range from birth to seven years).

Historical contexts

One way of locating the three adult generations historically is to consider how their lives were shaped by major historical events – though, as already noted, research participants less readily tied their own life stories to such external points of reference. Great-grandparents were mostly born during or soon after the First World War, when the British Empire was at its greatest extent, although already seriously weakened by the huge costs of the conflict. The majority of inter-war immigrants came not from the colonies but as refugees from Europe. The welfare state was a minimal presence, old age pensions for example having only been introduced in a rudimentary form in 1909 and with no national health service or financial support for children. State education was only beginning to reach into adolescence: statutory school-leaving age was raised from 12 to 14 in 1921. Most of this generation would have lived their childhoods or youth during the 1930s Depression, with its high levels of unemployment. Marriage and early parenthood, in many cases, coincided with the Second World War.

The next generation, the grandparents, were mostly born during or soon after this War, growing up with rationing and shortages, but also the establishment of the modern welfare State including a national heath service, family allowances (cash benefits paid to parents) and widening access to secondary education. The principle of free secondary education for all children was established by the Education Act 1944, with a two-tier system of grammar and secondary modern schools, and statutory school-leaving age was raised to 15 in 1947. Empire faded rapidly, but the late 1950s saw the beginnings of large-scale immigration from former colonies, which was to turn Britain into an ethnically diverse society. This generation's youth and early parenthood coincided with changing cultural and social mores, symbolised by the rise of television, the birth of rock and roll (in 1955), the legalisation of abortion (1967) and the spreading use of contraceptive pills from the late 1960s, and the beginnings of the Women's Movement. Yet it was also a generation that, like the previous generation, still mostly conformed to certain social norms: marriage rates peaked in 1971, cohabitation and divorce were still relatively uncommon. A range of household appliances and other products, such as cars, began to be available and affordable. It was a generation, too, caught in the Cold War, confronted both by the nuclear threat and an alternative political and economic ideology.

The parent generation grew up during the industrial unrest of the 1970s and the radical changes of the Thatcher years. This was a period of decline in manufacturing industry and rapid growth of the service sector, increasing privatisation and often high levels of unemployment: poverty and inequality grew rapidly, but so too did the incomes of many families. At the same time, from the late 1980s maternal employment began to increase rapidly, with far more women continuing in work on having children and fast rising employment rates among mothers with young children. While the welfare state in some important respects began to contract, state education expanded: school-leaving age was raised to 16 in 1972, a comprehensive system of secondary education mostly replaced the previous two-tier system, and higher education grew rapidly. Social change accelerated: cohabitation increased to the point where it preceded most first marriages; marriage rates fell and divorce rose; while births outside marriage, from being a relatively uncommon and stigmatised event as late as the 1960s, had come to account for nearly half of all births by the turn of the century.

The UK joined the European Union when this generation were still children (1973), while parenthood coincided with some immense changes of global proportions: the rise of 'market' or neo-liberal capitalism, an IT revolution and (perhaps not entirely unconnected) the collapse of the Soviet bloc, bringing with it the end of great power rivalry as the United States emerged as the world's only superpower.

The period that approximates to that covered by our three adult generations – from 1914 to the collapse of the USSR in 1991 – is described by Hobsbawm (1994) as the 'short twentieth century' in which a Golden Age of 'growth and transformation' is sandwiched between an Age of Catastrophe (two world wars and the inter-war years) and a period of 'decomposition and crisis' during the 1980s and 1990s.

The short Twentieth Century appears like a sort of triptych, or historical sandwich. An Age of Catastrophe from 1914 to the aftermath of the Second World War was followed by some twenty-five or thirty years of extraordinary economic growth and social transformation, which probably changed human society more profoundly than any other period of comparable brevity. In retrospect it can be seen as a sort of Golden Age, and was so seen almost immediately it had come to an end in the early 1970s. The last part of the century was a new era of decomposition, uncertainty and crisis...[I]ncreasingly it became clear that this was an era of long-term difficulties, for which capitalist countries sought radical solutions, often by following secular theologians of the unrestricted free market (pp. 6, 10).

Nikolas Rose (1999) tells a similar story of transformation over the 20th century. He describes the emergence of what he terms the 'social state', in reaction to the failings and ensuing dangers in the order of 19th century laissez-faire liberalism: 'by the early decades of the twentieth century, politicians in many different national contexts were under increasing pressure to accept that government of at least some aspects of [the] social domain should be added to the responsibilities of the political apparatus and its officials' (p. 117). Based on principles of solidarity and pooled risk, the welfare state emerged (pensions, for example, being introduced under the Liberal administration of 1908–15), but only achieving its fullest expression in the Labour Government's reforms after the Second World War. But during the 1970s, new forms of economic and political liberalism – neo-liberalism and advanced liberalism – begin to gain ground: the 'social' wanes and 'the individual' waxes, with a new emphasis on the citizen taking responsibility for the management of risk, both for herself and her family. The state increasingly assumes a role of forming and facilitating this citizen. In this extract, Rose draws our attention both to changing conditions and to changes in the type of 'ideal' subject that the state and economy create at different historical moments.

In the styles of government I have termed 'advanced liberal', the conception of the citizen is transformed. It became commonplace in the 1980s to hear talk of the 'active citizen' who was to be counterposed to the 'passive citizen' of the social state – the citizen of rights and duties, of obligations and expectations . . . [This] citizen was to conduct his or her life, and that of his or her family, as a kind of enterprise, seeking to enhance on existence itself through calculated acts and investments . . . Whilst social rule was characterized by discretionary authority, advanced liberal rule is characterized by the politics of the contract, in which the subject of the contract is not a patient or a case but a customer or consumer (pp. 164, 165).

Such historical analyses suggest we can locate our three generations in particular historical phases. Our great-grandparents, in the early part of their lives, live through Hobsbawm's Age of Catastrophe and Rose's emergent social state; our grandparents, during the same early years of their lives, are witness to the post-war Golden Age and the full flowering of the social state; while our parents come to adulthood in a new age of crisis, accompanied by the resurgence of economic and political liberalism. While such grand designs are helpful in constructing a context for individual narratives, a note of caution is in order. People, as we suggest at various points, may experience their historical times in a very different light: some great-grandparents, as we shall see in later chapters, did look back on their childhood in Hobsbawm's Age of Catastrophe as one marked by great hardship but others who had a middle-class upbringing made no reference to the Great Depression. For some the Second World War was a period of change and emancipation; while the age of crisis of the 1980s and 1990s was to some an age of further opportunities in education, employment and lifestyles. Historical conditions can play an important part in shaping lives, but they do not determine everything and everyone, affecting people's lives differently according to the experiences and life chances, including those of the families to which they belong.

Moreover, people's lives do not fit neatly into historians' eras. Our grandparents, for example, may have spent their early years in Hobsbawm's Golden Age, but their more recent years have been lived in the following period of crisis. The historical influences on them, therefore, overlay one another and may create reversals and contradictions. Moreover, to return to our earlier discussion of time, looking back on the past is always from a position in the present, which will influence how the past is remembered and given meaning. From the present, the past may look much worse or much better than it was experienced at the time.

The shape of the book

In writing and ordering the book's chapters, we have had to wrestle with three problematics. First is the issue of the individual's life course. Thus we have chosen to begin with a chapter on childhood (Chapter 2) and then to proceed to chapters which address the life course phase of bringing up young children (Chapters 3, 4 and 5). We have chosen this phase of parenting as a focus since this was a constant across the generations: the current phase reached by the third generation (parents) and a phase which had been experienced earlier by the two older generations but who were currently witnessing it as grandparents and great-grandparents. For both men and women in the three generations, this phase overlaps with employment and the ways in which they interweave their care and breadwinning responsibilities. In contrast Chapters 6 and 7 span the life course as they examine relations between family generations at different phases in the life course.

Our second problematic is the relations between family generations. We have analysed the cases at the level of the family or kin group and sought to trace the relations, transfers and transmission processes *within* families (Chapters 3–7). However, in addition we have been able to analyse our individual cases in relation to cohorts or historical generations. For example, in Chapter 2 we examine childhood through the eyes of three cohorts of women and three historical periods. Thus we have had to cut our analysis of the material in different ways. We have also tried to manage a difficult balancing act, one which has to be faced by all who engage in case-study research, that is, the issue of moving from the level of the individual case to the larger case, in our study the multi-generation family. In writing the book we have sought also to do justice to the breadth of our cases while illustrating the relations and processes within particular families. Thus the chapters weave together intra-family analyses, analyses between families and analyses where we compare different cohorts.

The third problematic is the methodological strategy which hinges upon the particular biographical approach we have followed. This we have discussed earlier and involves making the theoretical link between biography and history. In seeking to achieve this aim, we have sought in our methodology to draw out and to integrate the contextual (historical) and biographical 'facts' of the individual family members with their subjective experiences and interpretations.

There is necessarily some variation in the way we have treated the cases. Much of the book focuses at the family levels (lines of mothers in a family, for example) or at the cohort levels (grandparents compared with parents and great-grandparents), the analyses of which are located in the macro-structural context that we have set. But at times we move to a more detailed analysis of individuals and the 'biographical work' they engage in both in thinking about their lives and in the course of the research interview (Chamberlayne and King, 2000, p. 131).

Writing up team research inevitably implies taking different theoretical slants and analytic strategies as each of us took responsibility for different parts of the analysis. One of us took responsibility for writing the first draft of the book and for weaving together the different slants taken in the analysis. Because of this and also for the reasons set out above, the approaches taken in each chapter differ somewhat.

Reflecting the beginning of the life course, in Chapter 2 we examine childhood. Since there were few men in the oldest generation we have focused on women and the changes and similarities in their historical and family experiences of childhood. Chapter 3 focuses on women's and men's changing careers in employment and childcare among successive generations, showing in particular the shifts that have taken place in women's employment patterns especially among the youngest generation of today's mothers. An examination of motherhood in Chapter 4 is concerned with two aspects: intergenerational transmission within families – how women through their understandings and actions appear to identify with or distance themselves from the practices adopted by their own parents; and negotiating responsibilities, how women as mothers work out the relationship between employment and motherhood. Chapter 5 focuses on fatherhood over family generations: the timetabling of the transition to fatherhood; men's normative discourses about fatherhood; and the types of fatherhood practice men engaged in and how far such types of fatherhood are transmitted within families.

Running through Chapters 4 and 5 is the link between action and interpretation: how each generation interprets the norms of the time about what it means to be a 'proper' mother or father, both in the context of their individual situations and the historical period. Disjunctures emerge between actions and what interviewees say 'ought to happen', illustrating the interplay between the lived life and the told story – between structural forces and individual agency.

Intergenerational relations are the nub of Chapters 6 and 7. Chapter 6 looks at the transmission of material and care resources: what these transfers consist of, how and why they flow and, most importantly, the meanings given to them by different generations. Then in Chapter 7 we attempt to give some shape to what has gone before by proposing a typology of intergenerational relations and transfers, based on two factors: occupational and geographical mobility. We also insert here the concept of ambivalence, the other side of the coin to continuity and transmission, by which members of one generation differentiate themselves, to varying degrees, from previous generations. Finally, in Chapter 8 we draw some concluding thoughts, relating both to theory and policy.

2
Changing Childhoods across Three Generations of Women

Childhood is a social institution, and a cultural invention (Aries, 1962; Kessen, 1979). In effect, what it means to be a child and what a child experiences in one era is rarely the same in another era. In this chapter we focus on women's childhoods in three historical generations. We have made the assumption that childhood is a gendered experience and of necessity we have chosen to focus upon the experiences of women. There were very few living great-grandfathers in our study (as in the general population) and thus we have few accounts of their childhood. Moreover, changes in *women's* lives have greatly affected childhood. Over time, women's educational qualifications and employment have increased significantly, trends also associated in present times with the postponement of childbearing and increasing risk of divorce (Elder *et al.*, 1993). We focus here upon the three adult generations of women: great-grandmothers (born 1911–21); 1940s grandmothers (born 1940–48); and 1960's/70s current mothers of young children (born 1965–75).

In referring to childhood, we speak about it in the plural – to signify its variability and different meanings (Mayall, 1994), both over time and within the same historical period. Our aim here has been to identify some emblematic themes in typifying both the historically located experiences of childhoods and the normative discourses drawn upon to describe them. However, the way we, as adults, construe children and childhood changes over time and it has been our task to try to clarify from which particular normative and experiential vantage points narrators are speaking. Recollections of childhood, while they can refer to the impact of context and structure, need not do so. We have been sensitive to the ways in which a grandmother may evaluate her own childhood in relation to the time and context of her experience and how she may shift to the childhoods of her own children or grandchildren.

In writing this chapter, we have been mindful that capturing the essence of childhood in different historical periods relies upon retrospective accounting. As noted already, accounts are given with the cognisance of the experiences that people have witnessed subsequently – by individuals' subsequent exposure to different practices and ideas about childhood that prevail in different periods. Moreover, it is as adults that interviewees reflected upon their childhoods and from particular life course phases. At the same time we have taken the view that the recollection of childhood is shaped by experiences in childhood, by the ideas and conditions that prevailed at the time, by the informants' cultural locations in time and place, and by their linkages to others' lives and their own agency at the time (Giele and Elder, 1998). Thus, in making sense of accounts of childhood, therefore, we confront an issue already flagged up in Chapter 1: the complexity and multi-faceted nature of time (see also Chapter 8). We need to address how informants' accounts are permeated by their own time perspectives as well as locating them in the broad historical landscapes of our own sociological understandings. We have also suggested some continuities and discontinuities in childhood within families although this has not been the main focus of the chapter.

Great-grandmothers: childhoods in the interwar years

Great-grandparents witnessed huge changes over the whole course of their lives: two world wars, increased prosperity, first the growth and then, later, the decline of the welfare state, major changes in gender roles. The interwar period was marked by greater socio-economic homogeneity compared with the present day in that a much larger proportion of the male working population was employed in manual occupations (Halsey, 2000). Especially among working-class people in the 1920s and 1930s, hard times were a common experience, not only in absolute terms but also relative to the present day. Given the uncertainty surrounding employment, especially for working-class families in the 1930s and the importance placed upon men as breadwinners, children's experience of their childhoods was heavily dependent upon their fathers being in work, even though many working-class mothers were employed. Great-grandmothers grew up with few educational expectations and opportunities and while many entered paid work at different points in the life course, none developed an employment career as such. Children's experiences also depended upon mothers' contributions inside the home in helping families to 'make do' and 'get by'.

In recounting their lives, great-grandmothers who were in their 80s described their childhoods as part of the *general condition of family life*, though not in the sense of families being bounded discrete units (Jamieson, 1987). Their stories of the past are public accounts, which focused upon the impact of external events rather than their own agency. They portrayed the structural features of their lives as broad descriptive landscapes (see also Nielsen, 2003). Working-class great-grandmothers recalled the period of their childhoods as a time of hardship and struggle for the family and remembered their *mothers* for keeping families together. They remembered that as young girls they had helped their mothers with the enormous burden of household work. What is striking here is that even though this generation has witnessed enormous subsequent changes in children's lives and in the value accorded to children and childhood, in evaluating their childhoods none described the past as involving a loss of childhood *per se*. Nor did they identify childhood as a specific phase in which children were given special treatment.

Brenda Smith, born in 1924, started her account (which lasted five hours over two visits) by positioning herself as a child growing up in an extremely poor family; she described listening to the adults talking from her own small space under the 'dining table' around which much of the indoor life of the family took place. Despite this positioning, Brenda's account focused not only upon the details of 'making do' and 'getting by' in a poor London family but, unusually, embraced the broad historical landscape of events and social change. In the first two hours of her interview Brenda scarcely paused as she described her earliest memories of growing up poor in London in the 1920s and 1930s which she set against the backcloth of the arrival of the Jarrow marchers in London during the General Strike. Her father was out of work for much of her childhood and did 'odd jobs' until he got a 'pitch' selling newspapers on street corners. Brenda considered the contribution of her mother and the children to family income as essential to the family's getting by.

I was the youngest of seven children, and, um, I seem to have spent – we lived in a tenement, you know, two rooms in a tenement ... as far as I can remember, right back ... I seem to have spent most of my young childhood under the table. Because the way poor people lived then – and I mean poor – they lived in two rooms, and in the main room there was usually a bed, and a table, chairs. Hopefully, a chest of drawers ... It was a square table, and I used to play under there a lot. Never got trodden on. I used to, um, ... make pictures and toys and everything. I was always under the table, and . . . I used to listen a lot. 'Cos sometimes I'd say something from years ago, and I think afterwards, it couldn't have been really me, it must've been me listening to the rest of the family. You know, my mum and my – her sisters . . . My father was a – God! My father – it was in the '20s. Life was very hard, no jobs and all that. So he didn't really have a – any profession. He used to do odd jobs. Until he got a newspaper pitch, and for the rest of the time he sold newspapers for a living. Um, he was a clever man with his hands . . . And when we were kids, she [mother] used to do – she used to do the washing. We used to go up to the theatres [in the West End of London] and get a big basket of washing, and she used to do the towels and the tights, and all the stuff in the theatre. And we used to go up there with the pram, with my big sister. Pick it up and, at the end of the week, take it back and . . . [My mother] had a terribly hard – people in those days had terrible hard lives. She had to get up, you know, about four o'clock in the morning, you know. And a few of her cronies, and they would go down Covent Garden, and they used to shell peas down there. Peel potatoes for the hotels, you know. Like, they do by machine now. And they used to do that, and they used to be paid sixpence! Sixpence for – five days, six days a week and get three bob. In shillings. And she used to take in washing. That's how we sort of lived. My mum used to take in washing. We used to go to the public baths, which was just across from where we lived. She used to go in at eight o'clock in the morning, and about eight o'clock at night. She . . . (had) a hard life. But I don't remember her buying anything for herself, new . . . ever. Not until she got old. When you compare that generation to ours, it's like a different world. It's – she was 93 when she died, mind you.

This generation, who grew up in a minimal welfare state, related significant life events which frequently led to families falling into poverty, to mothers having to seek paid employment, and to disrupted or difficult family relationships. In some cases, the trauma was so great that great-grandmothers had, on their own admission, 'blocked' or 'blanked out' these memories. Such events included fathers' long absences during wartime; deaths of and desertions by a parent in early childhood; having an indifferent step parent. Jessie Miller, for example, described escaping the dire poverty that might well have been her lot when her father died in 1918 when she was only six months old. Her mother found work as a seamstress and she depended upon the support of her own mother in bringing up Jessie. Jessie commented that they managed well because she was an only child, remarking on their good fortune compared with other members of the family who were 'extremely poor': 'I realised then just how fortunate I'd been – only for the fact that my mother worked so hard to give me a good life because I was an only child.'

Working-class poverty meant children had to help their families to survive. Brenda Smith, quoted above, remembered how, during the 1930s, she and her siblings stole tar blocks from the roads to sell as firewood 'and the servants would come up from the basements and buy bundles of kindling'. Similarly, another great-grandmother noted that, as the eldest daughter, at the age of 14 she took over the care of her baby sister when her mother got a full-time job during the war. Yet another great-grandmother, whose mother was a lone parent and worked as a cleaner, described how the four children each had their own jobs to keep the household going which left them no time 'to go out to play with other children'.

It is significant that members of this generation who grew up in middle-class families made no reference to the 1930s Depression. But even girls in such families often did household chores especially when they were the oldest daughters in large families. In the 1920s, Grace Horton, as the oldest daughter in a family of three boys and two girls, was expected to help her mother in the house. Grace remembered how, as a child, she had understood the pressure her mother was under when, following a fall in family fortunes they could no longer afford the cost of servants.

Memories of being a child in this generation were not all about working. Even for working-class children, there was also time for leisure. This was typically organised *collectively* in the community, rather than individually or by parents. Moreover, leisure demanded children's active participation – that is, they were expected to make their own amusement, a practice which some great-grandmothers contrasted with what they perceived to be the passive consumption of today's children. Schools, churches, the Saturday matinée at the local cinema were key institutions providing amusement for children. Dora Peters, born in 1920, commented:

A lot of our activities was with the school and, er, sports days and all different things like that. And ... in the chapel. You know, we used to have what they used to call – I don't know whether they do now – Methodist Christian Endeavour, and they used to have Band of Hope ... We used to do plays and singing competitions. You know? And then once a year they used to have – which they used to call the 'anniversary', and all the children … used to sing or recite … we were encouraged to do it. Do you get my meaning? … You used to be able to go to the pictures for a penny. You know. But that was Saturday matinée or something like that … But otherwise you used to make your own amusements.

In this respect, children's worlds were seen to have changed and this led some great-grandmothers to remember the past through rather rose-tinted glasses. Childhood was recalled as a time of freedom to roam in the physical environment and as risk free, in contrast with their perceptions of the physical restrictions and perceived dangers of the present times. Dora Peters again: 'We used to have nice times. Yeah. And you could go off, and nobody ever used to touch you, or you never used to have anybody stop or anybody – no fighting or people nasty to you. You know. It's where I often wondered what's gone wrong. You know?'. Dora went on to recollect that childhood was not only less risk-prone than it is today, but that there was also less waste and more thrift, even from children. She remembered her father having to work hard to keep the family out of poverty, and that what was no longer needed was passed on to other people: 'I mean, as far as, like, that part, like – as I said, my father was in work and that. But if we had anything that my mother didn't want, we used to pass on to other people.'

Great-grandmothers mostly left school early and rarely gained any qualifications. Most recalled 'missing out' on educational opportunities. However, they made it clear that the loss was felt more keenly in hindsight than at the time. For over the course of their own lives, they had witnessed the growing importance of education, especially for women.

Grace Horton, born in 1914 into a middle-class family, was one such case of 'missing out'. At a time when access to qualifications often depended on private means, she was forced to move from a private school to a state secondary school when her father's business collapsed in the 1920s. The family moved to a smaller house in a different part of London, a move that curtailed Grace's subsequent educational and job opportunities. Grace recalled a moment in her life when an adult spotted her academic ability: during a training course after she left school to work as a cookery demonstrator, the teacher said to her 'What are doing here? You should be at university'. However, at the time she made little of the remark feeling no different from her friends: 'And I didn't know what to say, really. I was very surprised. And, um – I mean, you didn't have a chip on your shoulder in those days because you didn't, because none of your friends did.' Only subsequently, did she come to regret the absence of educational opportunity.

Thus, great-grandmothers described their childhoods during the First World War in material terms, reflecting a heavily class-based society in which many families were typically large, working class and poor. The quality of children's lives was seen to depend upon the material viability of the household: male breadwinning and mothers' household management skills and sheer hard work. Where fathers were unable to provide adequately or had died, mothers' paid work became critical. So, too, was the presence of grandmothers who both looked after the children and took on a parental role (see also Attias-Donfut and Segalen, 2002). The household work of children was important and sometimes involved doing paid work outside the home. The pleasurable aspects of children's lives depended more upon local community organisations than upon the involvement of parents.

While being shaped by history, childhoods were also seen from the vantage point of the great changes which took place in the intervening years. Children's freedom to roam was contrasted with the risks that seemingly endanger and restrict modern-day childhoods, while a world of thrift was compared with what was seen as today's wasteful consumption. Great-grandmothers viewed with hindsight lost educational opportunities from the vantage point of what they see to be on offer to today's children and hence they implied how their lives might have been.

Grandmothers: childhoods in the post-war period

The 1940s grandparent generation grew up after the Second World War in a period of high male employment and during the foundation of the modern British welfare state. Some experienced the employment of their mothers during the war. But following the end of the war, new childrearing ideas, introduced by psychologists in the 1950s, emphasised children's need for mothers' full-time presence in the home in order to give children emotional security. (Later, when this generation became mothers themselves, bringing up their own children in the 1970s, motherhood was subjected to liberal ideas relating to psychoanalysis.) This is not to suggest that attitudes to childrearing were consistently influenced by the hegemony of such new philosophies (Jamieson, 1987). In fact only one great-grandmother, Grace Horton already quoted, reflected upon the importance of these new ideas in the post-war period.

Unlike the generation before them who evaluated their childhoods as good or bad, hard or uneventful, the 1940s grandmothers recalled childhoods that were 'psychologised'. They assessed children's lives in relation to the concepts of individualism and the 'secure child'. Above all else, childhood was supposed to be 'happy'. The importance of the material context of childhood and family life shaded into the background, while the emotional milieu came to the fore (see also Harris, 1983). Celia Hurd, born in 1941, grew up in a 'respectable' working-class family:

> I think I'm one of those people who thought the sun always shone, and errr it was very loving, very loving. Very – I suppose I was spoilt. I was the only child for about 10 years. Ummm. I don't know, I just feel that I was wanted and loved and well cared-for. I mean obviously a lot of this is what one gathers from looking at photographs, but my recollection is that it was a lovely time. I loved school, all through.

This memory of childhood is in sharp contrast to her mother's. Born in 1912, Doreen Hurd's father died when she was eight. Her mother had four children and 'a very hard life'. Doreen could remember little about her childhood: 'I think I had such a hard life, I decided to block it (childhood) out of my life.'

Just as the oldest generation saw their own mothers as crucial to their family's material welfare, so the next generation considered maternal presence and *mother's love* to be the very essence of good motherhood, and good childhood (and good adulthood). Unlike the great-grandmother generation, this 1940s generation accorded their parents, that is their mothers, psychological responsibility for children's lives. Making reference to the post-war ideology – 'mothers' place is in the home' – they evaluated their own mothers according to their efforts to 'be there' for their children, that is, at home rather than at work. They saw mothers' job to be at home when children were young (few were consistently at home as we shall see in Chapter 3) and to ensure their children did not come home from school to 'empty houses'.

For example, Priscilla Peters, born in 1948, was quick to suggest that her mother was 'there' for her when she was growing up in the late 1940s and 1950s. Her mother, in fact, took a job as a home help when her children went to secondary school. Nonetheless Priscilla insisted that her mother was 'always there, with a cup of tea and a biscuit. Listen to all our problems'. Pauline Smith, Brenda Smith's daughter born in 1947, noted 'we [children] were never ever alone . . . We never came home to an empty [house] – although my mother went to work and my father went to work'. For the grandmothers, therefore, to say 'my mother never left us' was to lay claim, at a normative level, to a 'proper upbringing' and to define the condition for providing individual children with psychological security. The previous generation's concern about having too little space in the home (overcrowding) was replaced in the following generation with the fear of children having *too much* space – *emotional space*, epitomised in the recurring image of a poor upbringing, the child coming home from school to an empty, motherless home.

Many working-class mothers were employed in the war and some left work after the war when the government was encouraging women to return home. Yet the 1940s grandmothers rarely referred to their own mothers' paid work directly, as if still anxious to protect their mothers' reputations as 'good mothers' at that time. When work did crop up, it was often remembered as fitted around the demands of family life, to ensure children did not lose out. Kate Miller, born in 1940, remembered her mother working as a cleaner early in the morning and late at night, but emphasised her presence at home during the day: 'Y'know my mum was there during the day or whatever. Didn't miss her. Y'know she was only doing a little part-time job.' The emphasis on the smallness of the job – its marginality – serves to make her mother's presence even more vivid. Kate continues in this vein, explaining that her mother got a job as a school dinner lady 'to be home with us in the school holidays'.

Later in her interview, Kate went on to reflect that she herself had worked during much of her children's lives and was rather proud of this now. Yet she evaluated her mother's employment according to the mores that applied during her childhood rather than according to the mores of the time when she herself was a full-time working mother (the 1960s). Interestingly, her own daughter, Alison, chose not to work while her children were young and made this decision during a period (the 1990s) in which the employment of mothers of young children was rising sharply and becoming more acceptable. Kate, now a grandmother, was indeed rather critical of Alison for 'running herself ragged' in pursuit of her children's welfare. But Alison had consciously rejected her mother's practice: she now wanted to 'be there' for her own children (see Chapter 4 for a fuller discussion of the women in this family).

Working-class great-grandmothers remembered their grandmothers for the care they gave them as children. So too working-class grandmothers remembered their grandmothers. Pauline Smith noted that as a child she never came home from school to an empty house because

'Granny was there, Nan was there, and old aunt D . . . There was always people'. The social stigma of being a 'latchkey kid' was thus avoided. As Attias-Donfut and Segalen (2002) suggest, grandmothers also represent continuity; they are a source of symbolic support as well as practical (childcare) support – the backbone of the family – and provide a sense of 'genetic security'.

The experiences of two grandmothers are cases in point. When Thelma Hillyard's father was killed, the family went to live with her maternal grandparents. It is perhaps significant that although her mother was working at the time, she did not refer to it. Her account conveys the emotional security provided by her grandparents:

> They loved us very much, my nan and granddad. They had a nice big house. And a lovely garden. And I can remember in the summer we used to – they had a garden, they had a yard, 'cos they – my granddad was a builder, so it was working premises – and they had a garden at the top. And I can remember we used to sit up in the (?) to dry our hair in the summers with our nighties on, and that sort of thing . . . And then, when Mum got married again – we didn't live far away, we still lived in Y. And we used to go to Nan's every . . . for tea, which we used to look forward to after school. And Nan and Granddad were – they were the ones that sort of – well, all nans and granddads do – look after you. They used to take us on Sunday school outings, we used to go on the train from X, because the train was running then. And, um, one of the highlights, I can remember when we were tiny, was they'd take us out in the car to the pub on a Sunday [laughs]. That was quite nice. Er – yes. They were very – very happy days, all my sort of younger days.

Carol Masters' parents and her older sister shared a council house with her maternal grandparents and an uncle until she was five. She was very close to her grandmother whom she regarded as 'the mainstay of the family' and a source of support with respect to difficulties caused by her father. 'My grandma was a real, dominant character in my life. I absolutely adored my grandma . . . At times it wasn't a very happy environment, but we always went back to Grandma. So she was the mainstay of the family.' In 1947, the family moved to a 'prefab' (a prefabricated bungalow put up by councils as a quick and cheap way to re-house families after the war). Their new home was close to Carol's grandparents, but the family moved even closer when they got another council house in the same road.

Grandmothers also recalled their childhoods as being focused on the nuclear family in which mothers occupied a pivotal position. Indeed the post-1945 period witnessed the advent of the nuclear-family ideal symbolised in the growing importance placed upon the 'family holiday' among a wider population, due in part to the success of some groups of manual workers in winning a right to annual leave. For a growing minority the mass production of the motor car increased possibilities for family travel (Inglis, 2000). Holidays were not necessarily very expensive or taken far from home. Janice Brand, born in 1945, whose father worked in the local coop, described taking a family holiday with relatives:

> My Dad didn't travel very far, he didn't drive, he rode a bike every-where. So where we went was extremely limited. Ummm. We used to go down to X for our, for our holidays. But that was with an aunt and uncle usually. 'Cos they probably had then a car, and they could actually take us down, or we went on the train, or the bus, as the case may be...as I say, we didn't go very far – ...just X, and that was probably the limit of our holidays.

Going away was, however, only one small part of the long school holidays in which mothers' presence was remembered as crucial. We have already seen how working in a school ensured that Kate Smith's mother would be around in the holidays. The same was true for Janice Brand, who ended her remarks by stressing that her mother never worked during the school holidays: 'my childhood was, was just a very basic childhood I think, just surrounded by family, with a Mum and Dad. My Mum was always there. She had school holidays off with us. She never worked in, in, in the holidays.'

The grandmother generation reviewed their own childhoods through different lenses from the older generation: new psychological ideas and the growing importance of the nuclear family. But there are also continuities with the previous generation such as the importance of grandmothers and in their somewhat rose-tinted recollections, grandmothers, like great-grandmothers, adopted a comparative time perspective. They too contrasted the perceived risky nature of present childhoods with the remembered freedoms and 'simple pleasures' of their own past childhoods. Grandmothers who grew up in rural areas recalled being free to roam the countryside with their siblings and friends, and those who had urban childhoods spoke about playing in the street. Carol Masters offered a picture of a community of local children making their own amusements:

As I say, all the children were able to play in the street. The things that we played mostly with were – were one swing in the garden – I can remember that – which was made by – I don't know if it was my granddad or my dad. The children in the street used to put on lots of concerts that we used to go to, and we used to have to pay a farthing to get in, in the back yard of one of the children, whoever was putting on the concert. But mainly it was simple, really simple, entertainment that we – er, managed to get by with as children. We played in a big field at the top of the road, which I can't imagine our children at all going out of our sight, you know, in this day and age. But in those days I can remember this big field being called 'the Den' that we all accumulated in, and we played for hours there.

From the vantage point of *their own childhoods*, this generation subscribed to dominant ideologies of the period concerning how best to look after children. But this did not necessarily lead them to deny their own positive experience of being working mothers. Especially after their children started school, many women among the 1940s grandmothers returned to education and the labour market to build employment careers. We return to these themes of motherhood and employment later, in Chapters 3 and 4.

Mothers: childhoods in the 1970s and 1980s

The current mother generation was born into a Britain that had already entered a more socially liberal climate. While they grew up in the 1970s and 1980s, the economic climate became more neo-liberal, with an increasing emphasis on enterprise, markets and competition. Over their lives, this generation has seen a reversal in ideas, as values of solidarity and collective welfare have given way to the virtues of individual responsibility, informed consumerism and the stigmatisation of 'welfare dependency'. Unlike their forebears, this generation experienced and expects higher standards of living with respect to both adulthood and childhood.

At the same time, in contrast to the immediate post-war period, this generation's times have been marked by change and uncertainty in the economic sphere and considerable household change as partnering, separation and repartnering have become more frequent events. Like the two older generations, this generation grew up in a period in which employment by mothers of young children was uncommon and widely criticised, apart from 'little jobs' requiring short part-time hours often at times that permitted fathers or relatives to care of children. However, they took for granted the ideology of gender equality, which came to Britain in the 1970s: a sign of this, statutory maternity leave, was introduced in 1976. And, as we discuss later, by the time this generation became mothers in the 1990s it had become, if not yet normative, then no longer uncommon for mothers to remain in work when they had children (Brannen *et al.*, 1997).

Childhood for the mother generation was much closer in time than for the other two generations. This adds an immediacy to their accounts of childhood. Childhood also constitutes a large chunk of the life course of this generation who at interview were in their mid twenties to mid thirties. Moreover, this generational group was currently witnessing their own children's childhoods. They were reflecting upon their own childhoods from *the current vantage point of being a parent*.

The 1960s/70s mothers do show some continuities with older generations. For example, many considered their grandmothers to have been very important not only as a childcare resource but also a source of meaning and stability in their lives. Jane Smith, Pauline Smith's daughter-in-law, was born in 1965 into a close-knit working-class family and grew up in an inner-city neighbourhood of London:

My dad was working a lot. He worked hard, my dad. Well, my mum worked as well. She still does. But my mum was – I mean, my nan. We used to go to my nan's after school. My mum would be shopping after work, or something...Old Nan, yeah. She was the eldest of all her brothers and sisters, so – And their dad died young. So I think they – I think she held the family together. I think when she dies, it will – it's all spread out a bit. We won't see so much of aunts and uncles – well, my great-aunts and uncles, really. Her brothers and sisters. 'Cos there's hundreds of them!...I was always in [Nan's] after school, anyway, even if my mum was there. A cup of tea and a chat. We still do it now. Four o'clock, that's it. Tea-time!

But there are changes too, notably in ideas about motherhood. In the 1990s, as the British welfare state was restructured and trust in experts waned, the neo-liberal climate gave a new emphasis to individual agency and the ideal of 'the self-regulating subject' (Rose, 1990; Bernstein, 2000). This generation of mothers saw themselves as actively involved in creating their children's childhoods. (At the same time, it is important to stress that individualism in family life has deep roots (Jamieson, 1987). The concept of 'active parenting' (notably a non-gendered concept) has infused contemporary public policies towards children and their families, for example parent education, parental involvement in schools, parental responsibility for keeping their children off the streets (child curfews) and parents' (lone mothers') responsibility for their own employment and employability (the New Deal for Lone Parents). However, such emphasis on parental responsibility also reflects an interventionist state in the way it shifts responsibility on to parents while not providing many resources to help them to carry out such responsibility. Thus it may be argued that the discourse of parents constructing children's childhood is underpinned by institutional forces, as collective forms of welfare have been cut back to which parents rarely refer.

The current mother generation viewed the childhoods of their own children as a distinctive phase not merely as a time for 'growing up'. They saw it as a world which they, as parents, constructed for and in which they engaged with their children, while being silent about the state's role in bringing this situation about. However, unlike the previous generations, this active involvement did not preclude mothers' employment and did not imply mothers' presence on a full-time basis. In accordance with their present-day employment commitments, 'quality time' has supplanted 'quantity time' both as a value and a reality, or at least in some cases. The two discourses – of mothers as adult workers and mothers as parents – are kept separate in the accounts of this generation, as they are also in current public-policy discourse.

A current mother of two young children, born in 1969, Juliet Kent's childhood was a privileged middle-class one. Reflecting the normative views of the 1940s grandmother generation, Juliet was at pains to note that, though her mother had a part-time job, she was 'there' for her. However Juliet also evaluated her mother's engagement with her and her two sisters positively in other ways. She commended her mother for giving a sense of community and purpose to the lives of her children, and for encouraging them to participate in lots of extra-curricular activities. Her account graphically suggests her mother's occupancy of space and place:

> There was one corner where two roads met, and a second corner, and we would always meet at first corner or second corner, and I remember her arriving in the car and picking us up from school. I remember homework round the kitchen table, and I remember all the activities that we did from – we were all quite musical, so we all had an instrument, plus the piano. And I remember all this stuff that she used to take us to, and sit with us, and take us to exams and all that. So she

was very – definitely very – very proactive, and very, um – there was lots always going on. It was a very noisy, kind of busy house ... She always picked us up from school, so she worked funny hours. I was never aware of her – we had au pairs, we definitely had au pairs. I remember hundreds of au pairs. So I'm sure au pairs kind of had a part to play in all of that. But, er, I certainly have absolutely no recollection of her not being there, really.

But not all held a positive view of their own childhood and mothering. From the vantage point of being a currently 'involved parent', some of this generation of mothers looked back at their own childhoods and found them wanting. With one exception, this group did not criticise their mothers for being housewives, at least for part of their childhoods. More criticised their mothers (and sometimes fathers) for *not* providing a more child-centred childhood: simply 'being there' was no longer sufficient. Thus they evaluated their mothers and fathers according to *current* parenting mores while at the same time, according to the norms which applied during their childhoods, they were anxious to portray their childhoods as 'happy' and their mothers as 'being there' for them.

Janet Brand, born in 1970, grew up in a working-class family and scrutinised her parents' parenting. Through marriage and employment, she developed aspirations, wanting her new family of orientation to 'get on' in the world. In particular she was keen to help her young daughter in her schooling. Looking back to childhood, she reviewed her own parents' efforts in this regard. While emphasising that her own parents were 'good parents' and that her mother was always 'there', Janet now considered them too home-centred and too concerned with humdrum routines – not active enough. In seeing them as failing to help her and her sister with their schooling, she compared them unfavourably against her current ideals. By 'sitting down' more with her young daughter, Janet had hoped to inculcate skills and introduce her to new ideas and opportunities.

Janet contrasted the way her parents acted when she was a child with how they now act towards her daughter, their grandchild.

My childhood. Um – it was happy. But, um, I think, with my mother – my mother and father were – have worked all their lives, but they didn't actually have any ambitions to do any better than what they have – they achieved. So I think, really, sometimes I think they look at [us] ... and think, Ooh, I wish, you know, we'd achieved that. But it's trying to make them understand that, if they wanted it, it was there. It's just having the – the goal to go and do it. Um – but, yeah, it was happy. I mean, they're – they're lovely parents, they're very caring, but it's just that, perhaps homework-wise, and things that I wanted them to understand and help me with, they just had no idea, or no clue, how to do it . . . I found school terribly hard. I mean, we try and encourage [daughter] as much as we can. You know, If you have any problems, or if you want to do any reading, come and see us, and – you know, she'll sit down. But I don't ever remember doing that with my mother and father. Um – but, yeah, it was happy times. And, as I say, we get on – lovely now. And they absolutely dote on [grand daughter]. But they will actually sit down with a book with her. I'm thinking, Why didn't you do that with me?

There were other criticisms of parents for being insufficiently engaged with their children. Geraldine Horton, born in 1966 and from a middle-class family, said that her childhood was happy but questioned her own parents' wisdom in sending her away to boarding school. Again, she looked back at her own childhood from the vantage point of her own current hopes for her own children. 'I had a happy childhood. My childhood was just – because I went to boarding school, it just seems one big blur, really. I mean, I wasn't home at the night time. I didn't do after-school clubs with my mum and dad. They really weren't into all of that at all.'

Sonia Masters, born in 1967 and also from a middle-class family, questioned her parents' notion of a 'good' family life for children in similarly expressing regret that her parents sent her to boarding school; she found it difficult to understand why they were not more 'flexible' and had not explored 'other avenues'.

I just still to this day cannot believe how an institution can replace a family life. I mean I think family life is so *crucial*, and you know to be ripped so cruelly away from all of that, in my most formative years. Y'know, through puberty and all of that, as a young woman developing, I thought was really very damaging. Knowing how unhappy I was. Ummm. And I s'pose they in some ways, y'know, I can see now their hands were tied. Y'know there wasn't any alternative. They were concerned about my academic – . . . Yeah, I mean I can see . . . But I just sort of kind of wondered why they hadn't maybe explored other avenues . . . Thinking about my own children and their schooling, y'know. I s'pose it is difficult, because you know, y'know, you have the experience of your years to know what you think will be good for them. And I can understand that fully. Ummm. But I think there has to be some flexibility and some decision-making . . .

Women's fathers too came in for criticism, especially for failing to be sufficiently involved and active in their daughters' lives, as these two sets of comments about their (middle-class) fathers indicate. From the present vantage points of different normative discourses concerning fatherhood, mothers criticised their main breadwinner fathers (1940s grandfathers) for their commitment to work and for a lack of involvement with their children. It is worth noting that their own partners, fathers of their children, were similarly highly committed to their jobs; mothers did not criticise them for this as they were themselves working and committed to work. However, the current fathers in question considered developing relationships with their children to be very important, as we shall describe in Chapter 5.

Well, I'm the youngest of three children, and was looked after by my mum all of the time. My dad's always worked, although he had a period of unemployment when he sent my mother out to work [for a short time]. But then she still looked after us. I don't remember him ever doing anything for us when we were children. He worked, and that was it. In fact, I don't really have that much memory of him being around at all. He would go out to work at seven o'clock in the morning, and he'd come back at seven o'clock at night (Rachel Hurd).

My dad never used to come home from work until midnight most of the time, and when he used to pick us from school, he was always late, so it was always me and my sisters looking out of the window, waiting for Dad to drive up the drive. And he was always, always late (Geraldine Horton).

Parents who, as children, had experienced divorce and step parenthood did not blame their parents directly for this. (Despite the focus on intact families among those interviewed, one set of grandparents both of whom had been previously divorced was included, while divorce occurred among the grandparents who were excluded from the study design.) However, these parents saw divorce as having marred their childhoods. Alison Miller's childhood memories focused on her parents splitting up: 'I don't think of us as a family at all.' She remembered resenting the arrival of her stepfather and resisting his presence. She also fought against her mother's authority and that of the school, eventually moving to live with her father.

It always is sort of like the adolescent thing. But, I think because you do come from a split family, you, you've got an extra string to your bow, if you know, for want of a better expression. You can just sort of say, 'Well that's it, I don't care, I'm going over there to live with them now.' (Interviewer: Yeah. The other option.) Yes, that's right. 'I'm going to tell Dad you've said this,' or, 'I'm gonna tell Mum you said that,' you know you just...it all adds to the, as I say, you know, your stepparents telling you what to do and why should they?

The mothers did not lay all the blame on their parents for their upbringings. As in other areas, they also attributed agency to themselves. In another family, all three generations experienced poverty and disruptions in childhood. A current mother, Sheila Prentice, born in 1975, reflected on the difficulties which her parents had coped with and how she has since managed to come to terms with the disruptions. Again, grandmothers were remembered as key figures providing support in their childhood.

But it was nice, you know, you get spoiled when you go and stay with your grandma don't you, so that was...I enjoyed that, and the garden was a lot nicer up there as well, and...they used to grow all their own fruit and vegetables – potatoes and radishes, well all sorts really, 'cos like I said there was a lot of land there, you know, so you know,...and then there were loads of trees...it was dad's – my dad's mum. Yeah, she looked after us...both my grandfathers died..., just two grandmothers, but erm, my mum's mum, she was suffering from dementia, so she wouldn't really have been able to look after me, anyway, but my dad's mum, she was quite capable and able, and she lived till about 87 I think, and erm, yeah, I used to love spending time with my nan. Yeah, I bonded with her, better than I think I did with my mum to be honest, which I suppose – I don't know whether it's a shame or not really. I get on well with mum. It's not that I don't get on with my mum, but I've got on with my nan better because I suppose she was there when I was so young, when I was a baby, so it was a natural bonding instinct I think, yeah.

Sadly this grandmother died when Sheila was 13. However, even so, Sheila looked back now at her childhood, remembering how angry she once was, but also managing to find positive experiences and relationships in her past. It is significant that both Sheila and her partner Andrew were very actively involved with their young children and were determined to bring them up differently: we shall return to them and their contemporary parenting in far more detail in Chapters 5 and 7.

This generation's views of childhood involve close scrutiny of their own childhood from the standpoint of being relatively new parents. But they were also formed in the context of what Beck refers to as widespread social processes of individualisation (Beck, 1992, 1994; Beck and Beck-Gernsheim, 1995) and what Giddens (1991) refers to the reflexivity of late modern society. These social processes are reflected in structural shifts in British public policy, but also in the current generation's beliefs in their own agency and autonomy as an increasingly acceptable 'vocabulary of motive' (Mills, 1967), both with respect to parenting and their lives more generally. Such beliefs on the part of current generations are more evident among some groups than others (Brannen and Nilsen, 2002). However, they are typically accompanied by silences about the structural contexts and constraints in which agency is embedded (Nilsen and Brannen, 2002), a point that needs to be stressed. Moreover, such insights emerge methodologically in the way in which, during data analysis, the told story is linked to and interpreted in relation to structural and historical contexts.

Conclusion

The stories which the different generations of women relate about their childhoods reflect individual and collective experiences located in historical time. The stories also draw upon normative vocabularies. These differ partly according to the historical periods of lived childhood but also because interviewees were looking back at childhood from different life course stages and different normative climates. The oldest generation – great-grandparents born around the First World War – dwelt on the importance of families being able to provide children with external, materially secure childhoods and family lives. The middle generation – 1940s grandparents – stressed the importance of parents providing internal – psychological – security for the individual child. The youngest (current) generation born in the 1960s and 1970s stood out in their emphasis upon their own agency as parents in shaping their children's childhoods, as well as in their expectations of a more active and involved parenthood.

The two older generations spoke to a world in which children were free from external dangers and in which childhood was in some respects a collectivised community experience; this they contrasted with current concerns about protecting children from the dangers of the external environment. However, great-grandmothers, in contrast to younger generations, do refer to the historical context in their reference to poverty, material conditions and lack of opportunity (notably in education). The 1940s grandmothers in their emphasis on the importance of emotional security for children make no reference to high employment rates in the post-war period, economic stability and a growing welfare state. While the 1960s/70s mothers emphasise their own agency as parents, they are similarly silent about the economic uncertainties of the 1980s and 1990s and the pressure from government for individuals to engage with risk and take on increased responsibility for children.

While clear differences between the accounts of different generations emerged, there were also similarities. All three generations, but especially those from working-class families, referred to the importance of grand-mothers in their childhoods. In periods in which mothers worked when they were 'supposed' to be at home, grandmothers were seen as parental figures as well as carers. The importance of living near grandmothers at times of difficulty was also underlined. In some families who stayed geographically close to one another, grandmothers acted as a central focus for the family not only giving meaning to their lives but also acting as a cohesive force and a source of genetic identity.

3
Mothers' and Fathers' Work and Care Practices over the Generations

This chapter begins to explore the relationship between employment and care across the three adult generations in our study. It does so by focusing upon the practices and life course careers of men and women in paid work and parenthood – their 'lived lives' as mothers and fathers of young children, a critical phase in the life course when British mothers have typically worked less and fathers worked more. Our vantage point is to look at the great-grandparents, the grandparents and the parents as historical cohorts.

We describe the relationship between employment and childcare and the effects of having children upon men's and women's employment. We also describe the specific matter of childcare arrangements made by successive generations while mothers were at work, as well as each generation's views, from the viewpoint of today, on the best childcare arrangements for currently employed parents. We consider both the mainstream – what most did – but also the variations and extremes, the women and men who have gone against the stream. In the next chapters (4 and 5), we home in on particular families and look at how parents justify and give meaning to their practices.

Some caveats should be noted first. Although this chapter is about mothers and fathers, it devotes more space to the former. A main reason for this is that mothers' employment is both more varied and more subject to change across the generations: there is more to describe. This leads to our second point. As we shall show (Chapter 5), fathers' employment practices are relatively stable over the life course and their employment careers seem to follow similar patterns over historical time, at least when compared with mothers'. Both over the mothers' life course and over historical time, the story of mothers' employment is more complex.

In comparing mothers' varied patterns against fathers' predominant pattern, there is a risk of seeing the latter as normative, a standard against which women's employment 'progress' should be assessed. This is not our intent. Indeed we would argue that the contrast of men's and women's employment should serve to problematise all patterns of employment, and reveal men's to be not a necessity but just one possibility. This will become more apparent when, in Chapter 5, we introduce some current fathers who have transgressed the predominant male norm.

But before we turn to our families, we need to locate our analysis of their careers in work and care against the broad backcloth of change in the world of work in Britain in the 20th century, and within the context of policy and the welfare state.

Employment over the century

The 20th century witnessed strong changes in paid work, one of our two main subjects. The beginning and ending of working life has shifted. Lengthening education has led to later entry into permanent employment, while at the other end of the life course retirement from paid work has increasingly occurred at or around state pensionable age (Thane, 2000). According to the 1901 census, for example, when school-leaving age was still 12, 10 per cent of 10- to 14-year-old boys were 'engaged in occupations'; while in 1901 nearly 40 per cent of men aged 75 or over were still working compared to less than 10 per cent of men in 2001 who had reached the state pension age of 65 (Lindsay, 2003). Increasing longevity and the inadequacy of pensions may, however, lead to a reversal of this trend in future years.

Perhaps most striking of all though, has been the relative employment position of men and women. There is, it should be acknowledged straightaway, problems of counting. Especially in the early decades of the 20th century, it is likely that the amount of paid work done by married women has been 'grossly underestimated', one reason being that Census returns for this period 'ignore casual part-time jobs' (Roberts, 1986, p. 227) – which, as we will see when we get on to our families, were common among the great-grandmother generation, especially during the phase of childrearing. Even so, the broad picture is clear. Over the century, male economic activity has steadily declined, while women's has steadily increased. Thus in 1901, around five million women worked, making just over a quarter (29 per cent) of the total workforce; a century later the figure had risen to 13 million, nearly half (46 per cent) of the total workforce (Lindsay, 2003). The most striking increase has occurred from the 1960s, with the female employment rate increasing from 47 to 69 per cent between 1959 and 1999. During the same period, the employment rate for men has fallen 15 percentage points, from 94 to 79 per cent (Office of National Statistics, 2001, Chart 4.1).

Much of this growth in women's employment has been in part-time jobs. Although there has also been a slow increase in part-time working among men, the great majority of male employment remains full time. Much of the growth in women's employment can also be attributed to increasing employment among married women in general and women with children in particular. Between the Wars, marriage bars were introduced in certain occupations to stop married women entering (or remaining in) them, contributing to a large difference in economic activity between married and non-married women of the same age. In 1921, for example, only 9 per cent of married women aged between 25 and 44 years were employed compared to 32 per cent of all women in this age group; but by 1966 this gap had been greatly narrowed (38 per cent compared to 42 per cent) (Department of Employment and Productivity, 1971, Table 109).

Married women were also less likely to work because they were more likely to have children: motherhood continued to suppress employment, even as the effect of marriage *per se* faded in the post-war years. Even today, 'the presence of a dependent child in the family still has a major effect on the economic activity of women' (Office of National Statistics, 2003, p. 75). In 2000, when conducting our interviews, nationally just over half of all women with a child under 5 (54 per cent) were employed compared to nearly three-quarters (72 per cent) with no dependent children, and the former were less likely to be employed full time than the latter (Twomey, 2001, Table C).

Despite the continuing impact of motherhood on employment, major employment changes have occurred among the current generation of women with young children, especially from the late 1980s onwards. Just over a quarter of women with a child under 5 years (27 per cent) was employed in 1980; by 2002, this had more than doubled to 56 per cent (Office of National Statistics, 2003). Moreover, although most employed women with young children still work part time, much of the recent growth in employment has been in full-time work. In 1980, only just over a quarter of employed mothers worked full time: by 2002, a third did so.

These overall figures disguise varying experiences amongst different groups of women. Employment growth has been rapid amongst the more advantaged, in particular, women with high levels of education, living with employed partners and buying their own homes. It has been lower among women with little or no education, living without partners or with non-employed partners or in social housing (Brannen and Moss, 1998). In 2000, employment rates among women with a child under 15 years of age varied from 81 per cent among those with a high-level qualification to 65 per cent with a mid-level qualification and just 37 per cent for those with low or no qualifications (Escobedo *et al.*, 2002, based on European Labour Force Survey data).

The Women and Employment Survey (referred to below as WES) provides a unique insight into changes in maternal employment among women of our two older generations (Martin and Roberts, 1984). It plots the employment histories of nearly 5600 women aged between 16 and 59, born between 1920 and 1964. This survey confirms, and also elaborates, a number of the broad trends in women's employment outlined above: of overall growth and more continuity in employment across child-rearing years, but also of increasing differentiation between women. Over the period 1920–80, employment increased among successive cohorts of women aged 30 and over, mainly due to increased participation by women in their 30s and 40s and rising part-time working. Fewer women left employment at marriage; the proportion of those not working between marriage and their first childbirth fell from around 37 per cent in the 1940s to 12 per cent to the 1970s.

At the same time, interruption in employment following the birth of a first child continued to be widespread with only 14 per cent of women in the most recent cohort returning to work within six months of their first birth and hardly any women (3 per cent) with more than one child. Yet some changes were apparent in the employment behaviour of mothers: women, Martin and Roberts noted, 'increasingly tend to return to work between births and to return to work sooner after childbearing is finished, particularly if they have worked between births' (p. 137). And within this overall trend, some movement was discernible of more women returning to work within six months of their first birth.

So far we have dwelt on changing levels of participation by women and men in the labour market. But the changes in the labour force over the 20th century go further. There have been changes in the type of work undertaken. Industries which drove 19th century economic growth (coal, textiles, iron and steel, shipbuilding, railways, heavy engineering) have declined, while new industries (electronics, consumer goods, chemicals, cars) have grown – then often in their turn declined. Overall, manufacturing employment has slumped and with it manual work, including a large swathe of skilled jobs undertaken by men: accounting for three-quarters of the workforce in 1911, by 1981 manual workers made up just over a third (Halsey, 2000).

The growth of services and non-manual work has, however, more than compensated for this decline in manufacturing. One source of new jobs in the post-war years, which will figure strongly in the employment histories of women in our study families, was an expanding welfare state – in education, health and social services. Most of these new and mainly public-sector service jobs went to women, as have whole areas of new service sector employment in the private sector. But women have also made strong headway in longer established areas of employment. In 1911, clerical and sales work mainly employed men; but by 1981, four out of five workers were women. Though occurring later, women's share of jobs in management and administration has also risen, from 24 per cent of the workforce in 1981 to a projected 41 per cent by 2006 (Equal Opportunities Commission, 2001).

These changes in work have, in turn, produced shifting patterns of occupational mobility, that is, the extent to which individuals are able to move into higher status jobs. Across the whole population, men and women, Gershuny (1993) found a slowing down of upward mobility from manual occupations to higher status professional and technical occupations over the four decades from 1941. Aldridge (2001) concludes that the evidence points to a halt in upward social mobility. This, he adds, has been mainly due to a falling back among men, which is associated with slower growth in the number of professional and managerial jobs and a contraction in skilled manual work. By contrast, in recent decades at least, women have, to some extent, enjoyed more upward mobility than men: 'better education, increased labour force participation and improved opportunities at work have had a positive effect on women's social status' (ibid., para. 36). In short, as Payne and Roberts (2002) suggest, opportunities for men fell while they increased for women especially during the 1990s. However, this improved social mobility has mainly been 'part of a catching up process', and, to put it into further perspective, more room for women 'has been found in the "middle" rather than "at the top" (which may not really constitute a move up for working class women)' (Aldridge, 2001, para. 35).

This picture of faltering upward mobility is confirmed by a recent study of intergenerational income mobility, based on the experience of two birth cohorts, the first born in 1958 (10 to 15 years later than our grandparents), the second in 1970 (about the same time as our parents). Blanden *et al.* (2002) conclude that 'we see sharp falls in cross-generational mobility of economic status... [with] the economic status of the 1970 cohort much more strongly connected to parental economic status than the 1958 cohort' (p. 18). They suggest that one cause of this diminishing mobility is the greater advantage taken of expanding higher education by young people from richer families, 'an unintended consequence of the expansion of the university system that occurred in the late 1980s and early 1990s' (ibid.).

Public policy and the welfare state

Recent increases in maternal employment have been in spite of, rather than with the support of, public policy. Until the mid-1990s, such policy support amounted to a statutory right to maternity leave, introduced in 1976 and unusual, by international standards, for its length (long) and level of payment (low). The small amount of publicly funded childcare was limited to 'children in need', a concept which did not include parental employment as a criterion. Modest initiatives to support childcare for working parents began in 1995 under the Conservative government, and have been expanded under the post-1997 Labour administration. The change of government in 1997 was also significant for a change in the tone of policy towards mothers' employment: there was a turn from opposition or studied neutrality to positive encouragement, to the extent indeed of setting a target for increasing employment among lone mothers. The government, in its policy document setting out a National Childcare Strategy: 'welcomes women's greater involvement and equality in the workplace and wants to ensure that all those women who wish to can take up these opportunities' (DfEE, 1998, para. 1.6).

Given this history, successive generations of parents (in practice, usually mothers) needing or wanting formal childcare, and able to pay, have had to look to private providers, most commonly childminders, but also nannies and private day nurseries. These nursery places have increased rapidly from the late 1980s onwards in response to rising numbers of dual earner, higher income families, and Britain today has the highest proportionate level of for-profit nurseries of any country in the world (for a fuller discussion of the recent development of childcare policy, see Cohen *et al.*, 2004). However, study after study has shown that informal arrangements have in the past and still remain the main source of non-parental childcare, in particular grandparents (Bryson *et al.*, 1999; La Valle *et al.*, 2000). For successive generations of women, employment has most often meant part-time work that permits either fathers or family members to care for children.

Minimalist public policy can be linked to a variety of other phenomena, which individually and cumulatively have militated against mothers' employment (whilst, at the same time, working against fathers assuming more responsibility for childcare). The British welfare state has been described both as liberal, implying an orientation to targeted services, low benefit levels and an emphasis on individual responsibility (Esping-Andersen, 1990, 1999), and as maternalist: '[T]he "maternalist" assumption that the mother's primary and natural duty is to look after her child, and that as an extension childcare is and should be a "women's" issue, has been literally embodied in the political process, through a gender division of labour running virtually up to the top' (Connell, 1990, p. 183). The 'maternalist' assumption that young children should be in the exclusive care of their mothers, predominant throughout the 20th century, has influenced ideas about what care is appropriate for them, should mothers be unable or unwilling to fulfil their 'primary and natural duty'. Singer (1993) uses the term 'attachment pedagogy' to express the idea that mother care is needed for secure development and that, in its absence, non-maternal care requires to be modelled on a dyadic mother–child relationship (for example, care by grandmothers).

This mix of liberalism and maternalism has encouraged a popular discourse of childcare being a 'private matter' and a climate of opinion that has been hostile to mothers going out to work. For much of the 20th century *married* women's paid employment was seen as barely compatible with their domestic responsibilities including motherhood (Dally, 1982), and even when married women's employment became more acceptable, widespread opposition remained to the employment of women with young children. The 1980 WES study reported that 80 per cent of women held the view that mothers of pre-school age children 'ought to stay at home' or only go out to work if they 'really need the money'. This was somewhat fewer than the 95 per cent who held this view in 1965 but still an overwhelming majority (Martin and Roberts, 1984, Table 12.11). Nearly 10 years later, in 1989, two-thirds of respondents in the British Social Attitudes Survey (64 per cent) thought that women should stay at home when they had a child under school age, while a mere 2 per cent thought women in these circumstances should work full time (26 per cent opted for part-time work) (Social and Community Planning Research, 1992).

Indeed, even today, the question of the effects of *mothers'* employment on their children remains a subject of research (see, for example, Joshi and Verropoulou, 2000; Ermisch and Francesoni, 2001; Gregg and Washbook, 2003) and public debate. The assumption behind such studies and debates is that the employment of one parent (i.e. the mother) can be extracted from overall household employment practices and that its consequences can be treated in isolation. An alternative approach, which did not start from the presumption that mothers' employment was problematic, would be to compare families according to the number of employed members and their working patterns, which would focus attention on the part played by both parents in employment and childcare, and the interplay of father's and mother's employment.

Employment and care over three generations

Great-grandparents

With one exception, the great-grandparents had retired from paid work. They were therefore looking back on a part of their lives that could seem far removed both in time and from their current preoccupations. This, together with employment histories frequently dominated by parttime jobs, many of short duration, rendered the great-grandmothers' recollections rather sketchy: with each successive generation, employment accounts get more precise.

Ida Masters was born in 1914, and worked continuously from leaving school at 13 or 14 until she married at the age of 21, in a variety of jobs including shop work and cleaning. The precise details of her employment between the ages of 21 and 47 are unsurprisingly, hazy: 'Since I've been married I've gone out to, I've taken the kids with me and done cleaning... Yeah, I went doing this cleaning. Oh I've 'ad several cleaning jobs. I cleaned for a schoolteacher. And I cleaned for a chap that was in a jewellery shop. Who else did I clean for? I cleaned for another lady, that 'ad 3 or 4 children. Different times, y'know'. It is only at the age of 47, when her youngest child was 8, that her employment history becomes clearer. She reported taking a job as a kitchen assistant, then working as a cleaner, cook and dinner lady until she retired at 61.

Paid work was clearly a frequent practice for Ida while she was bringing up her children. Coming from a poor mining community in the north of England, and bringing up children in the 1940s and 1950s, she took it for granted that women had to work, even when they had children. With four children and a husband not earning a great deal, paid work was a necessity, to be combined with unpaid work – 'Well, you fitted yer work in didn't yer?' But whether she worked continuously is now impossible to say.

Brenda Smith, born in 1924, also from a poor working-class community, this time in London, shared this taken-for-granted attitude to paid work.

Now in her 70s, and still doing a few hours cleaning a week, she summarised her employment career: 'I've always worked'. Her working life spanned 60 years and she mentioned many occupations: working in a railway goods yard loading food, shop work, making curtains at home, working in a café and council lunch club, shelf-filling – and above all cleaning, an occupation which figured frequently in the employment histories of the two older generations. She also combined these jobs with unpaid childcare, looking after the children of her sister and daughters. Employment often meant fitting jobs around childcare, working early mornings, evenings – a recurring relationship across the generations, especially among the two older generations.

So, in the circumstances, it is hardly surprising that Brenda, like Ida Masters, did not offer a detailed employment history; she had long since lost count of the many jobs she had done. It may be that she had not literally worked continuously all her adult life – although it is not impossible. More likely, when Brenda said she had always worked, this meant that, like Ida, paid work was an expectation for economic survival amongst women living in her working-class community, and that she had spent much of her life earning:

We wanted things, just basic things. We needed things ... nobody resented – you know, everybody, the mums went out to work. You wanted something, you went out to work and got it ... [M]en didn't earn an awful lot of money – very few women was able to sit at home and wallow.

It was also difficult to get more than a sketchy outline of the employment histories of the *great-grandfathers*. Of the seven in the study, five started work at the age of 14 or 15. The work of many of this generation was predominantly manual and in some cases casual. Their employment histories were not only lengthy but also again complex making them difficult to recall.

As we show in Chapter 5, all great-grandfathers were sole or main breadwinners, although not without difficulty in some cases where employment was disrupted by events well beyond their control: a world war and military service; the Depression of the inter-war years and its attendant unemployment; and, in one case (a great-grandfather now dead), racial persecution in Nazi Germany and migration. Moreover, great-grandmothers' accounts also testified to fears concerning the commonplace risks for this generation that male breadwinners might become unemployed, sick or die (see Chapter 2).

Wartime service, common among great-grandfathers, interrupted employment careers, though it might also have positive longer-term consequences. Great-grandfather Bill Ashton, born in 1921, joined the RAF in the Second World War and trained as a radio navigator. After the war, he became a radio engineer and joined a publicly owned airline industry that provided 'a fantastic opportunity' and a job for life. But men's absence from home in wartime could also have serious implications both for their involvement in childcare and for their relationships with their children. Great-grandfather Miller (one of the majority of men in the great-grandparent generation no longer alive) was away for most of the war years. His son John, born in 1941, recalled his father returning from war: 'I said who is this strange man? He'd been away for five or six years, you see. Er, he came home once, but I never saw him. So there wasn't a bond between us. And over the years, it got thinner and thinner.'

Like the men, employment started at an early age (by today's standards) for the *great-grandmothers*, typically at 14 or 15 (Table 3.1).

Table 3.1   Women's work histories and childcare arrangements

	Great-grandmothers ($n = 16$)	Grandmothers ($n = 12$)	Mothers ($n = 11$)[a]
Age when started working	(1 never employed + 2 never employed after marriage)		
Range	14–18	15–21	15–22
Median	14	16	18
Age of youngest child when working	(4 never employed when had children)		(1 not employed since motherhood)
Range	Under 1–10 + years	Under 1–10 + years	Under 1–5 years
Median	Under 5 years	Under 1 year	Under 1 year
If employed after having children, if worked full time			
Never	6 (including 2 who may have worked)	3	6
Some	4	4	2
Most/All	2	5	2
Retirement age	1 still employed; 1 never employed; 14 retired	6 still employed; 6 retired	None retired
Range	22–late 70s	29–53	
Median	63	52	

Career progression	3	8	3	
Professional or managerial job	3	5	5	•
Childcare arrangements mentioned when employed full time				
Formal	3	2	3	
Informal	2	4	2	
Not needed	0	2	0	
Childcare arrangements when employed part time				
Formal	1	1	2	
Informal	3	3	6	
Not needed	12	9	5	
Childcare arrangements for full-time employed parents in vignette[b]				
Nursery	4	2	3	
Childminder	2	3	2	
Grandparents	7	4	3	
Grandparents + others	0	4	3	
Other	1	1	1	
No information	3	0	1	

[a] Twelfth interviewee in late pregnancy. Expected to resume work on part-time basis when child under 1 year.

[b] In a few cases more than one arrangement was chosen, so totals come to more than numbers in each generation.

Note: 'Childcare arrangements' include each childcare arrangement mentioned, so totals come to more than the number of women in each generation. 'Not needed' refers to non-parental care not being needed, often because working fathers cared for their children while mothers were at work. If fathers provided care while not employed, this arrangement is included in 'family/friends': this occurs only for the parent generation, and accounts for one arrangement when mothers were employed full time and two while mothers were employed part time.

As we saw in Chapter 2, a recurrent theme among these women was the lack of educational opportunities, spontaneously raised in 9 of the 16 interviews. Obstacles included the financial cost and parents' lack of encouragement to daughters. Eileen Peters recollected that her father had little ambition for her, and that at the time 'fathers looked after their sons more. The thing was that girls were going to be married. So they didn't need the higher education or the money spent on education. The boys did'. Her brothers went to the technical college and her father paid for them to go, 'whereas nothing was spent on my sister and I'.

Another obstacle to a good education was the grammar school admission examination. Passing this, however, was no guarantee of access to new opportunities. Doreen Hurd passed in the mid-1920s, but her family was too poor for her to benefit: 'my mother couldn't afford to send me to any other school...Cos you had to buy the clothes, didn't you? Of course...And she couldn't afford that, so I never went to another school. I stayed on at this one till I was fourteen.' However this was not the end of Doreen's unfulfilled academic ambitions. She wanted to be a teacher, and 'in them days you could carry on and be a teacher without going to college'. But the need to support the family financially came first: 'I would've loved to be a teacher, but you had to find a job where you earned some money.' So she became a nursery nurse. Even that was not the end, for though she says she loved her job, at 16 she had to move to a factory because it offered better pay.

Even going to grammar school could be a daunting experience for working-class girls. At the age of 11, in 1935, Brenda Smith, the youngest of seven children of a poor family, got a scholarship for a grammar school. She was quickly disillusioned: 'it was very class conscious... that's the first thing that changed my life...because there were rich kids there...[and] anything that was naughty, went wrong or anything, the nuns used to automatically blame the scholarship boys...the richer you were, the better you got treated.' She found herself 'out of whack' with both the children at school and the children where she lived – 'I lived two lives...a very mixed up life...so, on the whole that didn't do me any good'.

Maureen Horton also got a grammar school place, in 1930, but had to leave at 16 due to her father's incapacity and the consequent need to find employment. Her father went blind 'and so I had to – I left school and got a job'. This, however, was not the end. Maureen subsequently went on to train as a nurse, then as a teacher. She was the only great-grandmother to achieve a professional qualification.

Four of the 16 great-grandmothers had very short or no employment careers: one was never employed, two never worked after marriage and a fourth never worked again after having children. The remaining 12 had an interrupted employment career in which they resumed employment for some time after a break (Table 3.1). Seven reported going back to work when at least one of their children was under 5 years of age, two when they had a child under 2 (a third great-grandmother *may* have done so, but her employment history is not detailed enough to be certain), in both cases as a consequence of special external conditions – wartime. For Mildred Ashton, born in 1921, the war had an impact on her life that went far beyond employment. Married at 19 to an army officer she had known only briefly, she was soon both pregnant and aware that the marriage was a mistake. She saw little of her husband, who was serving overseas, and went to work in a munitions factory when her daughter was 1½ years old, first using a childminder then, following a near miss from a bomb, sending her child to live with a relative. Towards the end of the war she met Bill, her current husband. They began to cohabit, followed by Mildred giving up work, bringing back her daughter to live with her and, in due course, getting divorced from her first husband and marrying Bill.

Not only did the passage of time influence great-grandmothers' memories of employment, so too the negative social climate towards mothers working may also have shaped recollections. Doreen Hurd, born in 1912, spoke of resuming work in 1952 as a shop assistant when her oldest child, Celia, was 11 and her youngest child aged three. But Celia, her daughter, remembered her mother doing paid work at home before she went into shop work: 'my recollection is that my mother always had some kind of work, either within or without the home ... either sewing type or cleaning type work or catering type work ... she used to launder somebody's shirts ... she served food at dances.' Celia was in no doubt that the reason her mother did this work was 'purely financial and purely motivated by what she could find that she could do in the home.' In the circumstances, we cannot tell whether Doreen failed to mention this earlier return to employment because it had slipped her mind or because she did not see such work as a 'proper' job or because she preferred not to admit to returning to work at an earlier stage of motherhood.

Employment for great-grandmothers after having children was mainly part time (only two women reported working full time for most of the rest of their working lives). None maintained a continuous work record. In other words, consistent with the larger-scale picture presented by WES (Martin and Roberts, 1984), going back to work when there were young children was more likely to be for a short period followed by other breaks in employment.

Only one great-grandmother was in a professional occupation. We have already mentioned how Maureen Horton trained and worked successively as a nurse and teacher. Two other women had been managers, one junior, the other senior running a family firm. In the former case,

Josephine Prentice spent much of her working life in low skilled jobs, including office work and cleaning. In her 40s she became a part-time play worker, and successfully worked her way up to a management position in the local authority play service: she attributed this to her hard work and the many courses she attended. Then having taken early retirement, partly because of personal problems, she went back to a series of casual and low skilled jobs, which left her financially insecure and uncertain when interviewed about whether or not to give up paid work.

Both Maureen and Josephine came from working-class backgrounds. Maureen followed two well-trodden paths for women of her day into higher status work, nursing and teaching. Josephine, the youngest great-grandmother among our families, born in 1935, took another path opened up through the expansion of new kinds of public services in the 1970s before she fell back to her previous occupational status. In contrast, Margaret Kent, the third great-grandmother to have professional or managerial employment, came from a middle-class German Jewish business family. Fleeing Nazi persecution, she came to Britain as a refugee. After the War, she came in middle age to run a family firm, starting in management when her husband became ill then continuing to run the firm after he died.

These three great-grandmothers were the only women in this generation to show any career progression, Maureen over the course of her working life, the other two only later in life. The employment histories of the other great-grandmothers followed a similar pattern: a string of jobs, short term, often casual, with part-time hours frequently worked early or late in the day and at weekends to ensure the 'family care' of children. Typical occupations to which these great-grandmothers returned in the post-war period, during or after bringing up their children, were to be found in the growing public sector – as dinner ladies and cooks in school kitchens, and as home helps and cleaners. Most were 'little jobs' involving cooking and cleaning, shop work and making clothes and furnishings. These are just the type of jobs to be overlooked, in official statistics and people's memories. In any case, employment is discussed by this generation as part of a larger mosaic in which paid work is interleaved with family life, difficult to separate out as an employment career and to place into a neatly ordered sequence. Unlike the great-grandfathers, employment among this generation of women was organised around care responsibilities, mostly involving children.

If great-grandparents started working at an early age, this was not matched by early retirement. Four of the seven great-grandfathers who were interviewed had retired at 65 or older. While of the

12 great-grandmothers who had worked since having children, one was still doing some cleaning in her 70s and nine others had retired over the age of 60.

Grandparents

When interviewed, each generation in our 12 families was at a different stage of working life – retirement, nearing retirement and entering mid-working-life. In our grandparent generation, though nearing retirement, six of the 12 women and 11 of the 12 men were still employed. We do not therefore have complete employment histories for this generation.

This generation, as we outlined in Chapter 1, left education rather later than their parents, entering work on average at 16 (Table 3.1), and more had qualifications. However, despite the extension of state education, there was again a widespread sense of missed educational opportunities among women and for the same reasons – gender discrimination by parents, general lack of parental support and family circumstances. Like her mother Brenda, Pauline Smith's education was thwarted. Born in 1947, in the mid-1960s, she secured a place at art college to study industrial design, but was not able to do the course: 'at that particular time my dad got very ill and my mum needed a wage. My brother was just taking his O levels and in those days it was far more important for boys to have a higher education than girls.' Like her mother, Pauline's sense of missed opportunities was expressed, and perhaps felt more strongly, in the current context in which girls have surpassed boys in the education stakes: 'the things you regret most are the things you didn't do ... I didn't go to art college, I wanted to go and I didn't go. I wouldn't be stuck in this horrible council job now, I'd be doing what I wanted to do.'

Half of the grandfathers stayed on at school beyond 16, mostly going on to get higher qualifications. They developed 'careers' in the sense that they progressed up organisational ladders, some significantly improving upon their own fathers' employment record. Several went into public-sector professional occupations which offered security and promotion opportunities (Thompson, 1997). Born in 1943, Richard Samuels, whose own father had been a bank cashier and had started work at 14 or 15, went to university and became a university lecturer, gaining several higher degrees in the process. Born six years earlier, Michael Hurd, whose father was a fitter and later ran a small shop because of ill health, won a scholarship to university; he became a professional engineer progressing to management level in a large public-sector organisation. George Masters, born in 1942, failed some A levels and, because his mother was a widow, felt compelled to find a job, following his father's footsteps to work in the local power station. However, he pursued this occupational route to a higher level, studying part time and eventually completing his professional examinations. With one exception, all had unbroken work records, most staying with the same employer for many years and having few spells of unemployment. Michael Hurd was unusual in experiencing unemployment, in the early 1970s; although lasting only a short period, he said it was a great shock at the time, a period when unemployment at his occupational level was uncommon.

The grandfathers who left school at 15 or 16 without qualifications and without skills present a very different picture. All but one started apprenticeships but not all finished them. None pursued 'careers' as such, while several changed course occupationally. Moreover, some experienced interruptions in their employment histories though later rather than earlier in their employment careers, reflecting the employment trends of the times. Joseph Ashton, born in 1948, started an apprenticeship as an electrician in the mid-1960s but did not finish; he went on to a string of unskilled jobs, ending up as a window fitter. Peter Smith, born a year earlier, went straight into unskilled work and was a bus driver when interviewed. Paul Prentice, born in 1951, did an upholstery apprenticeship but was made redundant on its completion. Upholstery not paying enough to provide for his large family, thereafter he did a variety of short-term jobs before settling down: first, as a milkman supplemented by some evening youth work with the local authority and then, after a long spell on the 'sick', he became a postman. Two further grandfathers completed apprenticeships and worked for themselves in their own businesses.

The grandfathers' employment careers, like their fathers', were affected by parenthood in the sense that they were main breadwinners and family providers (discussed further in Chapter 5): parenthood confirmed their engagement in the world of paid work, though for most this did not mean working long hours of overtime. Grandmothers' employment was also affected but, like their mothers, this took the form of breaks in employment and, when employed, an increased likelihood of part-time work. At the two extremes, one grandmother had only the most minimal employment career after marriage, while one worked continuously.

Fiona Prentice, born in 1955, left school at 15, did a series of unskilled jobs such as cleaning and shop work, reduced to part-time work on marriage at 18 then stopped work when her first child was born, also at 18. Subsequently she had worked only for a short period, as what she called an 'au pair' (looking after her employer's children in their own home), when 29 and her fourth child had started school. She gave up this job for a number of reasons: her husband's opposition to her working, her son's aversion to staying for school meals, and because Fiona herself disliked the job and did not feel strongly motivated to work. Aged 45 at interview, the youngest grandmother in the study, she had not worked for 16 years and would have liked to do so – but was now not fit enough due to arthritis.

A second grandmother – as it happens born and raised in the same working-class area of London as Fiona Prentice – was at the other end of the employment spectrum. Pauline Smith, born in 1947, had worked continuously since leaving school. In some respects, she had a very similar employment career to her mother, Brenda – although she had only one child compared to Brenda's three. Like Brenda, Pauline said she 'always had to work because [my husband] never earned . . . big money . . . I always needed to work'. Both generations took it for granted that women had to earn to sustain the family income, and Pauline was very aware of the continuities in attitude and practice between herself and her mother as well as with other women in the family:

> everybody worked in some way or other. I mean, a lot – most women in my family did cleaning. I mean they did early morning and late-evening cleaning. Because that was the times you could – there was someone to mind the children. The older ones looked after the younger ones . . . My mum used to do it, my mum's only ever done cleaning, I can't remember my mother ever doing anything else . . . my nan must have been in her late 60s when she gave up scrubbing . . . my mum wouldn't understand anyone not working, if you need money you've got to go out to work for it and that's it.

Mother and daughter, however, differed in one important respect: the type of work they did. Great-grandmother Brenda had a string of manual jobs, mainly part time. Her daughter, Pauline also had a string of part-time jobs when her son was young, including office cleaning, bar work, with a detective agency and bookkeeping, sometimes freelance. But from the time her son went to secondary school, she had had a full-time job with the same public-sector employer.

The employment careers of 10 other grandmothers were marked by interruptions. Like Pauline, but unlike Fiona Prentice, the 1940s grandmothers had all worked for substantial periods since having children. Having left employment when they had their first child, they resumed work or education, most when they had young children below school age, and the majority when they had a child under 1 year. If we include Pauline Smith, the continuous worker, 9 out of 12 grandmothers had worked at some stage when they had a pre-school age child (Table 3.1). Only two, however, resumed employment permanently at this stage.

So there are some similarities between the patterns of employment of great-grandmothers and grandmothers. Overall, in terms of length, most had substantial employment careers, with interruptions mainly around childrearing and frequent part-time work – although full-time work after having children figures more with grandmothers. While a more continuous resumption of work usually occurred once children were at school, in many cases women did some paid work when their children were still under 5 years of age. In both generations, working hours and employment histories were shaped by the demands of childcare.

But generational change emerges when we look at employment from another perspective. For the 1940s grandmothers, work in the public sector was increasingly significant: and linked to this, employment 'careers' emerge more strongly, with more upward mobility into managerial or professional work. Three great-grandmothers achieved professional or managerial occupations: among grandmothers the figure rises to eight. In contrast to their husbands (see Chapter 5), such upward occupational mobility took place later in the life course, in the post-motherhood phase (Table 3.1).

In some cases, this later upward mobility matched the upward mobility already achieved by husbands. Diana Horton, born in 1946, came from a professional family and, although not encouraged by her father to follow in his footsteps as an architect, she did go to college to study art. She worked in a shop and a graphic design studio for a year before stopping work when she had her first child. Subsequently, while her children were young, she had a string of part-time low skilled jobs (bar work, shelf stacking, cleaning). After a third child was born, she retrained as a teacher, entered the profession and, in her fifties went full time. Her husband Bernard, whose father was in manual work but whose mother, Maureen Horton, had progressed to teaching after motherhood, had also gone to art school then entered a career in teaching straight after graduating. Diana only caught him up professionally in her fifties.

A similar example is Marjorie Samuels, also from a middle-class family. Born in 1942, Marjorie left school at 15, went into a secretarial job, married at 19, then left work on having her first child at 20. For the next five years she was a full-time mother, interspersed with what she refers to as 'odd jobs for pin money' and taking in paying guests. But when her youngest child was 3 years old she embarked on six years of education, A levels followed by a diploma and degree. Armed with this, she worked continuously in a series of full-time jobs, culminating in a senior management post in the National Health Service. By contrast, her husband Richard, who we discussed earlier in this section, pursued an upwardly mobile career following the end of his university course, which he took straight from school.

There are examples also of career progression among grandmothers with no or few qualifications and who did not return to education. Shirley Ashton, born in 1948, after working in offices, in a warehouse, and as a cleaner and a shop assistant, typically on a part-time basis when her children were small, eventually went on to become a sales support manager in a food company, albeit in a very junior management position, but working full time. Her husband, a window fitter, did not experience a similar occupational rise.

Six of the 12 grandmothers were still employed at the time of being interviewed, so a strict comparison of retirement cannot be made with their mothers' generation. However, half had ended their employment careers, one (Fiona Prentice) hardly having ever worked but the other five through 'early' retirement, on average in their early 50s. As we shall describe in Chapter 6, this was in part at least related to care commitments.

Parents

The working lives of the parent generation were still in midstream, making a full comparison with the older two generations impossible. As we saw in Chapter 1, this youngest adult generation had left school at an older age and were rather more likely to have some form of qualification, in a context of growing credentialism and expanding higher education. Not surprisingly, this generation made little reference to thwarted educational ambitions.

While the youngest generation of fathers was more likely than their fathers to have gained a degree or professional qualification (one was still doing so), those in higher status occupations had fathers who had also achieved high status or skilled occupations. Five working-class fathers followed their fathers into low skilled work while a sixth went into the family building business as his father and grandfather had done. Before doing so, however, he gained a vocational qualification in building management.

Most of the higher qualified fathers, had pursued 'careerist' paths, with management responsibility, for example a father who was a professional engineer in a large utility; a self-employed TV producer; a sales director of a big insurance company; an accountant in a private-sector company. One graduate father, who did not follow a conventional career route, pursued his interest in music, eventually setting up his own small record-distribution company. There was some movement of sons into private-sector employment where their fathers (in law) had been in public-sector jobs. For example, Patrick Horton, born in 1967, worked in the independent television industry, and Stephen Samuels, born 1962, ran his own business: both had fathers who were teachers.

Those men working in professional and intermediate professional jobs dwelt on the fact that they had to work long hours. Moreover, as we will discuss in Chapter 5, this contrasts with the experience of some of their own fathers who, at a similar point in the life course, worked standard hours. Reactions to working long hours were mixed. Sean Brand, who had taken over running the family's building business, generally welcomed the pressure at work, yet felt overextended. Mark Peters, an engineer with a utility, said he wanted to resist the demand to work long hours although he was at the time still actively seeking promotion and complying with his employer's demands. James Kent, a director of an insurance company, seemed to like the pressure of his corporate job and also ran his own business in his own time, but had temporarily cut down on his hours in order to become more involved with his children – while envisaging stepping up the pace again when he started a new senior management position. Douglas Masters, an accountant, was rather ambivalent about his long hours since, he said, it meant missing out on his children but he was still anxious to 'get on' in the company. Thomas Miller worked in the finance sector and was responsible for a large geographical area; he was ambivalent about demands to be constantly on call but accepted it was part of the job.

But at the same time as some fathers seemed to work substantially longer hours than older generations of fathers, there were also signs of significant change in the other direction. Three fathers – all from low skilled occupational backgrounds – had made major changes in their employment, to enable them to assume more responsibility for children: for the first time, therefore, we find some men assuming major care responsibilities and making major employment changes in consequence. We will discuss this group in more detail in Chapter 5, just noting the cases at this point. Luke Ashton, born in 1969, changed his working pattern to fit in with his partner's (both worked full time) and shared the care of his two young children. Graham Hurd, born in 1960, gave up a low paid job to look after two young children, which he combined with studying for a degree at university. Andrew Prentice, 16 years younger, also devoted himself full time to parenting for some years after becoming a father at 18.

The effects of motherhood on women's employment remain strong for this generation, but they are substantially less than for the older generations. As with the grandmothers, there are two extremes. Two women were not working *before* becoming pregnant with their first child. Both were from working-class backgrounds and left school at 16, but both also had somewhat unusual histories. Jane Smith, born in 1965 and raised in inner London, had worked after school in a number of low skilled jobs, before leaving home to travel (in itself, a new departure compared to previous generations of women). Having lived in Greece for more than 10 years, where she had a variety of jobs mainly in shops and bars, she returned to London at 29, where she took up a childcare course, which she completed while pregnant. She had not sought work after the birth of either her first or second child, in striking contrast to her partner's mother and grandmother – Brenda and Pauline Smith – who were from a similar background but, as we have seen, worked continuously after the birth of their children.

Sheila Prentice, born in 1975, had not worked from the time she left school at 15 until the birth of her first child at 19. Five years of non-employment and another child followed, before she took a part-time shop job when her youngest child was 3 years old. During this time, she and her partner, Andrew, brought up their children together, living on state benefits.

At the other extreme were women who had worked continuously with only a short break after childbirth, that is resuming employment within 12 months after giving birth. However this extreme, followed by only one member of the grandmother generation, accounts for 7 of the 12 mothers, while an eighth woman, Sarah Hillyard, seven months pregnant with her first child when interviewed, intended to resume her job within a few months after the birth. Both of the other two mothers had had a break in employment of more than a year, but both had worked for a period when at least one of their children was under 1 year old (Table 3.1).

This generation, therefore, reflecting wider trends in employment among women having children in the late 1980s and 1990s, were coming back to work earlier than the older generations, and were showing fewer signs of interrupted employment careers – at least at this stage of motherhood. A distinct feature of this generation is the availability and use of maternity leave, introduced as a statutory right in 1976. Six mothers had taken their entitlement for at least one pregnancy. One had returned full time to her former job after both of her pregnancies. In her case, therefore, maternity leave had been used to maintain continuity of full-time employment over all births.

In the other cases, the picture was not so clear cut. One mother, Annabelle Peters, took maternity leave with her first pregnancy as an insurance policy in case anything 'went wrong', but did not go back to her former employer or, indeed, to any type of employment until her first child was 3 years old. Two mothers negotiated a part-time return to work either after their first or second period of maternity leave. The fourth case, Rachel Hurd, was not eligible for maternity leave with her first child, having worked only a few months with her employer (eligibility conditions were very restrictive until 1998). But when interviewed, she was on maternity leave after the birth of her second child. She was planning to go back to work when the leave ended, although there was some question about whether she would return full time or part time and whether or not she would go back to her current employer or find a new job.

The final case, Naomi Samuels, took maternity leave with her first pregnancy and resumed full-time employment seven months after her son was born. But with her second pregnancy and expecting twins she decided she would give up work altogether and not take maternity leave. She was, she said, disillusioned with teaching, could not face the cost and effort involved in making childcare arrangements and also felt that 'I can't go into schools and tell people how to bring up children while I'm putting mine at a childminders'. Yet within five months of the birth, Naomi was back, not in her former job but doing part-time supply teaching at her old school, having been asked to return by the head teacher. One reason for returning to work was the need for money to enable the family to move house and area:

> I could never work again. Here [where they now live, in a rural area], I could just stop [work]. Because I can walk and walk and walk, and – and – you know. So there was an element of still pushing on, that we still – every day that I did would be another bit that we'd put away to move somewhere else. You know, there was always an element of that.

Some other mothers resumed work soon after giving birth, but without taking maternity leave. This was because they were not entitled, such as Geraldine Horton who was self-employed, or because of a change of mind about resuming work.

As the examples suggest, for this generation resuming employment within a year of childbirth did not usually mean remaining in full-time employment. In fact only one of the 12 mothers remained continuously in full-time employment whilst having her two children, and could therefore be said to have an employment career uninterrupted by motherhood (at least up to the point of the interview). A second mother, currently on her second maternity leave, planned likewise to go back to full-time work. The other five 'continuous' workers went on to part-time work either after their first child (in three cases) or after their second birth (in two cases): out of 16 returns within one year of giving birth, 12 were to part-time jobs. So, despite coming back to work earlier, most maternal employment (as among the previous two generations of mothers) was part time. In this respect, therefore, fathers and mothers continued to have very different employment histories: thus far in their employment careers only two mothers were continuously equal or main earners, one with a continuous full-time employment record, the other a teacher whose partner was studying for a degree.

Five of the 12 mothers in this generation had gained access to managerial or professional jobs, with four in these jobs *before* becoming mothers: the careers of three had already progressed. This contrasts with the upward mobility observed among grandmothers, which mostly occurred *after* having children. But it is too early to know how many mothers will similarly experience upward mobility later in their working lives and whether, over their working lives, this generation will show significantly greater upward occupational mobility than their mothers.

Childcare for working mothers across the generations

Table 3.1 shows the main childcare arrangements whilst mothers worked across the three generations. Great-grandmothers and grandmothers report very similar arrangements, usually seeking employment with hours that were consistent with their beliefs about motherhood, especially the importance of 'being there' for children – at the least during certain perceived key times in the day. Most common, therefore, was to find jobs in which childcare by 'outsiders' was not needed: working hours when partners were around to provide care or when children were at school, or taking children with them to work. This was often described in terms of 'fitting work around the family'. Next comes relatives and neighbours, followed by six great-grandmothers and grandmothers who had used some form of formal care: two great-grandmothers had done so while bringing up children on their own in wartime (a nursery and a childminder), one grandmother had used a nursery, and three had had some form of paid help in the home, including one great-grandmother who had also sent her children to boarding school.

Two families illustrate this management of childcare and employment through a mixture of part-time work, 'non-standard hours', partners and relatives, across the two older generations. We have already seen how both great-grandmother Brenda Smith and her daughter Pauline took it for granted that women had to work to supplement the family income. Work was a necessity. But it also had to meet certain conditions to make it compatible with ideas about motherhood and children's care.

Brenda felt non-parental childcare was acceptable for part of the day, 'as long as the mothers are there in the morning and in the evening, with the bathtime and bedtime and the feeding and the playtime.' Pauline, like her mother, worked almost continuously while bringing up her one child. But she would only work part time until Neil was at secondary school, when she felt able to take up full-time employment. Part-time work enabled childcare to be managed within the family, with a variety of arrangements: Brenda had Neil sometimes, Pauline had jobs when her husband was at home, she worked for a detective agency where she could take Neil with her, she worked around playgroup and school hours.

Maureen Horton was the only great-grandmother to have worked in a professional job when she had children. Born in 1919 and initially qualified as a nurse, she did not work when her first two children were young, but did some nursing when her third child was under 5 – but only in the evenings when her husband was at home. Then her older sister's husband was killed in a car crash, when Maureen's youngest child Catherine was about 6 years old. This made Maureen very uneasy: what would happen if her husband (a taxi driver) was killed and how would she and the children cope financially? Developing her nursing career was incompatible with her view that being a good mother required her to 'be there' when her children were not at school: 'So I thought, well what am I going to do? Nursing I can't do, because in those days it was just you know, ordinary shifts, you couldn't have flex-itime or anything like that. So I've got to have something where I'm home for the children.' As a result, she decided to train to be a teacher, her main motivation being so she could be at home after school and in the holidays: '[it] meant that it didn't make much difference to them really that I was working, because I was there at the same hours they were.'

Maureen's daughter-in-law, Diana, took a variety of part-time low-skilled jobs when her second child was six months old, which enabled her husband (a teacher) to care for the children; this despite the fact she had trained at art college. She then trained (like her mother-in-law) to be a teacher and completed her probationary year, at which point a third child, Matthew, was born. When he was 18 months old, Diana returned to supply teaching, working part-time, leaving him in the care of a friend. But after two terms she gave up teaching, unhappy at Matthew's response to being left, and, until Matthew started school, again took a variety of low skilled jobs where she could have him with her and avoid the need for non-parental childcare: jobs such as cleaning, and doing a school run for a taxi company. Only once her third child had started school did Diana feel able to resume part-time work as a teacher, freed of worries about leaving Matthew: 'It was great! Matthew was at school. It tied in very well. You know, I haven't had to sort of leave anybody and neglect them.'

Although the overall pattern was similar among current mothers, more had needed non-parental care. Furthermore, and unlike the previous generations, more childcare had been provided by fathers who were either not employed or who had otherwise taken time off work (as opposed to mothers and fathers, both employed, juggling their work hours to ensure parental care). Three of the mother generation had already used formal care (a nursery, a childminder, and paid help in the home) by this stage of their parenting lives. This modest shift reflects the longer and more standard hours worked by some women in this younger generation. However, it should be emphasised just how small a role formal care played overall: of the 12 families, only one had used formal care across all three generations, a nanny in each case.

Current time perspectives on non-parental care

Through the use of two vignettes[1] involving the parents of a young child (twelve months old) both of whom worked full time, we explored the views of women and men in all three generations about 'ideal' options where non-parental care was necessary. This provides a very different perspective on beliefs about childcare than accounts of childcare arrangements actually used by parents of young children. Not only are the situations decontextualised and hypothetical, with a wide range of possibilities and few constraints, but the time frame is different. Older generations, for example, are being asked to make choices in the present day when it may seem far more acceptable for mothers to be employed than it did in the past when they themselves were mothers.

Formal care was chosen by a majority of both grandmothers and mothers, but combined with grandparent care in half the cases (Table 3.1). Indeed, for all three generations, grandparents – either alone or in combination – were the most frequent choice. The attraction of grandparents was that they were family, and therefore could be trusted and were close to the child:

> Oh, I think – I think within the family. OK, we know that things go wrong there. How many times do we say, it's a member of the family? But, if grandparents are capable and willing, I don't think that you can possibly have anything better. [What can they do that other forms of care can't?] Well, I think there's the bond, isn't there? Well, there should be. Most – more often than not, there is, isn't there? It's that bond, once more, of love, which is so essential, to my mind. And, um, I think that is the best [Edna Ashton, great-grandmother].

> I think their main learning comes out of being with a one-to-one adult ... they need that bond ... [Grandparents] have an invested emotional interest in the welfare of the child ... to leave them with their grandparents is the next best thing to us ... it's their flesh and blood (Sonia Masters, mother).

Yet reservations about grandparent care were also often voiced. While many opted for this care in their response to the particular vignette, a frequently expressed concern was that caring for a young grandchild was an unfair imposition, especially when grandparents today often had the freedom in retirement to follow their own interests. Far from insisting grandparents had an obligation to care, concern was expressed that grandparents should not feel obliged to provide care: there was a sense in several responses that this generation had both the right and the resources to enjoy retirement without taking on fresh childcare responsibilities. Claire Ashton, a mother with a continuous full-time employment record so far, whose sister provided full-time (paid) childcare, decided in the vignette that a childminder would be the best option, because it was more 'one to one' than a nursery, while grandparents have 'other things they want to do, you'd be tying them down'. Fiona Prentice, a grandmother who was not working but looked after her grandchildren frequently on a part-time basis, opted for a combination of nursery and grandparent care in response to the vignette, arguing that children were too young to be 'left' all day in a nursery. Perhaps reflecting on her own life, she added that being with grandparents full time would 'completely take their [the grandparents] life away'.

Formal services also figured more in this hypothetical situation than in real life. This was partly a consequence of a reluctance to expect grandparents to provide childcare. But some spoke of the positive benefits of nurseries and childminders, being with other children in the former case, individualised, one-to-one care in the latter. Yet what is perhaps more striking is that from the perspective of 1999, at a time when Britain had its first National Childcare Strategy, there was still a wariness of non-family care, at least until children had reached a certain age when some form of part-time group experience is considered (at least today) normatively appropriate: typically, this is now around 3 years of age, when many children enter a playgroup or similar setting. In all generations strong terms were frequently used to express distrust, even distaste, for non-familial care: 'leaving children', 'putting children out to a childminder', 'dumped in nurseries', 'wouldn't let them (childminders) mind a dog', 'children survive at nursery', 'can't trust childminders', 'sling it (child) out to a childminder', 'lots of people are childminders who should not be', 'childminders can't be trusted', 'we all have those horrors of dropping children off at nurseries', 'these people who get paid to do childcare and they're terrifying sometimes' – plus frequent use of the terms 'stranger' or 'outsider'.

Over the three adult generations, whether in response to the vignettes or indeed elsewhere in the interviews, the welfare state simply was not mentioned – a silence to which we have alluded in Chapter 2 concerning the structural givens within society and which is explained in part by the liberal and maternalistic regime that has prevailed for so long in Britain. Similarly, employers were hardly mentioned as being either supportive or unsupportive of working parents – at least until the youngest generation. Three mothers in the 1960s/70s generation spoke of their employers being helpful or sympathetic in particular about maternity leave, in two cases negotiating extended leave and/or a part-time return. However only one mother had a consistently good experience, with an employer who was supportive over two pregnancies. The second mother distinguished between the employing organisation (helpful) and her manager (rather unsympathetic), while the third spoke of her employer becoming less sympathetic over time. A fourth mother had experienced unsympathetic employers both times she was pregnant – once in the private sector, the other time in the public sector. Overall, therefore, our mothers' experience – such as it was – consisted of limited and variable workplace help in managing employment and childcare.

Conclusion

This chapter has looked across the generations. In sketching the practices of three generations of parents – the lived lives of mothers and
fathers with respect to employment and care responsibilities, it has
traced patterns of both continuity and change. For the men, there are
continuities in that all three generations of fathers were similarly affected
by fatherhood. Over the century public policy presumed a male breadwinner model while the trade union movement fought for a breadwinner
wage. Even if many women made a contribution to breadwinning, most
fathers have been main breadwinners throughout their working lives.

It is among the middle of our three adult generations, born into post-
war Britain, that continuous employment has been most guaranteed for
men, with considerable employment uncertainty in the interwar period
for the oldest generation of men and in the 1990s for the youngest
generation. For the great-grandfathers there were also the disruptions of
the Second World War. Among the youngest generation, as we will see
in Chapter 5, there are hints of a different type of change, with some
current fathers taking more part in the care of their children, subverting
the 'typical' male employment pattern. How far the few 'new fathers'
represent a lifestyle that is chosen and how far it reflects structural
change in the labour market we will discuss later.

The story of women's working lives over the generations is more
complex and one of change and continuity. Women's lives continue to
be marked by motherhood in all three generations: both practical matters
of arranging care and beliefs about motherhood define how much
employment is possible and permissible. Yet despite these constraints,
there is still a good deal of employment during the life course phase of
childrearing, even among the great-grandmother generation whose
employment careers were more fragmented, more marked by interruptions, and whose jobs were mainly low-skilled, part-time and invisible.

The oldest generation of women, mostly born after the First World
War, like the same generation of men, were employed mainly in manual
work. The grandmother generation, mostly born after the Second
World War, benefited from increased education and better employment
opportunities, the latter typically later in the life course rather than
before motherhood. By contrast, the 1960s/70s generation of mothers
looks set to show the strongest attachment to the labour market thus
far, often resuming employment within a year of their children's birth,
reflecting increased educational opportunities, longer investment in
work prior to having children, and the growing use of maternity leave

in Britain. Nonetheless, the theme of part-time work still has a strong presence among them, with only one mother having a full-time employment record throughout her life course.

Across the generations, part-time working has been the common strategy for reconciling employment with ideas of good motherhood, in particular a belief that mothers should 'be there' for their children. For successive generations of British mothers it has also been the means for managing the demands of paid employment and childcare, solving the problem of finding childcare, with fathers and grandmothers filling in the gaps. The idea of childcare provided by 'strangers' has been met with deep suspicions if not outright hostility. Yet, just as the male pattern of full-time, continuous employment begins to show some signs of wear in the current father generation, so the idea of careers for mothers, as for women in general, has taken hold. Not only do more mothers today resume work following maternity leave, but more work full time – although, as in our study, many still do reduce their hours. Part-time working may be a source of new tensions as women wanting careers agonise over the consequences of not working full time.

This chapter is an introduction to the relationship between employment and childcare, not the final word. In Chapters 4 and 5, we approach the subject through a focus on the 'told story': the meanings and rationalities according to which mothers and fathers negotiate motherhood and employment.

Note

1 Vignette 1 was worded thus: Brian and Lucy have just had their third child. Lucy worked as a teacher until taking maternity leave and loves teaching. Brian works as a sales manager. Once her maternity leave ends, Lucy would like to return to work full time. The couple could manage quite well on one salary – either Lucy's or Brian's. Finding childcare may be a problem. What do you think they should do? (1) Lucy and Brian should work full time, with their child cared for by someone else; (2) Brian should give up work and provide childcare while Lucy works; (3) Both Lucy and Brian should try to work part time and share the care; (4) Lucy should not return to work until her child is older; (5) Lucy should work part time rather than full time; (6) other. Why?

Vignette 2: Lucy decides to return to teaching full time. Their son Adam will be seven months old when she goes back to work. He is an easy-going baby and settles well to new situations. There is a nursery nearby which has a good reputation. A local childminder who they know has offered to look after him and Brian's parents who have recently retired could possibly care for their grandson. However they have many interests and hobbies which they enjoy and which keep them busy. Whom should Lucy and Brian ask to look after their son? (1) nursery; (2) childminder; (3) grandparents; (4) someone else/some other arrangement. Why/why not in each case?

4

Motherhood: Intergenerational Transmission and Negotiation

In the last chapter we described the employment patterns of women, and showed how these patterns varied across successive historical cohorts. This comparative approach emphasises broad patterns of change. It can also give an impression of lives mainly determined by structural forces – demographic, economic, social, technological and so on. Neither broad patterns of change nor structural forces, however, tell the complete story.

For if we focus instead on particular families and the individuals within them, we find a great deal of diversity and complexity in women's employment and parenting practices, as we will illustrate in the cases presented in this chapter. Certainly in some families we find women's employment careers reflecting the broad historical changes that have occurred over generations of British mothers. But we also find exceptions to the rule, for example families where there is no linear increase in mothers' employment over time. Such variation suggests other influences in addition to the forces of structure, influences which imply a space for personal agency in women's decisions about the relationship between employment and care, and which mean that structural forces are not uniform in their effects.

While the structural context remains, our attention here shifts to the ways in which women tell their stories and how we as researchers seek to understand the intergenerational influences upon them. First, we explore the transmission of motherhood as an identity, in particular how far women follow or reject the role models provided by their parents. Second, we explore how women made sense of their work and family lives, and in particular how best to meet various and sometimes conflicting responsibilities, focusing on the decisions and 'choices' they made.

In these endeavours we draw upon two concepts: processes of identity transmission within families; and the negotiation of responsibility for work–family careers.

Thus we will suggest how structure and agency – biography and history – are linked when we examine women's interpretation of norms and values concerning work and care, those which obtained in different historical periods and in particular family contexts. Such an endeavour has to engage not only with the historical moments in which decisions were originally made but also with the location of women's interview accounts in present time and with their situations in life course phases which follow the arrival of motherhood. For this theoretical challenge of understanding the negotiation of family and employment responsibilities underpinned the original aims of our study.

Transmission

The ways in which identity transmission occur are various. Kellerhals *et al.* (2002) argue that complex processes are involved. Account must be taken of various transmission channels and practices, the type of relations and interaction between those involved in these different channels, and what they term 'forms of normative reference marks', that is persons, groups and institutions with whom individuals identify or those from which they distance themselves. These markers or reference points too vary, but families are important players. For, as each generation in a family grows up, family members gain a sense of whom they are from their predecessors.

Relations in childhood, in particular with our parents, shape our feelings and practices when we become adult and when we become parents. Individuals identify with or reject the models that their parents and other family members offer them as role models or ideals. As we have seen in Chapter 2, parents and grandparents emerge as key reference markers in childhood for all three generations. Such identification between members of family generations occurs in a number of ways. Interviewees referred to emotional identification – as being 'close' or 'not close' to their mothers and fathers. They also identified (or not) with them via value orientations, identifying with values that operated in their families during childhood and, sometimes simultaneously, subscribing to rather different values that apply in the current life course and historical period.

Even when identification is strong, of one family generation with another, the transmission process is not necessarily simply one of straight replication. Even where values are transmitted, notably from parents to children, the younger generation needs to justify what is transmitted in terms of 'being themselves': having their own convictions and preferences, not just those of their parents, enabling them to develop a sense of self, as being separate from their parents and which persists over time and across contexts (Gullestad, 1997). There is a need to stamp their own mark on what is transmitted, adapting their values to their particular conditions and desires.

The transmission process is not only played out as a tension between individuals and their families, it takes place across life course transitions and over historical time. Thus the grandmother generation grew up in a period – the 1940s and 1950s – in which it was normative for their own mothers (the great-grandmother generation born during and after the First World War) to be at home with their children (although, as we have seen, many did not in fact do so). But they later encountered when they had their own children, a culture in which it began to be more normative for mothers to take advantage of increased employment opportunities, especially part-time work.

Their daughters, the generation of mothers born in the 1960s/70s, lived their childhoods in an historical period in which being a housewife was still commonplace among their mothers but by the time they became mothers they witnessed a very different climate in 1990s' Britain in which work for all became a goal of government. Yet, as we shall see, this youngest cohort of mothers rarely confronts in their interviews the contradiction between their childhood experience and their adult practice, although such contradictions may become apparent in comparing different parts of their interview accounts. Thus it becomes important to examine evidence holistically, namely interviewees' accounts of actions as well as the explanations they give, that is, if we are to assess how far identification with, and reaction against, a parent in *childhood* bears upon the decisions people make in *adulthood*.

In our analysis, we have identified a number of patterns of identity transmission, involving both replication and change. In shaping their identities as mothers, women identified with or reacted against their mothers but fathers could also play a significant role. A working-class grandmother, for example, reacted against her father when she was young when he discouraged her from continuing her education but seems to have drawn inspiration and support in pursuing a work career from her mother and grandmother albeit they had not enjoyed such opportunities themselves. Below, we give two examples of fathers who act as reference markers for women since the main case studies that follow later in the chapter focus on transmission between mothers and daughters. In both examples, grandmothers suggested that they had identified emotionally with their fathers in childhood and later, in their own orientations to education and work, followed in their fathers' footsteps, even though their fathers had not encouraged them when they were at school.

We introduced Diana Horton and Marjorie Samuels in the previous chapter, as examples of upward mobility occurring later in the life course that matched the upward mobility already achieved by their husbands. Both women, from middle-class families, identified with their fathers in making the decision in the life course phase of motherhood to go to university. They also rejected the models of full-time motherhood offered by their mothers. Diana, born in 1946, described a cushioned middle-class childhood. Although 'close' emotionally to both parents, she idealised her work-orientated father (an architect) even though he did not encourage her educationally despite the fact that she had inherited his artistic talents.

> Neither of us [daughters] were really pushed to go into anything of any consequence, you know, and – we weren't, by our parents. I don't think we were advised. I think my mother didn't work you see, so she didn't come from that sort of – I don't know. I think if I, obviously now, with a daughter, I mean I would be insisting on encouraging them to get a good whatever – go into a good profession or whatever, but ummm. They certainly didn't. I don't know what they expected us to do actually.

When she became a mother, Diana said she had been determined to bring up her children rather differently from her own upbringing, encouraging them to develop their talents while putting on hold her own ambitions until later. Bringing up her children (all boys) in the 1970s had clearly been a central 'project' for Diana, although she had been very inventive in finding part-time work, which she fitted in around the family.

> I was determined always to spend lots and lots of time with my children, and to encourage them to do as many things as possible. To play as many instruments and to play as much sport and, um, just to give them as many opportunities as possible. But then I think that was the times, more than anything. There was more for them to do,

than there was when I was their age. Errrr. Maybe not. Maybe not, actually. No, I did learn the piano, but not very well.

Her own mother did no paid work following marriage and, in her interview, expressed frustration with her lack of educational and work opportunities. It was Diana's identification, later, with her father and his artistic talents that shaped her decision, following a late third child, to return to education and develop a teaching career in a similar field to her father's.

Marjorie Samuels is similar in some respects. In deciding to pursue a career after the birth of her two children and wanting to bring up her own children in a different way, she seems to have reacted against her mother as well as having identified with her father. Like Diana, Marjorie 'adored' her father despite the fact that he seems to have discouraged her academically when she was at school. But unlike Diana, she had a difficult relationship with her mother. In particular, she was critical of her mother for *not* working.

After giving birth to two children, more or less immediately she set herself on course to build a 'career'. In reacting consciously against her mother, Marjorie seems also to have found some inspiration, in helping her develop what she refers to as her 'independence', in her grandmother who had died when her own mother was a child: 'Her own mother was an unusual person, as well, given that she was – she'd left her home and she had become a nurse ummm, and she was a serious nurse, I mean she was a theatre sister, that sort of stuff. So there was some modelling there of an independence.'

The significance of the theme of independence emerges elsewhere, for example in Chapters 6 and 7 with respect to how families transmit resources to help individuals break with, as well as carry on, family traditions. Marjorie sought in turn, during the late 1960s, to make her own children 'independent'. When she and her husband became parents they consciously adopted a different course from both sets of parents, including moving away to another part of the country in part to put physical and emotional distance between them and their kin. Influenced by ideas of gender equality the couple sought to share the household work and expected their children to pull their weight also: 'We worked on the premise that there are four people in this house, and we are going to learn to live with each other co-operatively. It's not going to be at the expense of any one member of this family. And they thought that we were quite hard, that we were quite tough.'

Negotiating responsibilities

In order to understand the ways women enact motherhood and combine (or not) employment and care, as well as the explanations or justifications women give for their decisions, we have drawn also on another concept of negotiating work–family responsibilities (Finch, 1989; Finch and Mason, 1993). In their discussion of family responsibilities, Finch and Mason argue that responsibilities for family members are created over time and through negotiation, sometimes explicit but sometimes not, rather than consisting of the application of fixed rules or norms of family obligation. Parent–child relationships, they further argue, are in some respects different from other kin relationships. In particular, 'parents are allocated responsibility for young children . . . [with parent–child relationships] defined as relationships in which parents take responsibility for the material and emotional welfare of children' (ibid., p. 168). However, even parent–child relationships are 'located within the framework of "developing commitments", rather than the idea that fixed rules of obligation cover parent–child relationships' (ibid., p. 168). Seen from this perspective, making decisions about employment and childcare involves interaction and negotiation, not the simple application of universal codes.

There are three aspects to negotiating responsibilities. First, the process is relational: variations occur because 'responsibilities are a product of interaction between individuals over time' (ibid., p. 168). Second, it is context specific: negotiations are embedded in concrete, particular and local situations and informed by knowledge of this context and of the other actors. Third, it is ethical, having a moral dimension: 'By "moral dimensions" we do not mean moral rules . . . [W]e mean that people's identities as moral beings are bound up in these exchanges of support, and the processes through which they get negotiated . . . People's identities are being constructed, confirmed and reconstructed – identities as a reliable son, a generous mother, a caring sister or whatever it might be' (ibid., p. 170). Thus, in negotiating family responsibilities, women make *moral* judgements.

The concept of negotiating responsibilities towards others recognises the agency of women. Agency in negotiation is not simply a matter of calculating the best individual solution: indeed, negotiation problematises the language of 'choice'. Decisions are framed not so much in terms of individual preferences between a range of possible choices, but as actions decided on the basis of what seems 'right' in given conditions: decisions about responsibility which contain a complex mix of ethical,

relational and contextual considerations. The emphasis here is on responsibilities rather than rights. Making these decisions requires weighing up
many considerations – including normative beliefs, personal and family
circumstances, preferences and resources – to arrive at particular, situated
decisions, rather than applying universal rules or being subject to
immutable structural forces. Decisions are negotiated, both through
dialogue with others and through having to interpret and assess these
different considerations, including constraints and opportunities, personal preferences and responsibilities.

As the product of human agency, negotiating responsibilities is
closely linked to identities and their construction and transmission, as
discussed earlier. It involves constructing moral and personal identities:
What does it mean to be a 'good' mother? How can I best meet my
caring responsibilities and balance these against my need for personal
independence? The desire to be similar to my mother or grandmother
may be a strong influence, but so too may be a desire to be different.
Women, as we have already seen, may also be influenced by their fathers
especially with respect to occupational aspirations. In many cases, women
pull or are pulled in different directions, generating or generated by
ambivalences.

Negotiating responsibilities also provides one way of understanding
tensions within an individual's interview account between, for example:
a woman's general normative beliefs about whether mothers should
work; her personal actions – going out to work herself as a mother or
not; and her particular judgements about and the support she offers
a daughter or granddaughter who works when she has young children.
Tensions between these beliefs, judgements and actions not only suggest
ambivalence, they involve carefully differentiated positions, each negotiated in relation to a particular time, place and reference group. Older
generations of women might still espouse certain beliefs or standards
that were normative when they were themselves mothers of young
children (most commonly, that mothers should not work); but these do
not have to cloud their contemporary evaluations of how their own
daughters and grandchildren should live their lives in the present
context or their current decisions about what support to offer them.

Negotiating the ethic of care

The moral dimension in negotiating family responsibilities within
specific contexts has much in common with the concept of 'the ethic of
care' as developed by Tronto (1993). As Tronto puts it, 'the moral question

an ethic of care takes as central is . . . how can I (we) best meet my (our) caring responsibilities' (p. 137). Tronto locates the concept of an ethic of care in a tradition of contextual morality going back to Aristotle, and more recently, the Scottish Enlightenment thinkers. Sevenhuijsen (1999b) notes connections to Levinas (and his 'ethics of an encounter') and to Bauman, whose explorations of 'postmodern ethics' welcomes a repersonalising of morality, and the release of morality from constructed ethical codes: 'personal responsibility is morality's last hold and hope' (Bauman, 1993, p. 34). Responsibility for the other is one of several tenets proposed for the ethic of care, the others being attentiveness, competence and responsiveness (Tronto, 1993).

The ethic of care contrasts with a universalistic approach to ethics, in which ethical judgements are based on universal, impartial and decontextualised principles (see Sevenhuijsen, 1999b). Rather it focuses on judging the particular in context: '[it] demands reflection on the best course of action in specific circumstances and the best way to express and interpret moral problems. Situatedness in concrete social practices is not seen as a threat to independent judgement. On the contrary it is assumed that this is exactly what will raise the quality of judgement' (ibid., p. 59).

In many ways it seems to us that 'negotiating responsibilities' and the 'ethic of care' are two sides of the same coin. They both adopt a similar stance around the question of how responsibilities are defined and practiced, foregrounding active processes of decision-making informed by three connected dimensions – social relations, context and ethics. However, to avoid confusion we have used the language of negotiation in this and following chapters.

We do not mean to suggest that people necessarily see their own decisions about employment and care in terms of conscious negotiations (or indeed ethical decisions). Some may simply speak of a difficult decision, which once made may still leave feelings of uncertainty or discomfort. In other cases women suggest that there is nothing to be decided, the course of action adopted being entirely taken for granted. No contextual conditions arise to disturb normative beliefs, or so strong is the transmission of identity from mother to daughter, for example, that other possibilities for change are never considered. Yet, whether a conscious process or not, whether complex or not, the concept of negotiation provides a useful way of understanding the relationship between employment and care, implying that even in the most apparently straightforward case, responsibilities are constructed, and are not givens or mandatory. As we shall see in the cases that follow, comparisons between families and within families can suddenly show up what may appear to be taken for granted action as, in fact, a decision between possibilities.

A word of caution is necessary before we move to look at some cases, harking back to our earlier comments about time. The study involves a biographical approach, and participants covered large swathes of their lives in their accounts. The method generates retrospective accounts of decisions, actions and events, often in distant parts of life courses, and in the contexts of particular situations, relationships and moral judgements pertaining to these times. Not only may recall falter, but the evaluations of those decisions and events are made with reference to *present* time frames, even though informants seek to recall the past and how they thought and felt then. It is, in practice, impossible for a raconteur to stand outside the present when considering the past. Such issues must be constantly borne in mind, therefore, in how we as researchers try to unpick how people from different generations make sense of their paid work and care; such accounts are inevitably incomplete and partial.

Three case studies

We have selected three cases from the five families in which there are biological ties between lines of women over all three adult generations (in other cases, at least two of the three generations of women were related through marriage). The mother–daughter link provides the strongest conditions in which to study the intergenerational transmission of motherhood. The case studies have also been chosen to demonstrate three intergenerational patterns concerning the transmission of women's identities in relation to care and paid work: a pattern of continuity; a pattern of discontinuity; and a mix of both continuity and discontinuity. In analysing these cases, therefore, we observe similarities and differences in mothers' and daughters' employment and care careers.

The Peters women: a case of continuity

This family falls into, or rather just into, a group of families which we will typify in Chapter 7 as 'solidaristic', in terms of its pattern of intergenerational relations. Over time, the family exhibits a pattern of continuity, involving close identification between mothers and daughters; so mothers transmit to daughters that which was transmitted to them by their own mothers, and daughters reproduce these transmitted identities. Such transmission processes occur over the life course, for example, ideas about motherhood are transmitted in both childhood and parenthood.

The Peters women consist of great-grandmother Dora, born in 1920, aged 80, and a mother of four; Priscilla, born in 1948, aged 52 and a mother of two; and Annabelle, born in 1971, aged 29, and also a mother of two children, aged 2 and 4. In addition, we interviewed Eileen, the mother of Priscilla's husband, born in 1921, aged 79 and a mother of four. The two great-grandmothers, and their husbands, and Priscilla and her husband George all lived in a town in East Anglia, while the mother, with her husband Mark and two children, lived at a two-hour drive away to the west of London.

Dora was born and brought up in the West Midlands and Wales. Her father was manager of a plant producing tarmac for roads. Her mother ran a second-hand clothes shop from the time Dora was about 5 years old, and her grandmother was an antique dealer (who also often bought up clothes for Dora's mother to sell). Her mother died at 42, just after Dora was married. Dora left school without qualifications at 14, in 1934, the height of the Depression, which she was aware of but which did not impinge on her life: 'my mother had the shop, my father was working, so we didn't know anything about the Depression'. There followed a variety of manual jobs, including factory work – painting china, trim work in a car factory – and driving a bread delivery van. Her father, however, was very clear that she should not be a domestic servant. When she did get herself a job as a kitchen maid, her father forbade her to take it up: 'You're not going to do it, you're not going to be a skivvy.'

She married at 20, in 1940, and soon found herself with a baby, and a husband away in the Army. In these exceptional circumstances, left to bring up her daughter by herself, Dora went to work as a cook in a nursing home for mothers and babies, using a day nursery for childcare. What is striking is how unproblematic this period is recalled to have been: there is no sense of personal conflict or mention of problems 'balancing' work and family life. Indeed, Dora suggests that combining work and bringing up her daughter was easy: 'she was a lovely little girl . . . you would sit her down there like this and you would get yourself dressed and she wouldn't move away. She'd never get dirty.' Her cousin also worked as a cook at the nursing home and they both had accommodation there. Another person working at the nursing home was a widow with two children, 'and sometimes she'd say can I have [the baby] for the day?'

Also striking is how little apparent effect this period had on Dora's later employment: it is like a short stay in another world, with different customs, with no connection to what went before or what came after – a quite different context calling for a particular negotiation of responsibility towards her child which set no precedent for the future. When her husband Wilfred was demobilised in 1945, she gave up work and had three more children in three years, including Priscilla, after moving to the town in East Anglia where her husband had been born and raised. He worked as a fitter with one of the main local manufacturing companies.

Dora's return to work, some 15 years later in 1960, when her youngest child was around 11 years old, was the consequence of an event in the family, and the limitations of the welfare state. Wilfred had an accident at work, forcing Dora to take a job to keep the family afloat financially:

> We were getting no money coming in...[T]hey said to go to the Public Assistance as it was then to see if I could get so much money on that...[and because the PA said we had got] things in our house that wasn't necessary, and we'd had these things since we'd been married, so they didn't give us anything...So what did I do? I left them, I went to the hospital and I scrubbed the hospital for a shilling an hour.

Dora did this for a year, then worked for six months cooking and cleaning for the commander of the local garrison. She was found another domestic job by the commander when he left, did not like this new job, then became a home help working for the local authority. After 10 years as an ordinary home help, she took a course and became a 'family home help' – 'looking after problem families' – a job she liked and did for 11 years before retiring in 1984 at the age of 64.

We can see here not only the role of a burgeoning public service sector in providing part-time work (and Dora always worked part time after resuming employment), but also how this sector took up the slack in providing unskilled domestic work for women with little or no educational qualifications as private domestic service declined after the war (the 'skivvy' for a middle-class family has become the 'family home help' working for the local authority, no doubt better paid and with a modicum of training).

We can also see a recurring pattern of childcare: part-time work, with hours that ensured maternal presence. Dora determined that the right thing to do as a mother was to work, but to only do so at times when the children were at school: 'So I used to go out after they'd gone to school in the mornings and I was back here for lunchtime...I never

ever worked so they came home to an empty house 'cos I didn't believe in it.' Wilfred looked after the children when Dorothy worked occasional evenings, another acceptable way to ensure care responsibilities were properly met.

Priscilla, Dora's third child, was born in 1948 in the same East Anglian town where she has lived ever since. She left school at 15 with no qualifications – or rather, like several grandmothers, reported that she 'had to leave school...my father wouldn't let me stay on to take A levels'. This was obviously an important turning point. She said she would have liked to stay on, get A levels and then have trained to be a teacher: 'I would've loved to have done. But it wasn't to be.'My father was quite – you know. Because my two older sisters didn't want to stop on, I didn't have a choice. It was one of those things where if one didn't do it, the others couldn't do it.' She had no recollection of her father Wilfred ever visiting her school and the only reason he gave for not letting her stay on was 'the others didn't do it so you don't'.

Even in her 50s, she remained ambivalent and regretful about being denied this opportunity: 'I would've loved to have been given the opportunity to have been a teacher, but it wasn't to be, so there we go...[T]hat's my one regret, I think, in life.' She situated this episode in a time, the early 1960s, when paternal authority was still supreme, when early school leaving was normative and the labour market was buoyant. She observes that, in those days, 'you were not taught to stand up to your parents, and I wasn't a rebellious person'. Leaving school at 15 was also common then, 'the sort of norm really, everybody was doing it...that's just what happened. Nowadays it's quite different, isn't it? Everybody's staying on and if you don't go to university, then you're the odd one out.' She had no idea what she wanted to be, but went straight into work – 'then jobs were easy to get. You didn't really need any qualifications...[T]he technology wasn't there, so you know there was always jobs to do'. Her parents were happy as long as she got a job, 'I don't think they knew much about higher education and that sort of thing'.

So in 1963, aged 15, Priscilla went to one of the town's large manufacturing firms, which took many school leavers at the time, and where her father, future husband and other relatives worked. She started on a series of office jobs. Marriage at 21 (only a year later than her mother) to George (who along with his father Donald and son-in-law Mark are discussed in the next chapter on fatherhood) proved a turning point in her employment. Within a few months she had moved to work for a company closer to her new home, again doing office work, then after six months went to work part time for a local newspaper. Both moves enabled her to 'negotiate' her new domestic responsibilities as a wife: 'I could nip home and finish off doing stuff that I hadn't done before I went to work.' Priscilla occupies a halfway point between women leaving work on marriage (more common in her mother's day and what her mother-in-law Eileen did) and on having a first child (increasingly common after the war).

She says that 'I've liked work all along, really, but I did like the job at the paper'. However, that made no difference to her leaving this job and employment altogether, when pregnant with her first child. There was no maternity leave then, but in any case she took it for granted she would not go back to work after the birth: 'it never even entered my head that I would want to go back to work . . . I just saw myself as being a mother then . . . I just didn't visualise going back at all.' There followed 15 years as a full-time carer, until her second and youngest child was 11 years old, when in 1986 she began working part time (just 1¼ hours a day) as a dinner lady at the local school: like her mother, Priscilla re-entered employment via low-skilled work in the public service sector. At the same time, she started voluntary work teaching swimming at the school, which lasted for seven years. Both pieces of work came about through an informal offer: Priscilla and her husband George were visiting their daughter's school for a parents evening, when 'the head-master said we're looking for volunteers . . . to teach the children to swim, [and] we've also got a vacancy for a midday assistant – would you like to have it? So I didn't have to go for an interview . . . it was offered to me'. She said she had not considered going back to work until this offer was made.

Priscilla enjoyed the voluntary work and the job, both working with children. She continued her paid work for 14 years – with a year out to do a computer course, 'which I did enjoy . . . what I would've like to have done when I was 15', again hinting at an unresolved feeling of unused potential. She admitted to having had other periods of doubt while working as a dinner lady: 'I suppose when I was about 40 . . . I sort of thought, Well, I don't know, life seems to be passing me by, maybe I could have done something different, but I didn't really know what I would've liked to have done had I done something different. That was no use to me.'

At the time of interview, Priscilla had recently given up the school job, retiring completely from paid work at the age of 51, 10 years earlier than her mother. Care responsibilities and her identity as a mother had been main considerations in her decision to take early retirement.

Priscilla wanted to make herself more available for her daughter Annabelle and her grandchildren, emphasising the transmission of ideas about the importance of maternal presence, the importance of 'being there' even for adult children:

with the grandchildren coming, and Annabelle living away, when she asked for help, I wanted to go, *because that was what I was brought up with, if you wanted help from your parents, they would be there.* And I felt I wanted to do that for Annabelle, so that I could just go when she needed me. And it was difficult being at the school, I could only go school holidays (emphasis added).

She was also influenced by the care needs of her ageing parents. Priscilla was already providing some help for them and anticipated her care responsibilities would increase as they became more frail: 'health-wise [they] are declining quite quickly at the moment'.

Priscilla's participation in the labour market had been less than her mother's, not going back to work when either child was very young, retiring sooner and working rather shorter part-time hours. Employment was contingent on care responsibilities – for husband, children, grand-children and ageing parents. Nor were there any external pressures to earn, as with Dora – no war, no husband out of work. Indeed, Priscilla's husband George enjoyed continuous employment, with readily available overtime, as a technical designer in a multi-national manufacturing company: 'I'm one of those people who are fortunate enough where my husband is in the higher wage bracket . . . that's the reason I was able to stay at home.' Recent financial pressures on the family due to their youngest daughter going to university were met not by Priscilla increas-ing her work hours, but by George working overtime. Under less financial pressures than Dora, Priscilla worked shorter hours, but used some of her 'free time' for voluntary work.

Yet behind Priscilla's acceptance of a limited employment career there remained a doubt, a sense that things might have been different if she had been able to take another direction at the age of 15. There was an unrealised ambition and the thought that she was capable of doing more with her life. She may have committed herself to a marriage career, but she could still on occasion envisage herself committed to a work career. What at the time was taken for granted, considered an inevitability, can be glimpsed from the present as a decision and one possibility.

Priscilla's oldest daughter, Annabelle, left school at 16, in 1987, after six months at Sixth Form College, with one O level (equivalent to a Grade A–C in today's GCSE). She had a Saturday job with a chain store when at school, and on leaving education was offered a full-time job by the company as a shop assistant. When married at 21 (very similar in age to Priscilla and Dora, and like them, but unlike most of her peers in the study, not cohabiting before marriage), she transferred to another branch of the store, where she worked until she had her first child at 23. She took statutory maternity leave, but only as a form of insurance, having no intention of returning to work when her leave ended unless something had gone wrong with the pregnancy. She also did not want anyone else looking after her child, her identity as mother, as her mother and grandmother before, being bound up in the provision of full-time care at least when children were young.

At the time of the interview, Annabelle was working part time as an organiser in 'Bouncy Babies', which she described as being like 'a baby gym'. She started this work in 1998 when her first child was 3 years old: she had been taking him to 'Bouncy Babies', and on one visit saw a notice asking if any mother wanted to work (the same informal job access as her mother's). At the time of interview, she had done this job for about 15 months over the course of the last two years, working short part-time hours, initially Saturday mornings, with her husband caring for their child, then taking on a second morning each week. This decision by Annabelle to increase her hours, even by a small amount, was conditional on finding an acceptable childcare arrangement: her child being at nursery class for most of the time, then taken by a friend until Annabelle could collect him. After a short period of working these longer hours, Annabelle took time off, first because of illness, then to have her second child. At the time of interview, she had been back with 'Bouncy Babies' for a few weeks, working Saturday mornings again.

Like her mother, she took up work because it gave her an opportunity to get out of the house, while at the same time her job enabled her to be at home for her child during the summer holidays. She also saw another benefit: it gave her elder child (a son) an opportunity to spend time with his father. The money was not a consideration. The family could manage on the salary of her husband Mark who, like her father, had a steady technical job (as an electrical engineer) in a large national company. Annabelle described herself as not academic: she did not want to go to university, and enjoyed shop work. She had no regrets, indeed would not have changed anything. She had no plans to go back to more demanding work until her youngest child (a few months old) was in full-time education.

Like her mother and maternal grandmother, Annabelle had minimal educational qualifications, left school early and worked in a predominantly female occupation. Although she resumed employment after having children well before her mother, like her (and Dora) she judged employment acceptable only under strict conditions: short part-time working hours, not requiring a formal childcare arrangement. Like her mother, she found work in a service sector concerned with children. But rather than the public sector, she entered a new growth area: a branch of the private childcare sector, offering recreation and entertainment to young children whose parents could afford the cost.

There are striking continuities across the three generations – in the women's education and employment (few qualifications and, post-war at least, work in lower skilled service sector jobs), in the continuity of their husbands' employment (all working in skilled manual or technical jobs in large companies), and in understandings of what it means to be a good mother. Indeed, there is a clear transmission of values across the three generations about the importance of care, expressed through exchange of support and a strong belief in the importance of being available to children (even when grown-up), and an unproblematic downplaying of employment. Employment comes a clear second to care, not just care of children but also of husbands and parents, and is judged acceptable only if certain stringent conditions are met or in extreme circumstances – in Dora's case, war and her husband's accident.

When offered a 'care scenario' (see Chapter 3, footnote 1) of a contemporary working couple with a young first child, both deeply involved in demanding jobs, all three Peters women responded in similar fashion: Lucy, the 'scenario mother', should not return to work until her child is older. There was, however, some variation to the second part of the vignette, on the best childcare option, expressing different decisions about responsibility for care. Priscilla, the grandmother who had recently stopped work to devote more time to caring, chose grandparents 'because it's family oriented'. Both Dora and her granddaughter, however, opted for a nursery, Dora because grandparents would be too old, while Annabelle argued it would not be fair to ask grandparents.

There is also an awareness of the identity-transmission process. Priscilla liked 'to think I've been here like my parents and my [parents-in-law] were here for me, I'm here for this next generation coming'. There was a strong identification especially between Annabelle and her mother. In going straight from school to work, Annabelle explicitly suggested an understanding that she was carrying on the tradition of her mother and grandmother. So too in bringing up her children, Annabelle thought she was carrying on the same pattern, speaking of following in their footsteps. Asked who influenced her most as a parent, she referred to her mother and grandmother: aspects of their parenting styles have varied, but what she regarded as the basics, looking after your own child, were unchanged. She had an unambiguous sense of continuity in childcare practice, being the latest in a line of women who stayed at home: her mother and maternal grandmother Dora, but also Eileen, her paternal grandmother, who left employment at the age of 22 when her first child was born, and had never returned.

But there is an interesting twist in the story illustrating how generational relations can be marked by convergence and divergence so that the same generation can display both continuity and change. What seems, from one perspective, like a straightforward story of transmission and identification becomes more complicated if we look at the wider kin network: from this other perspective, the taken for granted and inevitable life course becomes a decision to opt for one of the several possibilities. For Annabelle's younger sister, Sophie, has followed a quite different and innovative course to the other women in the family. Having done well at school, she went to university to study medicine, and now at 26 was working in a hospital and living with a partner (in her family's home town, an element of continuity here). At an age when her sister, mother and grandmother had all become wives and mothers, Sophie was not married and had no children.

This divergence, however, was not interpreted as making her 'different' and, in important ways, had been absorbed within the family pattern of solidaristic relations. Sophie received support from her parents, both at university and now that she was working in a demanding hospital job – financial, practical and emotional. The contrast with her mother, Priscilla, is unavoidable. Sophie in the Peters family of the 1960s would not have had the chance to go to university, while Priscilla growing up in the 1990s could well have done so and had her parents' backing to be a teacher.

The Kent women: a case of continuity and change

Like the Peters family, this family is typified by solidaristic patterns of intergenerational support (discussed in Chapter 7). The Kent women consist of a great-grandmother, Margaret, born in 1917, aged 83, a widow and a mother of two; Miriam, born in 1942, aged 58 and a mother of three; and Juliet, born in 1969, aged 31, and a mother of two children aged 2 and 4. Unlike the Peters, all three generations lived close to each other, in the same part of London.

Margaret was born in Berlin towards the end of the First World War. Her father owned a leather tannery, her mother did not work and Margaret was looked after by a nanny. This secure, middle-class life was torn apart by two events in the 1930s. In 1935 her father had a stroke, and required a lot of care thereafter, leaving the family financially precarious. But they were also a Jewish family in Nazi Germany, and as such faced increasing persecution: 'I went to High School and very often I was told to get out of the class and sit outside as I was Jewish.' Expelled from school at 16, Margaret went to learn dressmaking at a leading couturier: 'my parents thought it was better for me to learn something with my hands in case I have to live off that.' In 1939 she fled to England as a refugee, leaving behind parents she was never to see again: 'My father died a natural death, he had a stroke and my mother was still there with my grandmother, my mother could've gone underground, but she couldn't leave the old lady there, so they went and they were put into a gas chamber . . . It was a terrible thought.'

Margaret arrived in England in 1939 as a refugee, with a visa procured by her brother (who had already fled Germany) for her to work as a cook. She lived with a family for nine months, working as a maid looking after a young child and doing domestic work (once again, the strong theme of domestic work in the lives of many great-grandmothers). She worked long hours, with only one day off a week: 'They didn't treat me very well, they had bad manners and it was so different from my growing up.' She got out of this situation when she married in 1940, aged 23. Her husband and his mother were also refugees from Germany, getting out in 1935. Margaret had met him a few times in Germany and renewed acquaintance in England when she went to visit his mother on her afternoons off. He now owned an engineering firm in London.

Marriage rescued Margaret from domestic service, and she stopped working altogether. She had her first child two years after marriage, in 1942, the second five years later. She says she 'didn't even consider [employment] . . . they needed me so I didn't cut myself in four parts'. She only resumed employment, after a 12 year gap, once her youngest child was at school, in the mid-1950s, working part time for the family firm: 'I could speak German so I did all the German correspondence, so I knew everything more or less which was a good thing.' Apart from fitting work around school hours, Margaret (like her mother before, and her daughter and granddaughter later) had domestic help. Her daughter, Miriam, refers to two staff, 'a nanny who looked after us and someone who did the cooking as well'. Margaret recalls that managing children and work 'wasn't difficult ... if you're organised ... [And] I had somebody who was staying here and was cooking and doing all these things, so that was much easier for me'.

Her involvement with the family firm increased over several years, when her husband became ill. She went daily to the office at this time, and the children were sent to boarding school when they reached 11. Margaret justified her decision in terms of negotiating conflicting care responsibilities. The children were sent away partly 'to grow up in the English way so that they're happy here', but mainly because her husband 'wasn't a well man and I had to look after him'. She had found herself 'cut into halves and quarters to be there for everybody, and that I think I found rather difficult, particularly when he was old – ill, and then, and the children – that was quite difficult, but everybody manages, so I did too'.

Margaret was 47, and her children 17 and 21, when her husband died in 1964. She took over the running of the business: 'I said to myself, if I can manage to do it for six months as people still feel sorry for you, and if I can't I have to give up. But I was very fortunate and I suppose with great willpower I suppose I ran it until my son was ready to come in.' Margaret, perhaps, rather underplays what was involved. Her daughter, Miriam, placed more emphasis on how challenging this must have been, not least taking over a mainly male workplace. Running the business meant working full time, long hours: 'I left in the morning at 7 and came home in the evening at 7, so that was quite difficult.'

Margaret continued to work full time until the age of 68, in 1985, then 'semi-retired' because she decided her son was old enough to take over (she talked as if she always assumed he would take over, and Miriam expressed no indication of ever being interested). However, Margaret still went to the office. Only in the last year or two had she cut this involvement because of her health, although still continuing to take an interest in the company.

The extent and nature of Margaret's involvement in employment represent a major change from what might have been expected for a young woman growing up in a bourgeois family in interwar Berlin: looking ahead in 1930, a life of non-employment, like her mother's, might have been taken for granted. What actually turned out can be understood in the context of a series of traumatic and exceptional events: the rise to power of the Nazis, her flight to England, meeting and marrying another refugee, and the illness and early death of her husband. Margaret showed great courage, ability and resilience in coping with life as a

refugee, then caring for her seriously ill husband and finally successfully taking over the running of the family business. She had to make
a series of difficult decisions, involving weighing up responsibilities to
her children, her husband and the family firm and her own unproven
capacity to run a business. She and her husband being refugees, perhaps
allowed her little choice; there was no one else around from either
family to take on the responsibility once her husband was ill. But, even
so, her initial decision to take over the running of the company after
her husband's death was very provisional.

Miriam, Margaret's elder child, was born in 1942, left school at 18,
re-sat her A levels at a 'crammer' (a private college for middle-class
school leavers needing to improve their exam results) before studying
briefly in Paris, followed by a shorthand course which equipped her for
a secretarial job in the City, started when she was 20. She got married in
1964, at 22, to Robert the son of another Jewish German refugee family.
Her husband's parents, from a family of big business, fled Germany soon
after the Nazis came to power, leaving behind their family business and
wealth to rebuild a successful life in England. Robert went on to become
a senior manager in a large company, before successfully starting and
building up his own business (Robert is discussed in more detail in the
next chapter on fatherhood, together with his son-in-law James).

Miriam clearly felt she had missed out during her childhood (she said
she had blocked out most of her childhood memories). She did not
comment directly on her mother's employment nor did she refer to the
historical context in which her parents, new to Britain, sought to rebuild
the family's material and cultural capital. But, in reflecting upon her own
different way of being a mother, Miriam referred to a rather 'lonely'
childhood. She was adamant that she would not send her children to
boarding school as her mother had sent her: 'my children have always
been very important to me. Um, so I've enjoyed their growing up. I did
a lot of things with them. Of course, if you don't send them away, you
have to fill in everything, which is what I felt strongly about, so all the
usual things like music and God knows what else, which I loved, and
they did a lot of.'

Having married comfortably, when Miriam became a mother she had
no financial need to work as well as little inclination. Moreover, since
her husband was often abroad, this further legitimised her not working.
So Miriam was happy to be at home in the early years of her children's
lives, resuming work when her youngest child was 4 years old, after a
break of about 10 years. Her mother, Margaret, asked her to come and
work in the office of the family firm, which she did part time: 'I went

there and did really rather dull jobs . . . I got a little bit of money for that and I got out of the house in the morning.' She initially worked three mornings a week, increasing her time as the children got older and were at school, building up to four days a week. This coincided with taking on more responsibility in the firm, in particular starting and running a new line of business. In addition to working part time and school hours, Miriam had help in the house from the time her youngest child was 3, from a succession of au pairs.

But Miriam never identified with her mother's enthusiasm for working in the family firm. She said she would have preferred not to go into the business: 'If one had one's time over again, I wouldn't have done it.' Miriam is also cooler towards paid work in general than her mother. She describes herself as 'not a career person', and contrasts her job with 'something that I do like doing' – which is her voluntary work. Nearly five years ago, in her early fifties, Miriam became an unpaid prison visitor: when interviewed, she was currently doing three days a week in the family business and two days prison work. She planned to retire from the family business 'in a few years time', but to continue doing her prison work until her 10-year stint was up. She had also done voluntary work when her children were young, for an organisation giving holidays to poor children.

The relationship between Margaret and Miriam as mothers was complex, mostly characterised by change but with some elements of continuity. The events of Miriam's biography suggest a reaction against that of her mother. Yet, at the same time, Miriam was at pains to emphasise emotional closeness to her mother and admired her as being a strong, capable woman. While Miriam sought to be quite a different kind of mother, she was reluctant to criticise overtly Margaret's model of motherhood.

Miriam's decision about employment can be understood in terms of negotiating her responsibilities to family members in a very particular context. In her case, the responsibility she felt towards her family meant working and giving time to the family business; without her 'strong sense of duty' she would have left the business long ago. Her daughter, Juliet, expressed this sense of family obligation when she said that her mother's work in the family firm was 'expected, loyalty, commitment . . . [S]he can't walk away and she's felt trapped . . . she has never seen any other office environment'.

Of Miriam's three daughters, only one, Juliet, had had children. Juliet differed from her mother and grandmother in three important respects. First, like many of her 1960/70s' generation, she went to university, where she met and started living with her future husband, James. He went on to a successful career as a senior manager, as well as running his own property business. Second, unlike Miriam, being a good daughter did not mean for Juliet going into the family business; she offers an example of a member of the younger generation who places her own mark (being herself) on otherwise transmitted values. Instead, she joined a large media company after graduating and did well, progressing from editor to senior editor, then to manager and senior manager until she became publishing manager which was her job at the time she had her first child. Third, she had built a career before becoming a mother and had subsequently worked continuously (including leave periods), unlike Margaret and Miriam who did not work until their children were of school age. Juliet's oldest child was 4 years old at the time of the interview, her youngest 2.

However, gender shaped Juliet's work career once she became a mother. She took statutory maternity leave with her first child, returning to full-time employment four months after the birth: '[I] absolutely hated it...it was just hideous...a nightmare of a very unhappy time.' The worst part of the experience was when her child was ill, continuously screaming and requiring endless medical attention. Work, by contrast, was a haven: 'I raced back to work after four months because I was probably going to throw him out the window otherwise.'

She took a longer period of leave (one year) on the birth of her second child, 'I felt sort of hard done to about [their first child's difficult early years], I felt kind of resentful I never had the cooing baby.' She did not feel pushed to return and was able to negotiate with her employer a return to work that was both delayed and part time:

> I had quite a big job by this point, I was running quite a large team of people on quite a large budget and I loved my job, but they said take a year and don't rush. I suppose they were worried I might not come back. So I managed to negotiate with them and they allowed me to come back part time on two days a week...I was thrilled...[it] let me keep my eye in until I made a decision about what I wanted to do.

On resuming work after her second period of maternity leave, Juliet managed to transfer to a new job in her company's head office, with a worldwide remit. At the time of her interview, she had negotiated a three-day working week, which included some overseas travel. Like much else about her employment, Juliet felt ambivalent about working part time. On the one hand, her current job was 'perfect for me at the moment, it's not what I want to do forever ... [but] it's exciting and ful-filling'. However there were 'status changes as a part-time worker ... you're not privy to everything that's going on and ... decisions are naturally made when you're not there ... [Y]ou just figure less in their minds by dint of the fact you're not there'. Her employer did not take advantage and there was 'no time sheet culture'. But, at the same time, in practice she found it difficult to maintain boundaries between work and home. She was constantly available on the phone – 'I should probably say Wednesdays are a free zone, but I also like what I do, so I don't want to be left out of the loop'. She felt she offered 'her services too freely, "I'll do that", "Yes, I'll take that", "No, no it doesn't matter, I can leave on Sunday morning", and then I suppose what suffers is here rather than there'.

Juliet said she was 'very lucky with my childcare ... [I have] absolute, total 100 per cent confidence and what that means is that when I'm at work I work'. When she went back to work after her first child, who was ill and quite difficult, she could afford to employ a full-time nanny, the fourth generation in her family to use this type of carer: '[She] was my sort of saving grace ... she gave me huge peace of mind, but also let me escape ... [S]he was massively qualified, an experienced and mature girl to deal with medicines and visits to doctors ... she just was a miracle worker. She got him into a routine, he absolutely adored her, she was with us for I think two years.' Juliet talked about how she and her hus-band sought to negotiate childcare responsibilities by 'throwing money' at them. But then it got too expensive so they arranged to share their nanny with another family.

Having gone back to work after her second child, but after a longer break and to reduced hours, Juliet and James used a variety of sources of childcare. There was an au pair (from Eastern Europe), who 'is a godsend ... the days I go to work she works full time, so ... she's more than an au pair, she's in sole charge from 7.30 to 6'. This au pair had just agreed to stay on an extra 8 months, Juliet '[bending] over back-wards to accommodate her needs, she gets the car at weekends and she gets lots of perks'. In addition there was help from her husband, both sets of parents, and her husband's cousin, who was currently living with them. She described her father Robert, now semi-retired, as 'probably the star ... my dad is really fantastic'. Her husband also described Robert as 'absolutely fantastic' and 'doing more childcare at the moment than I do'. Juliet's part-time work seemed to require even more complex childcare arrangements than full-time work: 'every day is a sort of military – we sit down on Sunday nights with diaries and Psions and mobile phones and literally work out menus, activities, who's doing what, bath-time, babysitting needs – everything changes halfway through the week, but everyone knows where everyone is.'

Despite 'wonderful childcare and wonderful family support', Juliet found life fraught. Her account was full of ambivalence, uncertainty and conflict. She liked her work and was getting more engaged as time passed – but 'it takes its toll'. This dilemma was getting worse, as the new part-time job became ever more demanding, with an increasing amount of travel: 'it's the juggling. Nightmare!'. 'Juggling' was a recurring metaphor – 'I think that juggling is actually what I am.'

Significantly, feeling that it was principally her responsibility to organise childcare, she internalised the problem and defined 'juggling' as a longstanding feature of her life and the sort of person she was: 'I always put too many things in my diary ... it's what I enjoy'. She wanted to do the job and the travelling, but '[James] finds that difficult because I am only part time, and yet the travel I do is very much full time'. There is an indication here that part-time work does not in her husband's eyes warrant such effort. Moreover, though her husband did quite a lot of childcare for the moment – more than she did, Juliet thought – this was unlikely to last when he started a new senior managerial job. His much valued participation was essentially discretionary: 'he chooses to do [childcare] when he wants to do it. *It's not his responsibility* ... he's absolutely fantastic, he's one of the most present fathers ... but it's just a different context isn't it? *For him, it's when he can do it*, he does it, but there's no written rule' (emphases added).

Because of, but also despite, these pressures, Juliet was beginning to think about resuming full-time work: 'the word "full time" is now back in my vocabulary, but it's only just started to seep back ... but I don't know if I've really thought it through.' She felt conflicted by the prospect: 'I would love to work full time, but I will also pay such a hideous price and miss my children ... [but] my career won't take off again until I go back full time.' Juliet wanted to be able to take her children to school and pick them up twice a week and thought this might be possible to negotiate with her company. For Juliet, picking up from school meant 'being there' for her children, and was central to her idea of a 'good' mother. It was a practice also engaged in by her own mother. Miriam had always collected Juliet and her sisters from school, and Juliet felt that this had helped to make them feel secure: 'Maybe that should influence me when – he will start school in September. I always remember my mother picking me up from school.' A central value of motherhood – taking children to and from school – was thus both transmitted from one generation to another, as well as being renegotiated from always to sometimes.

Juliet talked a lot about guilt, emanating from a belief that, despite her excellent childcare arrangements, her children really needed her to be with them more. 'I end up thinking I should be there ... I think guilt is what comes of motherhood ... I beat myself up a lot, I'm all the time questioning ... it just keeps going round and round, I think I'll always have that.' She feared that her children might be 'casualties', although she also hoped that 'I'm not doing any lasting damage, but my issue is – my relationship with my children suffers, definitely ... The big price that I pay is that they're pretty horrible with me when I get back from work ... it's [eldest son's] way of expressing that he's cross that I haven't been there all day.' Juliet contrasted her feelings with her husband's. James felt, she thought, no guilt about his absences, and these were not reported as affecting the children. Indeed, the children seemed to be quite different with James when he got in, making his time with them 'totally pleasurable, totally indulgent and wonderful ... I get moaning and whining and they don't let me out of their sight for a second'.

Juliet saw her 'choice' of maintaining her employment as exacting a price, even though from a gender equality perspective she saw such choices as being crucial for women: 'there is so much more open for women which is a great thing, but ... you pay somewhere along the line ... whether you pay with your relationships, or you pay with your children or you pay with your career or you pay with your earning capacity, everything.' She very much wanted to have the 'choice' but construed the notion of choice as one for herself to make and not for women to make collectively, a matter of individual agency without structural constraints. This led to her next evaluation namely that individual preferences can be potentially selfish.

> I'm greedy, I want it all ... That's what I could say about myself, is that I want it all, I'm not prepared to make sacrifices ... I want a bit of work and that might grow a bit, and I like a bit of the children and I like a bit of the domestic ... It's so clichéd but I think that's what's going on, is people want a bit of everything.

So how do the two older generations view Juliet's 'choices'? In response to the vignette (Chapter 3, footnote 1) concerning the employment decisions of a current couple with a young child, all three women responded similarly, choosing the part-time option. Margaret, consistent with her own high commitment to employment (though she did not work when her children were very young), was supportive of both her granddaughter Juliet and the hypothetical Lucy of the vignette wanting to work: 'I think [working] is quite a good thing otherwise they don't do anything but thinking about nappies and I think it's a very good thing that they keep their mind open. It's hard for her, I'm sure, but I think she's quite right.' But Miriam, consistent with her own work–family biography, is far more ambivalent. While opting for Lucy working part time, she added strong reservations: 'Why did Lucy want a child anyway?... I just feel if you want a child, then being as inflexible as Lucy just isn't right.' Her doubts, but not her expressions of disapproval, extended to her daughter, even though Juliet described her mother as her main 'emotional support', including discussions of her feelings of guilt. Miriam knew that Juliet wanted to work: 'I think it's important to her...I know her health suffers from it...I know if she didn't work, she wouldn't, she would be unhappy. I don't fully approve, I think at that age it might be better that the mother was there all the time.'

Juliet found the vignette particularly difficult to answer. Clearly it brought her own doubts and conflicts to the fore: 'I almost don't want to answer this...I don't feel comfortable about this.' If pressed, Juliet said she would opt for the mother working part time, but added 'it works for me but I know it doesn't work for a lot of people'.

On childcare in the vignette, all three chose different options. Miriam, the grandmother, opted (like Priscilla Peters) for grandparents – assuming they were interested. Margaret (great-grandmother) found it difficult to give a categorical answer as 'everybody is different', but rejected grandparents because 'they want to have their own life and don't want to be stuck with a little baby'. Juliet chose childminders rather than grandparents because despite providing the best care, 'they're recently retired and they've got those interests and I think that would be selfish'. Both Margaret and Juliet, therefore, share a view that grandparents today should be able to enjoy their retirement, which changes the negotiation of responsibility.

To draw some conclusions from this case, there are many clear elements of identity transmission and continuity between these three mothers/daughters. Since the oldest generation's arrival in Britain, all three women lived, with their families, in close proximity in the same area of London. It was a very 'close' family. There were strong ties of emotional closeness as well as a great deal of reciprocal support of a social and economic kind. Considerable value was attached to mutual care and support which are, however, rather less gendered than in the Peters' family. Miriam, the grandmother, together with her husband Robert, were pivotal, providing practical and emotional support to their daughter, while Miriam also provided considerable care support to her mother, Margaret.

All three women made substantial investments of time in their employment, including when they had children, and did demanding work. Yet, in all three cases, motherhood impacted on employment, producing breaks from work and part-time working. They married successful business men: this is a family with at least four generations of male managers and entrepreneurs. They had access to substantial resources not only familial care and support but also substantial incomes that enabled care and other services to be purchased readily. There was a recurring theme, going back to Margaret's childhood, of reliance on domestic service, which remained a feature of the lives of the next generations and related to high income and other material resources.

There is also, as with the women in the Peters' family, some overt feeling of continuity among the three women. Miriam suggested that her daughters might have been influenced in their attitudes to work because of an awareness of 'two generations of female workers, so I think they've always thought of females as working'. Although her daughters saw themselves as more into careers than their mother, Miriam explained this as a cohort change: 'that's partly to do with having a peer group and everything, that's a generation, I mean, that is different'.

But there are elements of discontinuity and change and lack of identification which make for innovation in the lives of these women. Events at societal and family levels produced new departures for Margaret, taking her from an upbringing where women of her class (including her mother) were not employed to a middle age devoted to running a company. Faced by extreme change in her circumstances, and a sense of responsibility to the family firm, Margaret had to make a new judgement about employment when her husband fell ill, then died. Both Margaret and Miriam, as members of particular historical cohorts, had little choice over their employment – or at least understood their situation in that light. They were drawn by a sense of kinship obligation into the family firm, which was both an opportunity and a constraint. Margaret's account though does not celebrate her business achievements.

Margaret and Miriam with ambitious, successful husbands who did not contribute much to the care of their own children, took back seats workwise when they had young children, only developing their employment careers after their children were at school, in a direction strongly influenced by a sense of responsibility to the family business. Miriam, however, rejected the path followed by her mother, deciding to prioritise motherhood over a career and refusing to send her children to boarding school, despite her husband's wishes, in reaction to her own experience as a child: 'I felt very strongly I wanted them at home, I wasn't at home at the most important time in my life.' Miriam's way of being a mother may be seen as a reaction in part at least to her mother and the kind of childhood she had experienced, albeit the choices she made to limit her work involvement occurred in very different conditions. The extent to which Miriam had a choice back in 1970s' Britain is itself debatable, with most women following Miriam's work trajectory. Rather Miriam made sense of her life in these respects in relation to juggling a lot of family commitments, from helping in the family firm to keeping her own household going with a largely absent husband, and making her mother part of her family. When interviewed, she still felt she was doing this: 'We have come in with childcare [for Juliet]. I enjoy it actually...but it's quite a lot of work.' Miriam's ambivalence about working in the family firm was in clear contrast to her unqualified engagement with voluntary work. She had less of a career – defined in terms of a career ladder – than her mother or daughter. Her métier turned out to be not management but social work.

Juliet's biography was very different from her mother's and grandmother's both in respect of education and employment career. She grew up during a period in which it was 'normal' for middle-class girls to go to university, to pursue a career progression and to try to maintain it as a mother. Equipped with a degree, Juliet took an innovative course, shaping her work career over the births of two children, albeit reducing her hours, but not giving up on a career. Indeed Juliet was seeking to consolidate the career progression she began well before having children. Unlike Margaret and Miriam, Juliet took it for granted she would resume work after maternity leave.

But, overall, Juliet did not contest the freedom to choose – in her words 'to have it all' even though currently it was costing her dear. Juliet was concerned that she might not be as good a mother as her own mother had been to her and her sisters. She faced a difficult decision in negotiating a relationship between employment and childcare. Despite a wide range of support available to her through high family income and her close-knit kin network, part of her felt that a 'good' mother should spend more time with her children than she did. She worried about lack of time with them, and about the employment consequences for herself of only working part time. Her employment pattern after having children was subject to considerable change, as she actively sought to find the right answer for her children and herself, that elusive balance between employment and care so much discussed in contemporary media. She was fortunate in being able to negotiate changes with her employer. Yet, remaining uncertain about her decisions, she experienced great internal ambivalence and conflict between her ambitions for motherhood and career. While she talked about choice, as both problem and opportunity, she also had considerable difficulty in deciding what was 'right' in the circumstances. Interestingly, she was silent about the individualised nature of her 'choices' and the solutions she depended upon: through negotiating individually with her employer; putting together a constantly changing patchwork of private childcare arrangements; and the apparent gendered responsibility of childcare, praising her husband for what help he chose to give and not expecting more.

The Miller women: a case of change

The Miller women's pattern of intergenerational relations reflects significant upward occupational mobility among both men and women in the family and geographical mobility. These produce less intergenerational support than in the more solidaristic families just described (see Chapter 7). The Miller women consist of great-grandmother Jessie, born in 1918, aged 82, a widow and a mother of two; Kate, born in 1940, aged 59 and a mother of three; and Alison, born in 1962, aged 38, and a mother of two children aged 6 and 10 years. The great-grandmother lived in south London, the grandmother in West London and the mother in a northern Home county.

Jessie was born in 1918, at the end of the First World War. Her father died within 6 months of her birth, a victim of the post-war influenza pandemic. Jessie talked about how difficult it was for her mother as a single parent – 'there was no social security in them days' – and how hard it was for families in the 1920s and 1930s: 'life was drab, you just about existed'. Her mother worked as a seamstress for most of her life and, through her mother's efforts, Jessie did not experience extreme poverty, though she saw it all around her (see also Chapter 2). Life, however, was hard for her.

Jessie, like many other great-grandmothers, spoke of frustrated ambitions. At school, she was good at art, and would have liked to pursue a career in this field, but could not do so because of the mores of the day and her social class. For working-class girls such as Jessie 'there wasn't no choices' except factory or shop work or domestic service. Her mother wanted Jessie to follow her into needlework, but having watched her mother work so hard this did not appeal. On leaving school at 14, with no qualifications, she went to work in a paper factory, assembling boxes and calendars, where she stayed for seven unfulfilling years: 'I didn't like it there, not really. It wasn't my sort of thing. But what I really wanted to do was out of the question.'

Jessie married at 21, in 1939, and gave up work, describing this as an expectation at the time: 'It was expected that you married – your husband kept you, and that job had to go to a single lady. Because there was such a lot of spinsters, because ... such a lot of men got killed [in the First World War] ... you 'ad to give your job up to that single woman, she had no-one to keep her.' (Although as noted in Chapter 3, most great-grandmothers continued at work until having children.) She had two children, when 22 and 26, during the Second World War. Her husband was called up when her first child was just three months and the family moved continuously in search of somewhere safe to live. Jessie was out of employment for 12 years, from the outbreak of war until 1951. During this time, her husband was discharged from the forces due to injury and there were times when he found it difficult to get work due to a severe limp.

Jessie returned to work when her children were 7 and 11 years old, to help meet the costs of a grammar school education (uniform etc.) for Kate, her oldest child. She took a part-time job with school meals, another example of the familiar pattern of great-grandmothers finding unskilled work in the expanding post-war education and welfare services.

Motherhood for Jessie, as for many great-grandmothers, meant being there for her children and fitting her employment around them. Childcare arrangements, she recounted, were never needed, returning to work only after her children were at school, then working part time and during school hours. She said that, at the time, she could not have envisaged increasing her hours from part time to full time because that would have been at odds with her idea of being a 'proper' mother: 'I made sure I only done part time, because – I, I wouldn't done full-time in any case, because I couldn't 've looked after my home prop'ly, and the children.'

In this respect, however, there was some difference in how Jessie and Kate remembered events (see also Doreen and her daughter Celia in the Hurd family, described in Chapter 3). While Jessie said that no one else looked after the children, her daughter remembered her mother paying a teenager to come in and sit with her and her brother for an hour or so when neither parent was home. Kate also recalled her mother working as a cleaner, first in the early morning and then in the evening, before moving to school meals. Perhaps Jessie, like some other great-grandmothers, had just forgotten these facts. Alternatively, she may not have mentioned it because this meant facing the reality, and contradiction, that she was not always able to 'be there' for her children.

Jessie was employed part time for most of her working life in a number of unskilled manual jobs, until she retired at 65. As well as kitchen work, she was on assembly lines and did cleaning for a police force, a job probably secured through the help of her daughter Kate. Jessie's only break in employment came in 1976 when, aged 58, she looked after her youngest granddaughter, then aged 2½, enabling her daughter Kate to take up full-time work. She did this for two and a half years and it was the only time that Jessie had worked full time since she was 21 – though she did not view childcare as a job and it is unlikely that her daughter paid her. As a pensioner Jessie had returned to her interest in art, taking up painting again.

Kate, Jessie's oldest daughter born in 1940, was evacuated in 1944, just before her brother was born. Although only away for about three months, she could still remember how she felt then and her time at a day nursery (not mentioned by her mother) before she was evacuated. Like her mother, Kate was attracted at school to the arts – and was similarly unable to pursue this interest. She was aware that her parents would not have viewed a creative/artistic career as a 'proper' job. Moreover, knowing that her mother had returned to work to help pay for her education, Kate was keen not to disappoint her by pursuing a career that she believed Jessie would not approve of.

Securing a place at a Catholic convent grammar school, the educational opportunities open to Kate were very different from her mother's. However, she did not do as well as she felt she could have: 'I should've done better than I did. I do regret really – 'Cos in the last year at school I really lost the plot a bit. I think I rebelled. From a religious point of view more than anything ... I should've stuck at it. And I should've gone on.' Kate left school at 16 with some O levels, did a year's further education in secretarial skills, then worked in clerical jobs until she had her first child, Alison, in 1962 at 22, the age at which Jessie too had become a mother.

Her husband, who worked as a printer, was earning a good income with overtime. However, they were struggling financially because, as Kate was to find out later, he was drinking heavily. Kate returned to work again, temping, when Alison was 2 years old, placing her in a day nursery, and continuing until her second child was born a year later. Kate stopped work again, but only briefly, returning within a few months to work part time as a shop assistant. Care of the children was shared between her mother-in-law and her husband, who was working nights.

In 1967, when her children were 2 and 5 years old, Kate divorced, a turning point that brought about major changes to her life. In new circumstances, she had to make a difficult decision: whether to work or stay at home to care for her children. Although awarded maintenance, she decided it would be better to work than rely on irregular payments from her former husband. She took a job working with children, at a 'one o'clock club' (a parent and toddler group) – another of the new areas of public-sector employment – so that she could take her son, who was now two, with her so negotiating an acceptable way of meeting her childcare responsibilities. Her son's entry to school prompted another change, 'when he started school I thought, I can earn some more money'. An interest in cooking, coupled with wanting to be at home during school holidays, led her to work in a school, preparing school meals, 'similar to my mother you see'.

But unlike her mother (or the other women in the study who found part-time work connected to school meals), Kate decided at this point to pursue a career in catering. She provides one of several examples from among the grandmother generation of upward occupational mobility after having children through a combination of working up from a low-skilled occupation and gaining further qualifications. Whilst working as a school cook, she attended night school twice a week to get a City and Guilds catering qualification. By this time she had remarried and her second husband cared for the children in the evenings while she was attending her course.

Her next move was to a local police force where she worked part time as a catering assistant until leaving aged 34 to have her third child, the first of her second marriage. This being 1974, there was no statutory maternity leave, and childbirth meant job loss: 'I was just getting into the stride of making a career for myself, and I found that I was pregnant with my daughter Annie.' Within three months of having her daughter, though, Kate returned to work with the police force – but to a lower grade job with part-time hours, from 4 to 8 p.m., which again enabled her husband to look after the children.

Kate continued in this job for about two years until a vacancy arose at the junior managerial grade she had been on before having Annie. However, the job was full time, creating a dilemma: how to combine a full-time job with her idea of proper childcare. This was only resolved when Jessie stepped in and offered to provide childcare, an arrangement which continued for over two years until Annie started school. Kate remained with the police force, working her way up from junior to senior management, but retired in 1993, at the relatively early age of 53. She took advantage of an offer of voluntary redundancy, but her decision was influenced by her health. Two years previously she had been diagnosed with cancer, which recurred after a year: 'I thought "I think this is a blessing in disguise", and I took it . . . So that was the end of my working career.' Kate remained very active in retirement. Like the other two grandmothers she did voluntary work, as well as adult education courses.

Alison was born in 1962. Like her mother, she rebelled towards the end of her schooling (they both use the same language of 'losing the plot') and did not achieve as much educationally as she might have: 'I just generally couldn't cope with being told what to do . . . just really beginning to lose the plot a bit I think.' She left school at 16 with O levels, moved to live with her father (her parents had been divorced for some years by then) and attended college to take A levels. Her father was keen for her to go on to university. Her mother, on the other hand, was not willing to support her on the grounds that she believed Alison would not put in the effort. Alison did indeed fail her A levels. However, she did not have the same regrets as her mother about not going on to University: 'I sort of almost wished that I'd done the work and gone . . . but I wasn't devastated . . . I sort of thought, "Well that's it. That's that little holiday period finished with, and now I've really got to sort myself out".'

Leaving college at 18, in 1980, Alison 'got any job that I could while waiting for a decent job to come up'. She worked as a cashier at an airport for 10 months while waiting to get into the Civil Service. Kate then helped her secure a job as a payroll officer with the police force where she (Kate) worked; the grandmother in this case, therefore, seems to have played a role in getting jobs for both her mother and daughter. Alison stayed there for the next 10 years, working up from a clerical to an executive grade, before leaving on the birth of her first child in 1990, when she was 28.

Alison recalled deciding at the age of 7 that she would not work when she had young children, in explicit reaction to the experiences of herself and her younger brother, in particular (as she remembered it) being left to their own devices. Alison's memory is of her mother 'never being there' for her, although she acknowledged she probably was – 'but you don't think of it like that'. She remembered having to look after her brother and, later, her half-sister during school holidays: 'We used to look after her in the holidays a lot . . . It always seemed a little bit sad to me, even at the time.' Jessie and Kate were appreciative of their mothers working, in particular for the economic benefits. Alison, in contrast, did not see that Kate's work brought her any benefits (see also Chapter 2).

So, though eligible for maternity leave, Alison resigned at the first opportunity. However, things did not work out as planned. Alison and her husband Thomas had moved out of London so that they could live on one income, but found they were still unable to manage. Alison had to renegotiate her motherhood, taking a job in a supermarket, working 2 days a week, when her first child was just a few months old. Everything was wrong about her return to work. The days were long, over 10 hours with travel, and she hated a job she did not want to be doing. A baby who was difficult did not help and she had little practical support from her husband. She was also somewhat unhappy about her mother-in-law caring for her daughter.

After four years, promotion for her husband and an improved financial situation provided the opportunity for Alison to renegotiate motherhood and stop working: 'All our problems were solved in one swoop really and I've not worked since.' With a second child, and a husband moving rapidly up the managerial ladder, Alison could be a full-time housewife and mother. However, full-time motherhood was not entirely satisfying: 'I did go through a really bad downy patch where I just thought, y'know, really, there's nothing here at all for me.' She described a housewife as not much more than 'a dogsbody'.

Alison decided to retrain as a teacher. So after a four-year break, when her children were 4 and 8 years old and both at school, she did a two-year part-time access course before starting a degree in English Literature. When interviewed, she had another two years to go, then a further year to qualify as a teacher. Talking about her future she once again displayed some ambivalence towards being a full-time housewife: 'I will definitely do something... I couldn't envisage myself sitting here day after day when the children were properly at school... That would just drive me mad, just to sit, dusting.'

There are certain continuities here across all three generations of women, especially unfulfilled schooling with some making up for missed opportunities later in life. Resuming work after having children was also driven by strong financial needs: in Jessie's case, Kate's education and perhaps her husband's injury; in Kate's case, her husband's drink problem and, subsequently, divorce; in Alison's case, the inadequacy of a single wage. Both Kate and Alison had to negotiate difficult decisions about employment and childcare, in which financial responsibility was probably the determining factor: Kate whether to resume employment after divorce and whether to take a full-time job, and Alison whether to resume work soon after having her first child despite a strong preference not to work.

Jessie started work in a factory and her granddaughter, Alison, worked in a supermarket, a sign of changing forms of unskilled employment. But in between there was a linking thread of public-sector service work in traditional female occupations: school meals, childcare, catering and clerical work in the police force.

The differences, however, are more striking, in particular their employment histories. Jessie, the great-grandmother, left work at marriage, had a long break from employment, then a long spell, over 30 years, of part-time employment. Kate also worked seven years between leaving education and stopping work, but did so when pregnant with her first child. Her subsequent employment history was very different from her mother's. Until her early retirement (12 years earlier than her mother's) she had been less than four years out of employment, the longest period being 2½ years when her first child was born; unlike Jessie she was back at work before her youngest children were 3 years old. She also resumed full-time employment with her final child; neither Jessie nor Alison had worked full time since having children.

Her daughter, Alison, had a longer period between leaving education and stopping work (10 years), and was initially thwarted by financial pressures from taking a sustained break from employment on becoming a mother. However she did so, once the family finances improved. This was explained as a specific distancing from her own mother's decision to work when she and her brother were young, a divergence reflecting generational ambivalence. Yet at the same time, she suggested that full-time motherhood was not totally satisfying, hinting at some underlying identification with her mother's situation: Kate, her mother, described herself as 'not a housewife', while Alison described being a housewife in pejorative terms.

Kate, the grandmother, showed the strongest attachment to the labour market, at least until illness and a voluntary redundancy offer persuaded her to take early retirement. She also showed a strong career progression in later working life. With the help of extra qualifications, and her mother's offer of childcare at a critical moment, she was able to re-establish herself in the full-time position she had before the birth of her third child, then move up to a senior management position in the catering service of a large police force. Her mother, by contrast, had unskilled or semi-skilled jobs throughout her working life, while her daughter took a low status job after a forced return to work – although she may in due course, through gaining a qualification, again at a later stage of life, also be able to progress occupationally.

This generational fluctuation in employment (both occupation and employment patterns) is matched by other divergences to do with generational distance but also divergence in lifestyles and values. Alison (from a working-class family) married into a middle-class family. Alison and her family were living some distance outside London, where both Jessie and Kate continued to live. Her husband Thomas was doing well in management, and with the encouragement and help of one of her husband's relatives they were sending their children to a private school, a decision greeted with some ambivalence by her mother.

How did the different generations respond to the contemporary dilemma of working parents? All three women offered different answers to the first part of the vignette (Chapter 3, footnote 1). Great-grandmother Jessie thought that the vignette mother (Lucy) should stop work, rationalising this on grounds of gendered abilities: 'I would always say the woman [should stop working] because the woman makes the home ... I can't see a man wanting to do all the shopping, the cooking, and the cleaning. Whereas a woman would automatically do that.' This view is no doubt shaped by Jessie's own experience as a mother in the 1940s when her husband had little involvement with housework or childcare. Yet, despite this normative view, Jessie was not critical of her daughter and granddaughter working when they had young children, accepting they both had to work from financial necessity.

Kate, like her mother, said one of the parents should stay at home if they could manage on one salary. But she believed it immaterial whether it was the mother or father. Alison, on the other hand, chose the current normative trend namely both parents working. Just as it was important for her to be at home because this was what she wanted, so it was important for the vignette mother to do what she wanted and go out to work: avoiding personal dissatisfaction was the first consideration.

Both Jessie and Kate opted in the vignette for grandparents as carers. Jessie believed relatives provide better care than 'strangers', while Kate argued that the child was too young to be 'left' with someone else. Pushed further, she reasoned that grandparents could come to the child's home, maintain the child's routine and provide the child with individual care and attention. Alison, on the other hand, chose either a nursery or a nanny. Like the two other mothers featured in this chapter, she passed over grandparents, though in her case because she thought them 'too old'. She also rejected childminders because their standards of care were not high: 'I've seen so many of them dragging their kids, other people's kids round Safeways.'

Conclusions

The actions and decisions made by women in these multi-generation families demonstrate both change and continuity. As part of the process whereby women forge identities as mothers, women identified with or distanced themselves from the models provided by their own parents. In some cases, women testified to the transmission of identity through the stories of the 'person' resources that were available to them and which they drew upon – whether in terms of wishing to emulate or react against the kinds of mothers (and sometimes fathers) with whom they had grown up. Such identification or distancing may emerge through their practices in education, employment and caring , but it may also be evident in their responses to their parents' attitudes and actions, for example to parents' encouragement, or otherwise, in these areas. Alternatively, identification may emerge more relationally in terms of women's emotional identification, expressed as emotional closeness to or distance from their parents.

So, in some cases, women made a decision and developed a pattern based upon conscious evaluations, expressed during their interviews, of their parents (or in some cases another family member), either of them as persons or of their actions. In other instances this is less apparent; as in the latter case (the Millers), women do not themselves suggest influences upon their actions. As researchers and analysts of the biographical histories of these family members we can, however, observe in their actions processes of transmission bringing continuity or breaks with the past.

Many of the post-war grandmother generation identified with models of full-time motherhood. Yet several changed the course of their lives by pursuing education and employment careers in the wake of motherhood and, by so doing, followed different paths to those taken by their mothers, often taking advantage of widening employment opportunities. Few of the current, youngest generation of mothers (born in the 1960s and 1970s) drew upon older generations for role models in making employment decisions. For, by the 1990s, it had become common for British mothers to remain in, or soon return to, work when they had children. The youngest generation stood out in their emphasis upon their own agency in shaping motherhood. However, this does not mean that they no longer faced structural or other constraints. Rather they remained silent about them, as in the case of Juliet Kent who empha-sised her individual solutions, the personal price she had to pay and the possible price for her children.

In this chapter we have examined the ways in which women made sense of their lives as mothers and the work and care decisions that make up their life histories. Some of these decisions – which we have interpreted within a framework of negotiating responsibility, which implicates moral or ethical judgements – seem, as recounted, to have been relatively straightforward, requiring little deliberation. Others were more complex, often because of unusual or unexpected circumstances: for example, Margaret Kent's decision to take over the running of her deceased husband's business, or Kate Miller's decision to work after her divorce or to work full time after the birth of her third child. Many were condi-tional, judgements that a course of action was justified by a particular situation. Some decisions were seen to come at a price and were subject to current uncertainty, for example Juliet Kent's decision to pursue her career part time.

The role of what we have termed 'negotiation' in arriving at decisions is in part an internalised process of deliberation, working out with oneself the 'right' thing to do. But it is also an external process, in which others are implicated both in the process of deliberation and in providing solutions. For example, Annabelle Peters decided to increase her part-time hours because of the willingness of friends to contribute to childcare arrangements. In Juliet Kent's case it is the considerable support provided by her parents and the latitude she had as a relatively high status employee to negotiate with her employer a reduction in working hours, while Kate Miller could take up full-time employment with young children because her mother was willing to provide full-time care.

As we have already flagged up, the approach we have adopted – nego-tiating responsibilities including an ethical dimension – problematises the concept of choice. In the neo-liberal climate of *fin de siècle* Britain, in which our study took place, choice assumes an independent, isolated human agent making rational or calculative decisions 'upon relative assessment of costs and benefits of "investment" in the light of envir-onmental contingencies' (Rose, 1999, p. 141). It takes as its model the consumer in the market place looking for 'best value' or the entrepreneur deciding which course of action offers the best rate of return.

We have posited, instead, 'a relational self, a moral agent embedded in concrete relationships with others' (Sevenhuijsen, 1999b, p. 56), who makes deliberative decisions about what is right in the context of particular circumstances and possibilities and faced by a variety of responsibilities. This moral agent also makes judgements about others. In so doing, she is able to distinguish between what is the right action for herself in her particular time and place, and what seems right for others to do, within their particular situations.

This study gave us the opportunity to apply such an approach to families with several generations who variously reflect upon their decisions and actions in respect of different life course phases and different normative climates pertaining over much of the 20th century. Older generations of women may hold norms which applied when they were mothers or when they were growing up, but they do not allow these to override their concern for and understandings of the circumstances and preferences of today's generation of mothers – their daughters and granddaughters. A great-grandmother may have held, when a mother herself, that mothers should not work, or only in very closely defined circumstances, and she may still hold to this belief today. But she can also accept the decision made by her granddaughter to go out to work, because she appreciates that bringing up children today is more expensive, and she recognises that her granddaughter and partner are good parents. In practice, employment decisions and others' views of those decisions represent a contextualised morality.

5
Timetabling, Talk and Transmission: Fatherhood across the Generations

This chapter turns its gaze from motherhood to fatherhood. It focuses upon fatherhood as practised by different historical generations and how practices change or are transmitted from fathers to sons in particular families. In keeping with the methodology we have sought to balance a concern with the life course and the significance of historical context with the interpretations interviewees bring to the recounting of their lives in work and care. This is a difficult task not least in presenting the analysis, given the wealth and depth of the material provided by members of the multi-generation families interviewed.

We adopt three types of analysis. First, we focus upon timetabling: the scheduling of fatherhood in the life course of three generations: when it occurs, the context in which it occurs, in particular the scheduling of fatherhood in relation to other life course transitions such as marriage, housing and employment. We then shift gear to focus upon 'talk' in particular the normative discourses men from different generations draw upon in negotiating their own positions with respect to what is still today a matter for critical debate in Britain: whether parents with young children should be employed and how children should be cared for.

In the third part of the chapter we look in detail at the transmission of fatherhood within the families. We examine the ways in which fathers in the 12 families practise fatherhood in the childrearing phase: in relation to breadwinning, on the one hand, and looking after and being involved with their children, on the other. Here we look more closely at four families to see whether and in what ways fathers and sons in the same families describe being fathers. Thus we begin to address the question whether ways of 'doing fatherhood' are transmitted. (Only two of the four families discussed cover three generations of men, a reflection of the small number of great-grandfathers who were still alive. Only two families contained strings of biologically related fathers and sons over three generations.) The last of the family case studies presented is discussed in the greatest depth with a more detailed analysis of the 'whole case' (the fathers in question); we tease out the biographical and historical 'facts' of the case first in order to provide an interpretative context for understanding how the fathers made sense of their lives (see Wengraf, 2001). The rationale for this is that this family constitutes a critical example of fatherhood being transformed in the current generation, involving the negotiation of a new male responsibility for children: from breadwinning to shared carer. But first we will present a brief overview of developments in British fatherhood in general and in public policy.

Fatherhood: a brief overview

Fathers have been the subject of much less attention demographically than mothers; official statistics typically have less, if anything, to say about fatherhood than motherhood. Fathers have rarely been a focus in public policy, in contrast to motherhood. However most research evidence suggests that changes in fatherhood have nowhere near matched the scale of the changes in motherhood: fathers' employment has remained overwhelmingly continuous and full time, still marked at the end of the century by long working hours (averaging 46 per week in 2001).

Historical research warns us against making generalisations about fatherhood in particular periods and across social classes (Thompson, 1977); this is also the case for fatherhood among younger generations (see for example McKee and O'Brien, 1982; O'Brien and Shemilt, 2003). However, this is not to say that there are no general trends. The authority and prestige of fathers as patriarchs declined during the industrial revolution in which men's work was removed from the household and citizenship took the place of fatherhood: 'By the end of the 19th century, middle class fatherhood had become a matter of evenings, weekends and certain calendared occasions' (Gillis, 2000, p. 230). Gillis argues that companionate marriage and women's feminisation in the home in the post-Second World War period weakened fatherhood, with men's link to their children being mediated largely through their wives. Fatherhood has historically been allied with breadwinning with some current studies continuing to report this (Warin *et al.*, 1999). But from the 1970s onwards, there is much reference to the 'crisis of the breadwinner father' (Gillis, 2000).

Some see this as a consequence of women's increased contribution to the workforce and the restructuring of the labour market. There has been a growth in non-manual and service sector employment and a decline in certain kinds of skilled manual work and in unskilled and semi-skilled work. Some of the major growth areas of the current economy, such as care work, are in occupations mainly employing women. On balance these changes in recent decades have eroded the employment of working-class men and thus their potential to be 'providers', while women's employment continues to be in the ascendant through the increase in non-manual and service jobs. They have also been accompanied by men taking more responsibility in the home, especially for children, with the time fathers devote to child-related activity increasing most rapidly since the late 1980s and among men with children under 5 years of age (O'Brien and Shemilt, 2003). Even though the division of domestic work and responsibility between mothers and fathers still remains unequal, this shift in fathers' childcare involvement suggests a response to the growth in the employment of mothers with young children that has occurred in this period.

Public policy reflects the type of welfare regime operating within a society, that is, the contract between capital and labour (Esping-Andersen, 1999), and the type of 'gender contract' that exists between men and women (Hernes, 1987). The notion of contract here implies a form of historical compromise which is implicit (Duncan and Edwards, 1999). In Britain, the bourgeois or strong breadwinner model (Lewis, 1992) has dominated over the last century, based on the ideal of a male breadwinner family and of the mother as the primary caregiver in the home. Such implicitly gendered assumptions about men's and women's responsibilities have permeated historical developments in British public policy, for example in social security, income tax, family allowances, wage bargaining and equal pay (Land, 1980). It has produced what we referred to in Chapter 3 as a 'maternalist' welfare state. Where working-class men were able to earn a 'family wage', this obviated the need for wives to go out to work, leaving them better able to attend to the very heavy demands of running a household.

However, as we have seen in earlier chapters, the breadwinner *ideal* of the husband as the sole earner, to which much social prestige was attached, was rarely achieved in the 20th century except in middle-class families. Women as wives and mothers often did paid work. Moreover, public recognition of and support for working mothers (apart from in wartime) and for fathers took a long time to achieve in Britain.

Only in the late 1990s has public policy begun to take a new direction but it still largely ignores or underplays fatherhood – beyond its insistence that fathers take financial responsibility for their children notably in the context of separation and divorce. Rather public policy ignores gender in its emphasis upon parents and on paid work for all. There have been few active public policies to counter the continuing gender divisions in childcare responsibilities and the domestic sphere. Conservative governments in the 1980s and 1990s rigorously opposed proposals from the European Commission, first tabled in 1983, for an entitlement to parental leave, which recognises and supports fathers' equal responsibility for childcare. When finally conceded in 1999, the parental leave entitlement was minimal – unpaid, inflexible, short in duration (Deven and Moss, 2002) – and hence unlikely to be widely used either by women or men. Since the end of our study, paid paternity leave of two weeks has been introduced, in 2003, but alongside an extension of maternity leave to 12 months post birth: in no other country does maternity leave extend so long after childbirth (ibid.). Government's choice of this leave initiative, rather than strengthening parental leave, suggests a continuing and deep-seated state adherence to ideas about the gendered nature of childcare.

The timetabling of fatherhood

Changes in men's demographic behaviour have received rather little attention. Looking at overall trends over the long term, in Northern Europe changes in parenthood across the generations appear linear, with fewer children born and first time parenthood occurring at older ages (Fagnani, 2004). But, when we compare the three cohorts of fathers in our study, there are (as with the mothers in our study) some striking contrasts which do not add up to a linear pattern of cross-generational progression. Rather, there is much variation in the patterning of their life courses in relation to the social transitions which constitute it.

First, on the issue of the age at which men became fathers, it is the *middle* generation of men born around the end of the Second World War who had children at the youngest age (a mean age of 24 compared with 27 and 26 years for the great-grandparent and grandparent generations respectively). Again, it is this generation who married at the youngest age (20 years compared with 23 years for the other generations). Second, there is the ordering of social transitions, in particular the premising of fatherhood upon marriage. Here the significant change is in the 1970s/80s generation who, in contrast to their fathers and grandfathers, lived with their partners (in all but one case) *before* marriage. (None of the grandfathers and only one of the great-grandfathers cohabited.) Indeed three fathers were still unmarried at interview and two had only married following their children's births. (See Chapter 1, Table 1.2 for an overview of when cohabitation, marriage and fatherhood occurred for the three male generations in the study.)

Third, there is the issue of the timetabling of transitions. For the middle generation of men especially, transitions into work, marriage and fatherhood fell thick and fast, within a very few years of each other. In contrast the transitions of the 1970s/80s generation are stretched out: they are staggered over time, reflecting this group's older age at becoming fathers and their extended youth phase – a time in which as 'young adults' they could experiment and try out different patterns of living (Brannen *et al.*, 2002). So too are some of those of the few great-grandfathers. Though the contexts differ for each generation, some issues are similar.

Housing, for example, was an issue which many of the 1970s/80s generation had sorted out before children arrived, reflecting the way in which having a home of one's own had become a normative precondition for parenthood in the 1990s. Indeed, nine of the fathers (again with the notable exception of the three unskilled fathers) had taken out mortgages on a house or a flat before their first child was born, while in another case the couple bought a house following the first birth. In contrast, among the grandfather and great-grandfather generations, buying a house was not a priority or a precondition for fatherhood. Only five grandfathers were homeowners by the time they had their first child while amongst the great-grandfathers only one had a home of their own before their first child was born. Indeed most of this latter generation either began married life living with parents or in-laws or were serving in the forces and living away (it being wartime) when their children were born.

The 1970s/80s generation enjoyed longer in education than the oldest generation (and the middle generation). But their entry into work was punctuated by uncertainty, as was that of the oldest generation whose employment and fatherhood were often interrupted by the Depression of the 1930s or the war that followed. In contrast, the middle generation enjoyed the economic stability provided by a high employment rate when they became fathers in the post-war period.

For the grandparent generation in the *Ashton* family, social transitions fell thick and fast around the transition to fatherhood in contrast to both the subsequent and older generations. Joseph Ashton (grandfather) was born in 1948. He left school at 15 with no qualifications and almost immediately gave up an electrical apprenticeship to work as an electrician's mate. Aged 17, his girlfriend became pregnant and they married just before Joseph's 18th birthday. After the birth of their son they moved in with Joseph's parents, and then into a temporary rented accommodation before they were granted a council flat. A second child was born when Joseph was 21, then a third child three years later. Several years later, after a move to a council house, they took out a mortgage (on the council house).

By contrast, Joseph's son, Luke, cohabited, got married, became a homeowner and settled into the labour market, all *before* becoming a father, with some time gaps between these transitions. Like his father he left school at the earliest opportunity and went straight into work. But unlike his father, he lived with his wife-to-be for a year before marrying at the age of 24, and the couple bought a flat together before marriage. Similarly and unusually Joseph's father, Bill (great-grandfather), cohabited before marriage (a situation which related to the particular conditions of wartime) and had a variety of occupations, including a period of wartime service and training, before becoming a father. Bill did not secure permanent (council) housing, however, until after their second child was born as housing was in short supply after the war. It took both Bill and Luke nine years from leaving school (both spent one year longer at school than Joseph) to having their first children; for Joseph, it took only three years.

The coincidence of social transitions in the grandparent generation can also be illustrated in the *Samuels* family. The life course trajectory of Richard Samuels (grandfather born in 1942) stands in sharp contrast to the staggered pattern of transitions of his son, Stephen, born in 1963. (We have no information about the great-grandfather in this family.) Richard began a relationship with Marjorie, his wife-to-be, while an undergraduate. They married (but did not first cohabit) when Richard was 19, and their first child was born soon after. Richard graduated two years later at the same time as they had a second child. The following year the family moved to the other end of the country where Richard started training as an educational psychologist. They then moved again when Richard took up his first 'proper job' and bought his first house. All this occurred within the space of five years.

In contrast, Richard's son Stephen, who also went to university, took a decade to go through a similar set of social transitions. Like his father, Stephen met his wife-to-be, Naomi, at university; but unlike his father, they cohabited first while both were at university (Richard's wife, by contrast, was not a university student at that time). Stephen and Naomi then lived separately for short periods because of the location of their first jobs, with Stephen returning to live at home for a spell. Six years after the start of their relationship, Stephen and Naomi married and bought a house before starting a family. From leaving school at 18, it took Richard only two years to become a father; for Stephen, it took nine years.

In both cases, the current fathers (Luke and Richard) portrayed many of their life course decisions as 'personal choices'. For example Luke had some difficulty finding stable employment in the 1980s and 1990s – he had two episodes of unemployment following redundancy – but talked about 'being in charge of my own future' when he got a particular job. Moreover, both of these current fathers had to contend with rising house prices and increased expectations of home ownership. But they did not describe these as limiting their scope for choice. In contrast, Bill (great grandfather) did not perceive at the time the training opportunities he was afforded in his wartime service in the RAF to be an 'opportunity' except in retrospect: 'I was just joining up' he said when asked if he saw it then as an opportunity. Joseph (grandfather) described his early entry into parenthood as similarly taken for granted rather than a choice; it was what many young men like himself did at that time. Neither did Joseph refer to the possibilities that the high rate of employment afforded in the post-war years – although it is clear from his account that he found jobs relatively easily. For example, he suggested having little hesitation about leaving an apprenticeship to take unskilled work, much to the dismay of his father (Bill) who had been a skilled worker.

Fatherhood talk: negotiating normative discourses over the generations

Is the way men talk about fatherhood changing over the generations? What do they consider to be appropriate practices for mothers and fathers who have young children to care for?

National evidence, based upon the British Social Attitudes Survey (BSAS), concerning attitudes to parenthood and work suggests that there has been a considerable shift, with recent cohorts of both men and women expressing more egalitarian attitudes than earlier cohorts (Scott, 1999). In 1994, 83 per cent of women and 78 per cent of men who were similar in age to the parent generation in our study, that is between 18 and 27, disagreed with 'traditional gender roles' (i.e. the husband's job is to earn the money and the wife's job is to look after the home), compared with only 27 per cent of women and 21 per cent of men over the age of 68, a group rather younger than the great-grandparent generation in our study. The middle-aged group in the BSAS (our grandparent generation) fell somewhere in the middle (Scott, 1999).

Such attitudes are captured in our study in responses to a vignette concerning parents' decisions about employment when they have a young child and their childcare preferences (see footnote 1 in Chapter 3). As in the BSAS, the two older generations in our study were conservative in attitude: great-grandfathers, like most of the great-grandmothers, thought that the mother rather than the father should be at home. Similarly, most grandfathers (8/12) but only one of the grandmothers favoured mothers staying at home. In contrast, though, fewer of the 1970s/80s generation of fathers (5/12) and only three of the mothers thought that mothers should be full-time carers or work part time when the child was young. Across the three generations, only one (a grandfather) explicitly endorsed the vignette option of both parents working full-time when they have young children.

As we discussed in the previous chapter, general attitudes are only part of the story of how people make sense of and make decisions about household employment and children's care. Looking more closely at the more radical views of the 1970s/80s generation of fathers, most talked about employment and childcare in a 'gender neutral' way while, at the same time, avoiding being overly prescriptive. Perhaps not surprisingly, given the newness of their current parental responsibilities, they fore-grounded personal choice in taking decisions about employment.

While the two older generations of fathers expressed a commitment to general principles about what it means to be a 'proper' mother and father, they also tempered their normative statements, taking into account the particular situations of family life in different social and historical conditions. As do mothers (see Chapter 4), men too make contextualised ethical judgements. In two families, we may see how fathers and sons negotiate different positions. Gordon Brand, grandfather, suggested that mothers' working was in principle 'wrong'. But he moved from a general normative viewpoint, which he linked to his own childhood experience of family life, to one which allowed for the possibility of reasoning differently in relation to the current context. Gordon talked about how his mother had so much domestic work to do when he was a child, so much so that she was 'totally occupied'; whereas he considered that mothers today could take work outside the home since they have more time and less household work to do. Thus, Gordon modified his position in adopting a present time frame and accepted that it may be right for today's mothers to work – because of modern conveniences in the home and the fact that some women can command higher salaries than men.

Well, it was the man that works, wasn't it? and, um – you see, in those days, especially in my mother's day, I mean, my mother never had time to work, with the house-cleaning and washing and everything. It was a full-time job, wasn't it? These days, there's washing machines and hoovers and things that – it's a lot different. I know these days women can earn perhaps sometimes more than men. But, um, it just seems wrong from the – for a man to look after children while the woman's working. But I suppose they can't help it.

Gordon's son, Sean, negotiates a position with a different result. Sean is careful to assert that he agrees in principle with women working, that is, according to present mores and practices, and is anxious not to be seen to be 'old-fashioned', that is, to be opposed to mothers' employment. In referring to the particularities of his wife's decision to return to work, he avoids making a specific judgement, going along with her decision: 'She said that she wanted to do it. I didn't have any – and I just supported what she wanted to do. Um, but in doing that, I always assumed that if there was a problem with [daughter] – you know, you chose to go back....' In fact in his response to the vignette, Gordon opted for the mother working part-time.

However, with respect to childcare Sean draws upon an explicitly gendered viewpoint. As the previous quotation demonstrates, he assumes that their child is his wife's responsibility. He feels it legitimate to assert that a child needs a mother's care, while recognising that this view might be considered 'old-fashioned' by today's standards. 'Mothers make better mothers than fathers...It may be old-fashioned...um, the baby's used to the woman's voice all the time, the smell, and everything. And as soon as that comes out, there's a bond, isn't there? I think. So I'm not sure that a father bringing up a child is as good for the child as a mother.'

Like Gordon Brand earlier, George Masters (a grandfather) expressed a normative commitment to fathers as breadwinners and mothers as carers, again suggesting how this belief was instilled by his parents. He described how his own parents had stressed the importance of finding a stable, secure job in order to be a 'reliable' family provider: 'Women won't work and you're going to be the breadwinner...Women were domestic in those days...the man was the money earner wasn't he really?' Moreover, it is significant that, after George's father died, as the youngest of six children he took on the provider role; his mother had never worked and did not expect to. George also noted how during his own childhood it was important for men and their immediate families to be self-sufficient, that is, *not* to have to rely on material help from other kin (outside the immediate family): 'We didn't have major aspirations except, as I said before, stability and – as long as you cared for your family and you didn't have to rely on other people looking after you, it was all you ever wanted ... [A] sort of fairly humble stable home, that was ... as big as your expectations could be.'

George in part repeated this pattern in his own marriage, being the main breadwinner. However his wife was an important secondary earner. His response to the vignette was consistent with his general (childhood located) beliefs although the grounds for opposing mothers' employment shifts slightly. Instead of stressing the importance of mothers as homemakers (consequent on fathers being providers), he emphasised the importance of mothers as carers of children in their formative years:

> I think mums are – any decent mum is the one that should be the – the chief. I think that – I think that people look up to their mum for, er, their formative years ... Mums look after kids better than dads ... they've got a natural instinct, mothering instinct. It's a bit like animal things.

As to fathers, George observed that 'I think they [learn different things] from their dads later on'. He also expressed concern about children being cared for by 'strangers'. Yet, it is significant that George did not opt for grandparents as the preferred childcare choice with respect to the vignette. Perhaps thinking of his own situation as a grandparent, he considered it 'unfair to burden grandparents' and chose the compromise of the childminder, albeit one who is 'a friend of the family'.

George's son, Douglas, unlike his father, distanced himself from a traditional gender viewpoint in not wanting to appear prescriptive (in the interview) about whether women with young children should or should not work. Like Sean Brand, he talked about his wife's 'choice', which complemented his own preference – *not* to care for his children on a full-time basis:

> Y'know I'm not a traditional old-fashioned person that says, 'No the woman must stay at home, and work.' I don't believe in that. I think [wife] is ummm very different to a lot of y'know girls that want a career these days, in that she did want to stay at home. Y'know she 'ad, and y'know, that fitted in with, y'know I was happy with that. But I'm not sure, with the, the shoe on the other foot, that I would've wanted to do that. I wouldn't've wanted to be the carer staying at

home. That's not something that I've sort of ... that's been in my y'know, something that I've wanted to do, from, from early on.

By carefully positioning himself as 'not a traditional man' in general terms, and being at pains to emphasise his wife's 'choice' to stay at home, Douglas could avoid making his somewhat traditional position too explicit. He could present a way of life freely chosen rather than governed by gender structures and constraints. In contrast to his father, Douglas attributed a greater sense of agency in shaping his career as a father, even though his own father was also driven by clear goals (providing security for his family). However, his father's goal was more 'basic', that is, to ensure the family 'kept its head above water' so that they did not have to rely upon others. Douglas's goal is of a different order: he spoke about 'psychologically preparing' himself for being the main breadwinner, as he moved upwards in his occupational career and gradually overtook his wife in terms of pay – stressing his ability to take on the mortgage on his own. Moreover, in developing his career he was careful to enlarge his work experience in case he did not pass his professional exams; this, he said, would enable him to further his career 'in another direction' (implying but not saying that his wife would still not have to work). In *not* referring to his wife's earlier contribution to breadwinning (his wife had been earning more than him in their first years in the workforce), Douglas was able to more easily legitimate his wife's decision to stay at home: how *he* was able to 'let' his wife make a choice about employment when they had children.

Some fathers in the 1970s/80s generation said that *both* parents ought to work part time. Moreover the final choice was seen to depend upon individual contingencies, for example which parent could earn more. But no father referred to the gendered structure of the labour market, whereby most men still earn substantially more than women. In *not* addressing this issue, they could assert that they were egalitarian in the sense that it did not 'matter' whether it was the father or the mother who 'stayed at home': it was, they implied, simply a pragmatic and personal choice, untrammelled by structural inequality or normative societal attitudes.

Such men could envisage other possibilities premised on fathers having the potential to be equally good carers of children. The father, for example, might care for children if his wife was a higher earner, thereby suggesting the norm was negotiable. Yet, among all the generations, there was a strong endorsement of the *parents managing it between themselves* so that at least one of them was 'there for the child' or so that they shared the care by working part time.

Thus over the generations (historically and in particular families), there appears to be a growing acceptance of mothers' employment. However such egalitarian views are negotiated in the context of gendered assumptions about what *children* 'need': that is, maternal care and certainly not care by 'strangers'. The youngest generation of fathers also distances itself from decisions about household employment – putting the choice on to mothers – a strategy whereby they avoid committing themselves to principles of gender equity, at least on this question. As the idea that we, as autonomous individuals, are expected to negotiate our own ways of 'doing family life' takes hold, such consequences are unsurprising.

The transmission of different types of fatherhood

We turn now to the difficult task of making sense of the different ways in which men over three generations negotiated being fathers of younger children. In order to do this we have conceptualised fatherhood as sets of 'practices' (Morgan, 1999) as encompassing both actions and meanings. While we have made inferences about what fathers did from men's accounts of the past, we have also drawn upon the accounts of other family members. In conceptualising fatherhood as a subjective construction, constituted by the meanings and interpretations that fathers bring to fatherhood, we have also had to engage with the fact that for some generations being a father of young children was a long time ago while for others it is current. In all cases fatherhood – past or present – is interpreted through the lenses of the present (see Chapter 2 for a discussion about time).

We have focused on men's involvement in the labour market and their breadwinner contributions to the household, and also on their involvement with their children and the running of the household. We also have looked in particular depth at how fathers negotiate particular types of fatherhood in the interview encounter (see the last case discussed below).

As depicted in Table 5.1, the practice of fathers acting as main breadwinners and mothers as supplementary breadwinners remains the prevailing pattern for all three generations during the childrearing phase of the life course, with a fall off in men acting as *sole* breadwinners between the great-grandfather and grandfather generations. Only two grandfathers were sole breadwinners throughout the majority of the childrearing years, with all but one of the others being the main breadwinner. In two of these latter cases, the mothers worked for a very short time, in one case when the husband was unexpectedly made redundant but only until he had found another job.

Table 5.1 Fathers' breadwinning practices in the childrearing phase

	Great-grandfathers $(n = 24)^c$	Grandfathers $(n = 12)$	Fathers $(n = 12)$
Sole breadwinner (most of the time)	8	2	0
Main breadwinner (all/much of the time)	13	9	7[b]
Equal breadwinners (both full time and some of the time)	0	1	1
Mother main breadwinner (some of the time)	1[a]	0	1
Both parents full-time carers (some of the time)	0	0	2
Not known/as yet unclear	2	0	1[d]

[a] After husband's death.

[b] The wife of one of these men was employed briefly.

[c] Only seven were interviewed; information was provided by great-grandmothers.

[d] The baby was not yet born.

By contrast with older generations, none of the 1970s/80s father generation was a sole breadwinner on a consistent basis. In this generation we see some emergent trends that suggest 'alternative' ways of organising parenthood. On the other hand, the majority pattern for this cohort of fathers is to work full time and for the mothers to work part time. The variant patterns include three cases where both fathers and mothers stayed at home for some time to look after young children and one case with both parents sustaining full-time employment and sharing childcare. The three non-employed fathers had no qualifications and two little in the way of employment records. At the time of interview, one was employed intermittently, another had entered full-time work and the third was combining childcare with a university degree.

In Figure 5.1, we have plotted the fathers in our study according to two dimensions. The vertical dimension refers to men's reported contributions to breadwinning: whether they were the main or sole breadwinners when they had young children, as against fathers who shared breadwinning equally or were only spasmodically involved in employment and income generation. The horizontal axis refers to men's involvement in family life and with their children. Thus we have typified fathers according to whether they suggested stronger or weaker involvement in and identification with fatherhood. Locating the cases in these ways distributes the

Main/sole breadwinner

B. *Family men and child-oriented fathers*	A. *Work-focused fathers (career men and provider fathers)*
Two great-grandfathers Four grandfathers Three fathers	Two great-grandfathers Six grandfathers Four fathers
Strong fatherhood involvement	**Weak fatherhood involvement**
C. *Hands-on fathers* Four fathers	D. *Non-employed fathers with a weak investment in fatherhood* No cases

Not main/sole breadwinner

Figure 5.1 Models of fatherhood (breadwinner contribution and fatherhood involvement).

Note: Two grandfathers move between types, so are excluded; one father is excluded since child was not yet born; three great-grandfathers from the maternal line are excluded.

men in the study into three types. Such a typology is of course crude with some fathers 'fitting' better than others.

Work-focused fathers

This group (2 great-grandfathers, 6 grandfathers and 4 fathers) includes fathers devoted to their professional careers and fathers we term 'family providers', a good provider being one legitimation for being a 'good father'. Those with careers were in professional jobs or management and had made their way up the organisational ladders. They described their work as being the most important aspect of their lives at the time, in having an 'expressive' orientation to work (Goldthorpe *et al.*, 1969). Given the nature of their work and the relatively high financial rewards involved, the career aspect took precedence in their accounts over the breadwinning aspects.

By contrast, 'provider fathers' had always worked in low skilled jobs and did not emotionally invest in their work. The nature of their work, the low level of skill, the low financial rewards and poor working conditions generated 'instrumental' orientations to work (ibid.). Moreover, putting in long hours at work by doing overtime was a key way to increase family income and maximise earnings which in turn might compensate for low job satisfaction (ibid.). For both types of fathers their work effectively took precedence over time to participate in bringing up children.

Family men/child-oriented fathers

For this group (2 great-grandfathers, 4 grandfathers and 3 fathers) the provider role was also important to them. However, when they were not at work they were family-centred. They included skilled workers who crucially could command 'decent wages' without having to work over-time. While their male identities depended in some large measure on being main breadwinners, their wives assuming the role of secondary earner, these 'family men' emphasised their presence in the family: 'being there' and doing things 'for the family' such as DIY (do-it-yourself).

Those we have termed 'child-oriented' in this group focused in particular on their relationships with their *children* as well as with their families. Three out the four child-oriented fathers were from the 1970s/80s genera-tion who currently have young children. They noted how they sought to resist the pressure to spend long hours at work to have more time with their children. This was often difficult, they suggested, and dependent upon the power to negotiate individually with their employer. However these men could risk placing so much priority upon children and family life since their wives had developed a strong investment in work which the family could always fall back on if need be.

Hands-on fathers

This group only includes men from the 1970s/80s generation (4 fathers). Work did not figure much in the identities of three of the four men; those who had been employed in the past had only ever been in low skilled jobs. Three fathers who were not employed for much of the time had relied upon state benefits, as did their partners when they were not in work. A fourth was employed full time, again in low skilled work, but shared breadwinning and childcare with his wife on an equal basis.

This model of fatherhood involves high levels of childcare in terms of time and a strong identification with fatherhood. It was a model which men actively embraced. However it was also a 'choice' made in a context where employment opportunities had receded for the low skilled. In effect, life on the dole or having a breadwinner partner provided the conditions for this new model of fatherhood to happen.

Non-employed fathers with a weak investment in fatherhood

We found no such fathers in our study although, undoubtedly, such fathers could be found.

As in the case of motherhood, so too with fatherhood: there is no simple linear progression across the generations. Work-focused fathers are found in all three generations and, similarly, those who are family or child orientated. Moreover, one type of fatherhood does not necessarily lead to greater involvement in the next generation. While there are some cases of continuity within families, there are more cases of discontinuity, suggesting that fatherhood can slip backwards as in the instances where 'family men' have sons who as fathers are work focused (our first example). On the other hand, 'work-focused fathers' have sons who are child oriented (our second example); while 'family men' have sons who become child oriented (our third example).

Our fourth example, which we elaborate in detail, concerns the transformation from two generations of 'provider fathers' to being a 'hands-on' father in the youngest generation. It is significant that 'hands-on' fathers are all from the current generation of fathers with young children. These cases show the greatest change in men's parenting practices and identities.

From 'family man' to work-focused father: the Peters fathers

Our first case focuses on Donald Peters (great-grandfather, born in 1911, aged 89 and a father of four), his son George (grandfather, born in 1943, aged 57 and father of two) and son-in-law Mark (born in 1969, aged 31 and currently father of two children, aged 2 and 4). Both the older men describe themselves very much as 'family men' (the women in this family form one of the cases in Chapter 4). They were highly skilled workers (in engineering) and, when their children were young, neither expected to work very long hours. They placed high value on family life and on providing emotional as well as financial security for their families. All three men were also united in a similar religious commitment.

Donald sought to involve his sons in his home-based leisure pursuits (he did not socialise outside 'with the boys') – working on cars and motorbikes and doing jobs around the house. When his children were babies, he talked about 'helping' his wife with night feeding. His rationale was expressed in terms of doing things for his wife – 'giving his wife a rest'. His rationale for breadwinning is couched in terms of 'supporting' his wife and family.

First of all, it made me sure that I kept my job. Because I had responsibilities. In other words, er, one didn't tell the boss off if you wanted to keep your job. And I think too my family affected me to this extent, that I never went out with the boys. I had a family to come home to. My family wanted me, I wanted to be with them. I've seen plenty of cases where the men have gone out night after night and left the wife at home with the children. I couldn't do it. Again, on the basis that I was brought up to look after my wife. If you can't support her, don't marry her.

Donald's son George, also a family man, testified to his father's commitment to family life as a 'practical man'.

Dad was always a family man. He didn't go off and play golf on Sundays, or anything like that. Um, he was always around the home, yeah. Great sense of – of family, and supporting Mum, and the children, and, um – and work with the church. He was like me, a practical man. He did a lot of jobs round the house and that, and – . But, no, he never felt it was right to, um, sort of work all week, and then at weekends go off and play golf on a Sunday. You know, leave the wife again with the family and that, so – …He helped us with our homework if we wanted help with the homework. And if we were – I don't know, repairing our pushbikes or something, he would do that. He let us use his garage and his tools. If we wanted to learn how to use them, he'd show us how to use the tools in the garage. Um, as I say, he always helped us with homework. If I had a problem, I always felt I could go and ask him. More like technical things like Maths, and things like that. I always remember the day he explained to me how an internal combustion engine worked.

George's account of fatherhood and family life was remarkably similar to his father's. Like his father, he said it was the wife's job to do most of the 'bringing up' but that he did 'his share' especially jobs around the house. Like his father, he mentioned doing a certain amount of practical care when his children were babies including taking on night feeding. However, as a father of two girls he felt he was less influential as a father than his own father had been with his three sons and one daughter. Unlike his mother, George's wife went back to work when their girls had both started school – though to part-time jobs involving short hours and no work during school holidays.

George's son-in-law, Mark, worked in a similar employment sector and was also a skilled worker, though unlike his father-in-law he went to university: but he was rarely able to return from work at 5.30 or 6 p.m. In climbing the corporate ladder in a very different historical period he was expected to work long hours. Indeed, Mark's account focused at length upon his employment career and very little upon fatherhood.

He offered this spontaneous portrayal of his family: 'I think we're quite a traditional family, in the sense that I'm the breadwinner, [wife] stopped going to work.'

Mark's account suggested highly segregated domestic roles in which he managed the finances and his wife organised the children, food and social arrangements. Although Mark looked after their two young children for a couple of hours on Saturday mornings while his wife worked at 'Bouncy Babies', there was not much other evidence of child-care involvement. Interestingly, part of his wife's rationale for taking on some work herself was so that Mark could become more involved with the children. Moreover, there was a lot of kin support in this family to fill the gap, especially from the maternal grandmother Priscilla, who came to stay whenever there was a need. Yet Mark portrayed himself as 'pretty domesticated'. On the other hand, he also suggested that he felt guilty about not doing enough.

From career-focused father to child-focused father: the Kent fathers

The next case concerns a grandfather and son-in-law (the women in the family also appear as a case in Chapter 4). In this case the grandfather had been a middle-class, work-focused father when his children were young. His son-in-law, despite being similarly career oriented, was much more participant with his children, negotiating an arrangement with his employer in order to do this (albeit on a temporary basis).

Robert Kent (grandfather, born in 1937, aged 63 and a father of three) travelled the world in the course of his work, even at one time commuting on a weekly basis to the United States. He 'rescued' an overseas operation of a big British company and became its managing director. Then he built up a number of his own companies and when one was taken over he 'made some money'. Yet, except in his initial life story, Robert's account focused rather little on his highly successful occupational career beyond reporting the main biographical facts. Instead, looking back from the current vantage point of being an active grandfather, he focused upon his employment as it had adversely affected his earlier fatherhood.

> I think it was all the difficult years, the early years of the children's lives. When I say difficult, you know when a father should be around, I don't think I was really much help. I was either fairly jet-lagged, or I was absent. And I think in fact, they say, the children would say, and I think they're probably right, that I probably wasn't a very

satisfactory father, in those early years. Certainly I wasn't here a lot of the time to be any sort of a father, I mean I really was away a lot. Ummm. And then, after I was – I spent a year commuting, fifteen months commuting to [the United States]...and then I was quite fairly sort of driven by business, and business opportunities. I always found – I was quite ambitious and I found them very motivating.

Robert's story is also organised around the theme of a very close-knit, middle-class Jewish family, whose great-grandparent generation had fled Germany as refugees: 'The family is the most important thing. And I grew up knowing that.' He now clearly regrets being so much of an 'absentee father' (his words) and is delighted to be able to devote semi-retirement to being a highly involved grandfather; according to his daughter he is 'really fantastic', 'a 'star' (see Chapter 4). Moreover Robert hopes that his daughter will say '[I am] much better as a grandfather. Ummm. So I think errr, yes, I think being an absentee father is not good. If you're an absentee father and then you're quite strict, and then you try and overcompensate because you get guilt complexes and all that – I think there was a bit of all that.'

Robert was very close to his son-in-law, James, born in 1965, aged 35 and a father of two young children. Currently James was spending some time alone caring for his children; he described 'making a choice' to become more involved, a choice which he said also fitted in with his own career. In the job he hoped to do next he would devote himself much more to work than currently. Like his father-in-law Robert, when his first child was born James buried himself in work, 'because it was easier', as also did his wife, Juliet: the child cried a lot because of a feeding problem. He now spent a great deal more time with the children partly because Juliet was stressed with too much work (albeit part time) and also because, as a senior manager, he was in a position to organise his own working hours to some extent. In this next comment, James portrayed himself as a participant father and partly defined himself in contrast to work-focused fathers who have little contact with their children on a daily basis:

I take [son] swimming on Sunday mornings, just let him swim for [unclear], and, er, it's called 'the Guilty Fathers' Club', 'cos there's only fathers take the little under two- under three-year-olds, and I suspect that most of them are quite guilty. They haven't seen the kids all week. It's known as 'the Guilty Fathers' Swimming Club'! I'm the only one who's there that doesn't feel at all guilty, 'cos I spend lots of time with the kids during the week. But all the others definitely – definitely take that approach. There's a couple of Guilty Mothers there as well, who have clearly spent too much time with their big law firms all week, and not been home. But there's definitely a guilty-looking bunch.

James's involvement was in the context of an extensive support system. He and Juliet employed a nanny and housework was done by paid staff. There was also considerable family support including from his father-in-law. Moreover, while James was child-focused, his practice of parenting placed his role as secondary to Juliet's and contingent on his employment situation. He observed that 'I broadly do as I'm told, and don't innovate, don't lead'. And while, at the time of interview, he thought he did 'a reasonable amount of childcare', probably more than Juliet, he expected this situation to change when he took up a new job in senior management. He was doing more just now not purely in response to Juliet's position but because the slight hiatus in his work life permitted it, and Juliet would need to adapt her work when he started his new job: 'it's just luck that Juliet happens to be very busy at the moment and I'm doing the work up here...but when I start my new job again, then I'll be back into needing to work very hard again, and that'll put a lot of strain on childcare and Juliet will have to start to relax and not work so hard.' James contrasted his own 'input' with the low involvement provided by his own (career-oriented) father. But at the same time he continued to assume a long-term gendered division of responsibility for childcare.

From family man to child-focused father: the Horton fathers

The third example, of a grandfather and a current father of young children (father and son), is in part a case of continuity: both men prioritise family life. But the current father articulates a strong relational involvement with his two young daughters. Bernard Horton, grandfather (born in 1943, aged 57 and father of three), became a teacher and had worked his way up to being head of department while doing a number of jobs 'on the side'. He was able to do extra jobs since teachers in the late 1960s and 1970s were required to put in less hours, that is, compared with today. He was the main breadwinner until quite recently, when his youngest child left home and his wife moved to a full-time position.

Bernard took his breadwinning role in the family for granted. Because of his several jobs he was aware of not having spent as much time at home as he might have done, but felt he compensated by spending the long school summer holidays taking the family on camping holidays. Bernard described being involved with his children, especially with his youngest son who was born much later than the other two. The main reason for his increased involvement was this son's health problem which demanded a lot of his parents' time. While Bernard was in some ways a traditional, work-oriented father who assumed his wife would take most responsibility for the children, he also had a 'sixties attitude' to life which made him more relaxed; he reported how he never smacked his children and that 'we always talked things through with them'.

A strong theme in his story was about how he tried to make his family life different from his own experience as a child. Bernard strove to create a sense of continuity for his children, living in the countryside and staying in the same area. In contrast, his own childhood had been marked by moves abroad and wartime separation from his father. Bernard also sought to ensure that he brought up his own children differently from the way his parents had brought him up, so that they had 'none of the angst I had to go through'.

In many respects Patrick, a TV producer (born in 1967, aged 33 and a father of two young children), was similar to Bernard, his father. Asked what had influenced his way of bringing up his children, his reply is unequivocal: 'My parents . . . gave us our outlook on the world.' What differentiates them was Patrick's recognition and reflection about what he saw to be a new approach to fatherhood – being close to his children – while asserting some continuity with his own parents at the same time. Significantly, Patrick's initial life story focused on memories of his own childhood which, he said, were triggered by becoming a father: 'You get changed by that whole experience of watching them grow up and their development.' Patrick's father, by contrast, sought an unqualified break with generational continuity.

Making time to be with his children was a conscious strategy for Patrick: 'I do try, I think, make an effort to, when I'm with them to, err, do things with them instead of just watching tele . . . When I get home at night, if I get home in time, I try and go upstairs and read them a story. We share, well [partner] probably would not agree, but I think we do share the burden.'

The differences in emphasis between father and son may be explained by two factors. First, Patrick was currently a father of two young children. Second, there has been a cultural shift in this generation towards a more relational approach to family life in which parents seek to create relations with their children (Chapter 2). Patrick said that it was best that either he or his partner worked part time in order to ensure that their *relationship* with their children did not suffer. In fact, the part-time worker was his partner Geraldine, unsurprisingly from a structural perspective. Yet from Patrick's perspective there was no intrinsic reason why the parent working part time should be the mother, it was simply a matter of circumstance and preference. As described earlier in the chapter, like the other fathers in this generation, Patrick was anxious not to appear sexist in relegating care and domestic work to women and he seemed genuinely concerned to spend time with his children.

Patrick hoped to be able to work more from home in the future. However, as a committed programme producer in the world of television, this may remain a dream.

From provider fathers to being hands-on: the Prentice fathers

We end the chapter with a fourth and extended example, this time all three generations in the same family: great-grandfather Jack (born in 1931, aged 69 and father of five), his son-in-law grandfather Paul (born in 1951, aged 49 and also father of five), and his son, current father Andrew (born in 1976, aged 24 with two young children). In this example we will seek to focus upon the biographical and contextual 'facts' of these fathers' lives and their implications for the kinds of fathers they become, and we will also explore in some detail how the men in their interviews put flesh upon these 'facts' in order to understand the processes of both change and transmission.

The Prentice family is an example of intergenerational continuity on the one hand and significant change on the other, entailing a profound shift in fathering in the youngest adult generation. The lives of all the members of the Prentice family are marked by low skilled work and by the absence of educational qualifications. There are strong ambivalences between the two older generations evident in disrupted social relationships. Andrew, a current father of two young children, emerges as a force for innovation and renewal in the Prentice family. Both his grandfather and father were traditional 'family providers': but Andrew has looked after his children with his wife on a full-time basis for the first years of his daughters' lives.

The biographical 'facts' and context

The three men's life histories are similarly structured in their beginnings. All three left school before taking any public examinations at 14 or 15, with the oldest and youngest missing large amounts of schooling (one because of the war and the other because the family was constantly in search of housing). All three then entered and stayed in low skilled work. All married young, in their early 20s, though only the youngest cohabited before marriage, at 17. Their first children in two cases were conceived premaritally.

The *work histories* of the three men are differently structured and reflect the decline in low skilled work that occurred over the second half of the 20th century. The two older generations started their working life as apprentices in manual trades and moved into lesser skilled work. The great-grandfather, the youngest of our sample, had changed occupations and jobs rarely, working with his father for many years as coal porters in a local coal merchant's. The early life of his son-in-law was punctuated by several occupational and job changes. Both also found extra jobs in the 1970s in youth work during the heady days of the Inner London Education Authority, prior to its abolition by Margaret Thatcher in the mid-1980s.

The young father, Andrew, stands in marked contrast to both men for, like his birth cohort, he joined the labour market at a time in which apprenticeships had largely disappeared. With changes in the youth labour market and the decline in jobs for young school leavers occurring from the mid-1980s, most young men of Andrew's generation were expected to continue in training and education after 16 (Furlong and Cartmel, 1997). But Andrew dropped out of school before 16 and did not enter the workforce for five years, that is, until the introduction of the New Deal for Young People in the late 1990s. Unlike his predecessors and most of his own birth cohort, therefore, his career trajectory started with several years of unemployment: his father also experienced unemployment, but later in the life course when his health broke down, while his grandfather's work portering coal was seasonal. Like his father and grandfather, Andrew's first job was in the service sector but was occupationally quite different: as a customer complaints assistant in a supermarket, his work reflects two icons of the current period – consumption and communications.

The *family careers* of the two older fathers reflect their historical periods. For their generation and social class, an early entry into fatherhood and a tight timetabling of life course phases were normative. Both older men were strongly committed to work despite being low paid and low skilled. This attachment was rooted in their status as family breadwinners – supporting non-employed wives and large families (both had five children) – and both Jack and Paul were guided during the peak years of fatherhood by the work ethic (Bauman, 1998). Despite living in London and in close proximity to some parts of their kin network, both the older men made the break from London. Paul moved with his wife and his four sons who were then in their teenage years to a rural area, with no job to go to and no local ties. His father-in-law made the break later in the life course (during retirement) taking two unmarried sons to live with him, but to quite another part of the country.

In contrast, in the mid-1990s, the work ethic of Andrew and similar poorly qualified working-class young men was undermined, in particular by the decline in demand for traditional male unskilled work (Furlong and Cartmel, 1997). Andrew was starting a family at a time of considerable family change and variation in ways of 'doing' family life (Morgan, 1999). However, his scheduling of fatherhood went against the normative grain; rather than a number of staggered life course transitions before embarking on fatherhood (described earlier in the chapter), Andrew cohabited at 17 and became a father at 18 while living at home and with no employment record.

In contrast to his father and grandfather, Andrew was no longer guided by the norm that children ought to be born in wedlock. Instead he married on the eve of the birth of his second child. Moreover, his decision not to be in paid work was linked to a positive decision to share equally in the upbringing of his children with his partner and later wife, Sheila. Such decisions were unheard of in his own parents' and grandparents' time. As a father, therefore, Andrew demonstrates a strong commitment to care and, as yet, a weak commitment to the labour market: he had negotiated a different set of responsibilities towards his family.

Andrew's innovative practice was not only about fatherhood, it was also about himself. Many young people in the western world seek to express and develop themselves in ways that were not only uncommon but unthinkable in previous generations (Brannen *et al.*, 2002). They seek adventure and self-development over an extended youth period and into other life course phases such as parenthood (see, for example, Frønes and Brusdal, 2000). These 'young adult' activities include taking a year out travelling to distant places, studying and practising different art forms and experiences, and often involve a struggle financially, rarely attracting more than minimum income support. However, taking up such life styles is strongly differentiated by social class. British young people typically depend upon family support, while in some Northern European countries young people may draw upon strong welfare states. A flexible labour market, as is currently the case in the UK, also enables young people to move at will in and out of work (Jones and Wallace, 1992).

Whether or not this represents a low commitment to work is debatable. Rather it may be understood as a cohort and period-specific phenomenon. In 'a risk society' (Beck, 1992) and in an age where more attention is paid to *life style* than to *life practice* (Jones and Wallace, 1992; Bauman, 1998; Sennett, 1998; Brannen and Nilsen, 2002), it is hardly surprising that young people seek to express themselves by whatever means are available to them. This said, the life styles referred to here are more available to young middle-class people than to working-class young people. Andrew is in many ways an innovator in his own family not only because of his commitment to fatherhood, which in many ways represents another form of lifestyle choice, but also because he has a strong interest in expressing himself through music and art.

In order to understand how men negotiate particular types of fatherhood not only in particular generational contexts, we turn now to the ways in which Andrew and his father and grandfather elaborated on these biographical 'facts' in the interview encounter.

Stories of fatherhood

Informants relate their stories of the past with reference to present time frames (Nilsen, 1996). How informants begin their narratives is often illuminating. Beginnings provide clues to the main themes that govern informants' accounts and thus are often indicative of the underlying structure of informants' stories. Two examples given in response to an initial invitation to narrative may illustrate this and shed light upon these men's identities as fathers, the first by grandfather Paul, the second by father Andrew:

> Let's see. Employment. I served an apprenticeship as an upholsterer, straight from, virtually straight from school. Ummm. I've always been employed, errr, and I had bit a, spell of sickness for 5 years, but other than that I've always found it easy to get a job. So I've never suffered errr that way. Ummm. Care. Are you looking whether you care for someone or whether you care about things? What sort of care? Ummm. I don't really know. I think as you get older you care more about your ummm, the way you live, society itself, or things like that (Paul, grandfather).

> It's hard to put it all into words I suppose. [*Long pause*] Well my childhood was quite good. I enjoyed my childhood, where I lived in X. Erm, I enjoyed going to Y school. It's a nice school. I mean like the building more than anything else for some reason. [*Interviewer*: really?]

And where we lived in erm, where was it called? ... I enjoyed living there as well. It was quite a nice place. Erm. Family life was a bit hectic at times, in those days, for my parents, I think, erm. But apart from that it was okay I think, really. When I look at it now, but erm, then, I kind of, you know, my views towards it were other [not clear] but, no it was okay. Then we moved – we did a lot of moving ... then we moved to S and I met up with old friends, and we started a band [... right], which was good, being able to express ourselves, how we felt. We spent a lot of our time writing songs and just discussing music and playing music, and I met up with [wife-to-be] again and we got together. In fact we've been together ever since then, which is around 8 years I think (Andrew, father).

Paul was a natural storyteller. Much of his life story was structured around a narrative of his work career. This is prefigured in his very opening remark: 'Let's see, employment'. His initial uncertain response to the issue of care is also revealing: 'What sort of care? Ummm. I don't really know.' Yet he admitted the possibility of change, as he gets 'older'. In his account, Paul was at pains to present himself favourably in the current interview context according to the criteria against which he judged himself as a man, namely skill (achieved through an apprenticeship) and his ability to provide.

Andrew's initial response was much less a narrative and more an evaluation of his life and of his childhood in particular. Moreover, his evaluation was positive despite the unsettled character of his childhood. He identified points of stability in his life in a sea of instability, emphasising his strong relationship with his wife and the band that he and his brothers set up (following their move from London to the countryside). The account suggested a process of reflection in which he had moved from a negative to a positive view of his past.

The unfolding accounts of fatherhood, especially those elicited in the later semi-structured part of the interview (which followed the life-story section), referred in part to the discourses of fatherhood current at the time that these three men were bringing up their children. However, important information about their practice of fatherhood was also revealed in the events of their life histories as already discussed. Jack, the great-grandfather, had few memories of being a father but readily recalled growing up in wartime London. This memory lapse is not surprising since work dominated his life 'by day' while extra-curricular activities kept him away from home in the evening. There was also little space at home. Indeed, for 10 years Jack lived with his wife and five children in a flat occupied by his wife's father – seven of them sleeping in one room.

> I can't think much about the years . . . mainly it might be because, as I say, I was always working. And (wife) brought them up to a certain extent. You know apart from the summer when I said we spent time together. But in the winter I never used to see her so she must have had a hard time really with the 5 of them. Cos we only had two rooms. The lot of us, 7 of us slept in one.

While Jack's position as the family breadwinner delineated his role as a father in the 1950s and 1960s, he was mindful of the present and the way fatherhood has changed today. Thus he was anxious to present himself as open to new ways of being a father, demonstrated in his use of the phrase 'it seems' which distanced him, as he was when interviewed, from past fatherhood practices. But he was quite clear that *at the time* he had not subscribed to these ideas: 'it was before all this business about your father would be there to see the birth'. Yet, asked a later question about who had influenced him most as a father, Jack was keen to present himself in a good light. He claimed to have brought up the children with his wife on a 'half and half basis'. He justified this on the grounds that, at his wife's insistence, he never hit his children and that he was considerate to his wife when she was tired and needed time off from the children. This reflects the division of labour of the time in which the 'male provider role' defined both ideals and practices of being first of all a good husband as well as a good father (Bernard, 1972).

It became apparent that Jack was very involved with external aspects of his sons' lives, although he did not refer to these in response to direct questions about fatherhood. Jack had a keen interest in athletics, developed during a period of National Service in the 1950s that he spent overseas. For his sons, but not his daughter, athletics constituted the main arena for the practice of fatherhood. He coached his sons very successfully using the facilities of the local play centre where he did voluntary youth work. Eventually this led to a second (evening) job in youth work.

The story which Paul, the grandfather, told was mostly about work and providing for his family including his efforts to take his family away from what he saw to be the increasingly threatening environment of inner London. Asked about becoming a father (at 21) Paul replied: 'You just got on with it . . . 'Cos the attitude then was that, if you wasn't married by the time you was 21, there's something wrong with you . . . you just did it, and that was part of life.' Asked about having more children, he distanced himself from current ideas of planning: 'I come from a different planet. I can't work out why people – "Oh we'll have one this year." – d'you know what I mean?' Rather than consciously planning fatherhood, Paul 'followed' the normative notion of fathers as breadwinners and the normative time scheduling for his time and social class, that is, to have children in early adulthood.

Paul was initially staggered when asked about influences on the way he had parented his children. It is not uncommon for men of these older generations to have difficulty in expressing themselves about areas of life that have traditionally been seen as women's domains (Nilsen, 2001). Other studies have concluded that men and women not only have different ways of expressing themselves, but also that the topics men and women speak about at length reflect different gendered interests and life experiences (Belenky *et al.*, 1986). On the other hand, Paul considered himself to be a 'gentle father' who had always 'backed' his children, clearly something that he felt that his parents had never done for him. He mentioned that he had supported his sons in their band (which seems to have been their full-time occupation for a while).

Asked if he was 'a hands-on father' when his children were young, Paul replied that he was 'there', adding 'I've never been a nappy man'. Asked about the important aspects of being a parent, he spoke in traditional gender terms about boys cleaving to their mothers. He added 'it's only now they wanna know their dad'. By 'now' he may have meant when his boys were older; but, perhaps, he was also thinking of Andrew being a father in the different cultural climate of the late 1990s. Overall, however, Paul considered that his children thought him to have been a 'good father'. Thus from the vantage point of the present and the judgemental context of the interview, he sought to defend his record of fatherhood.

Despite the great differences, Paul clearly admired the way his son Andrew was currently practising fatherhood. In his rather elliptical way, Paul spoke of his son with pride and the way Andrew and his wife were 'working at' parenting: 'They discuss with one another...I was brought up to think that "the man makes the decisions"...whereas...they would talk about it, whereas we never did...Dad was the man. I know my mum worked but he was the breadwinner. He was the one that made the decisions.'

Compared with his father and grandfather, Andrew gave a very different kind of account, different both in quality as well as content. His account suggested a journey to self-understanding and self-development that occurred at cognitive and emotional levels. While being intra-subjective, his account was *not* about constructing an identity for himself in the present and the future. Andrew's reference point was coming to terms with and reparation for his past. Through self-understanding and accept-ance, Andrew put a positive complexion on the past and so dispelled much of its negativity. This journey clearly affected the way he approached his relationship with his wife as well as fatherhood. Let us look now at his account in further detail.

Andrew actively embraced a caring identity in deciding to be involved with his children – 'I wanted to look after the children' – and to share their care with Sheila – 'we are a team'. After the first baby was born, they shared the care on a full-time basis for two years, they 'just split the whole thing down the middle'. In addition he noted two other goals: wanting to give his children a stable childhood (unlike his own) and to make a go of his relationship with his young wife. He suggests a process of negotiation with his wife and children: 'It's just about trying to find a balance of happiness with them and ourselves and what we're doing and where we are going . . . it's something to have to work at.' Asked how he managed to achieve that 'balance', Andrew referred to a process of reflection and self-understanding: 'by understanding yourself and how you feel about what you're doing . . . just trying not to bottle things up . . . just be yourself but at a level where you don't take your frustrations out on other people. You deal with them, er, keep level-headed.' Asked what was the spur to this he acknowledged a need to come to terms with his childhood: 'when I looked back on it and tried to understand it on a less personal level and just to see how it is and why people . . . and why I did the things I did, and just try and understand it.'

The route to self-understanding also included cultural interests: getting involved in art and setting up a band with his brothers. Reflecting on these artistic endeavours, he suggested how the exploration of self had led to an understanding of others: 'I just wanted to see what I could do, what I could create . . . just like a natural expression of the movement of my arm or how I felt, and how I projected my feelings, and then through being interested in what I was doing I became interested in others' work as well and understanding what they were doing and why they did it and how they painted.'

Andrew suggested a similar reflective process shaped his parenting: 'My own life, how I perceived that and, from looking at that, trying to see how I should bring up my own children. Watching other people and seeing how they do it.' He also provided an insight into how, when he became a father at 18, he was able to deal with the uncomfortable experience of his peer group giving the couple a wide berth after their first child was born. Rather than resenting this fact, he described how he sought to understand it and not let it intrude on his own feelings and experience.

In becoming a 'hands-on father', Andrew resisted the worker identity that was so central to his father and grandfather. His wife Sheila interestingly had a stronger orientation to the labour market than Andrew. Asked if he felt under pressure to become a breadwinner (he had recently found work in customer complaints in the local supermarket), Andrew briefly acknowledged the pressure to enter paid work: 'in some ways... you need money in your pocket'. But he still had reservations about working, in particular noting that he and his wife were no longer 'half and half any more'. Indeed when he took some time off because of a family problem, he found his employer distinctly lacking in family friendliness, reporting that a manager went round to his wife's place of employment to investigate the problem! Andrew significantly omitted from his account the external pressures of the state upon him to join the labour market. As he said, 'I just guide myself.' For this part of the story we had to draw upon his wife's account and our own knowledge of the policy context.

In contrast to his father and grandfather who defined themselves in 'positional' ways as breadwinners, Andrew's self-definition was *personal* (Bernstein, 1971). The structuring feature of his story was agency. Yet Andrew's account of the person he had become was less redolent of post-modernist identity construction, choosing from an array of identities. He was not a 'choice biographer' as in the theorisations of Beck and Beck-Gernsheim (1995). Rather the account he gave turned on notions of the processual self, in actively and creatively engaging with the conditions of his *past*. Interestingly, another new father in the study, Graeme Hurd, also from a working-class family, became the main carer while his partner was the breadwinner. His account also hinged upon the theme of reparation for a past that he did not want to repeat with his own children.

Andrew remained silent about the fact that this new form of fatherhood – premised upon equal sharing of parenting in terms of time and commitment – had been achieved in his case in the context of financial dependence upon the state (see also Nilsen and Brannen, 2002 for a similar phenomenon). Nonetheless the story is a remarkable tribute to teenage parenthood, disrupting some negative stereotypes prominent in recent public discourses. Andrew and his wife had succeeded in 'making a go' of parenthood with few material resources in a society in which young fatherhood is discouraged and stigmatised. But instead of becoming a non-resident father, and despite substantial material disadvantage, Andrew had become a very present 'hands-on' father.

The case as a whole is also remarkable in that it represents a major departure in intergenerational patterns of fatherhood, while also enabling us to see that some aspects of men's commitment to their children are transmitted down the generations, albeit taking different forms. For in many ways Jack and Paul were very committed to their children especially to their sons. Andrew's story differed from his father's and grandfather's in the way he expressed himself on issues of care. His language of care was both highly elaborated and expressed the practice of care. When his first child was born he said: 'I just wanted to do everything . . . like you know do all the looking after. I wanted to change all the nappies.' Later he described helping a friend who was having mental health problems, 'I was there a lot for him to talk to, and to talk to him.' He links this sensibility to being a father: 'You learn to deal with stressful situations. I mean you can't always tell what's wrong with a child immediately, so in that way you kind of learn.'

In contrast, for the older generations, care was embedded not in such negotiated practices but rather in family roles namely breadwinning and in activities carried out beyond the home. For these older men care was associated with women's gendered roles. It was thus excluded from the hegemonic forms of masculinity which shaped fatherhood in their own day.

Drawing the threads of the case together

The stories of these three Prentice men have important structural features. There are strong similarities in the occupational status and life chances of all three generations of Prentice men. At the same time, important structural shifts had taken place, in particular the decline in low skilled employment, which had weakened the work ethic of the current generation of fathers. Normative and structural changes in family life had also weakened fatherhood as an institution based upon family breadwinning. In this context, Andrew used the decline in traditional resources available to men of his social class as an opportunity to take advantage of new cultural resources which give legitimacy to men being actively and equally involved with their children. For Andrew had made fatherhood in the first years of his children's life a meaningful and rewarding occupation in the absence of paid employment. Moreover, in the future, he and his wife intended to share breadwinning.

We would agree with Bertaux and Bertaux-Wiame (1997) when they discuss the agency-structure dilemma, that the deployment of structural resources is key to understanding agency:

> Socio-structural components may be found in those decisions and acts apparently most clearly powered by will ... [T]he idea that a life trajectory may be determined – or rather, conditioned – much more easily by the supplying of a resource than by the imposition of a constraint lends an entirely new content to the concept of determination: one which includes both the socio-structural dimension and praxis (p. 95).

For Andrew, fatherhood constituted such a resource. Through his involvement in music and art, Andrew gained social skills and competences that were important in developing a positive sense of self. His father, moreover, morally supported him in this. The very fact that this was achieved through living off social security did not come across though in his account of events. For this generation of young people, the work ethic, in the traditional sense of the term, may not be as strong as it was in earlier times. Even so, the means by which they support themselves are typically taken as 'given' or become a 'taken for granted' aspect of life (see Brannen and Nilsen, 2002; Nilsen *et al.*, 2002).

The *enabling* aspects of social structure vary across national and social class boundaries. The resources available to Andrew – from the state – were meagre, but nonetheless important in enabling him to develop a sense of self and self-worth that had a positive impact on his practice of fatherhood. The fact that his wife had subsequently and willingly taken on part of the breadwinning was also a resource that was legitimated in the current historical period through a changed gender ideology.

The perspective we have adopted in this case and in the study generally has paid equal attention to both life course and life story. It has thereby made it possible both to explore how a wider understanding of changes in gender relations and class structures operate over time to influence individual life experiences, and to shed light upon the ways in which individuals interpret their own lives.

Our analysis of men's accounts of fatherhood and care in this multi-generation family has moreover uncovered not only differences in experiences and understandings of what care and fatherhood mean in different eras, it has also hinted at possible variations across generations in the ways men express themselves in this arena. Where in earlier times a more pronounced and sharper dividing line existed between the public and the private, between work and family, seemingly different ways of expressing opinions and meanings are associated with these spheres. The male sphere of employment, men's strong commitment to the work ethic and a hegemonic ideology of masculinity combined to shape the practices and experiences of the two older male generations.

These factors may also account for the lack of elaboration in men's accounts of care and fatherhood among the two older generations. Coaching his young sons in sport, as Jack did, constituted an important resource to pass on to his sons who could utilise it in a new way. (Jack's sons were not included because of the study's design but two of them had become very successful sportsmen.) However, this aspect of fathering was not emphasised by Jack. Jack associated this involvement with his children with 'life outside the family' and, as such, as being about leisure activities, voluntary work and, later, as a source of additional income. He did not mention doing well by his sons by fostering their interest in athletics, even though his account of parenthood was elicited in the current climate which stresses the importance of being an involved parent.

'Care' as a notion attracts different connotations and meanings over time (Wærness, 2000). Jack did not see sports coaching as *care*, suggesting that the concept of care may have particular connotations for men which limits its application to the domain of women and the home. When exploring issues of care in accounts from men and women belonging to different generations, the gendered aspects of care must be viewed through the lens of history. We must be sensitive to the notions and practices that have guided people's lives and life courses, in very different historical periods.

Conclusions

In this chapter we first looked at the timetabling of fatherhood in relation to the life courses of three generations of fathers. We showed that the middle, grandparent generation became fathers on average rather younger than fathers in the older and younger generations, while the current generation have by and large achieved a complex of staggered life course transitions *before* they embark on fatherhood. In contrast, for the generation of fathers born around the Second World War, life course transitions fell thick and fast so that marriage, parenthood and labour market transitions all occurred within a very few years. For the oldest generation born in the first part of the 20th century, their lives and fatherhood were disrupted by war.

The new generation of fathers differs from its predecessors in particular respects. For this generation marriage is not a necessary precondition for fatherhood. Unlike the generations before them, this generation has experienced an extended period of youth with time spent living independently, with peers or in cohabitation. Some of the present parent generation have yet to marry while others have married following the births of their children. For the two older generations, marriage was a necessary precondition for parenthood. The parent generation is also different in being the first generation for whom home ownership has become a commonplace expectation; public housing was sold off in the 1980s and 1990s and private ownership not only was easier to arrange financially but became central to a 'proper family life'. In terms of starting work, the youngest generation contrasts with the grandparent generation in facing an uncertain labour market in the 1990s, being in some respects more similar to the great-grandparent generation when times were also hard or uncertain.

The chapter then explored fathers' normative beliefs concerning parents' employment and the 'needs' of children. The new generation of fathers rarely made general normative statements about the 'right way' to organise employment and family life. Older generations are more likely to do so but also recognise the changed context in which the new generation is parenting children. However, while men's attitudes concerning equality of opportunity in the labour market have moderated over the course of time, as they recognise women's 'right to work', they are less negotiable concerning the needs of children. Assumptions about what children 'need' are still governed by gender assumptions in that children are still regarded as being best looked after by mothers. This is particularly the view of the older two generations of fathers. Moreover, the new generation of fathers, while espousing gender equality in the labour market and presenting themselves as 'modern men', does not explicitly address gender transformations. Some of the current generation of fathers draw upon a repertoire of 'excuses' (Finch and Mason, 1993) which effectively legitimate women's greater involvement in childcare, while not overtly appearing to do so. These 'excuses' relate to notions of individual choice, personality or circumstance.

We would argue, therefore, that contemporary family life is no longer governed by one set of normative principles in that fathers and mothers of different generations increasingly make judgements about what is acceptable and 'proper' in terms of particular decisions, situations and practicalities. However, while these practicalities and choices may guide action, structural issues of gender remain which are often hidden and unaddressed by the actors concerned. The ethic of care even among some of the younger generation of fathers continues to be shaped by traditional gender divisions though, as we have shown, there are some interesting exceptions to this.

We have also examined different ways of being a father. This typology is premised on two dimensions: men's breadwinner status and their involvement with their children when they are young. We found three broad types of fatherhood. In the first type of fatherhood which occurs in all three generations, men were highly committed to the labour market, overshadowing their involvement with their families and children: middle-class 'careerist fathers' in high status jobs providing high intrinsic rewards; and 'provider fathers' who held low skilled jobs which offered few intrinsic rewards and required them to work long hours in return for a 'decent wage' (there were no provider fathers in the current generation). A second model covers those we have termed 'family men', all from the two older generations. These men were the main breadwinners but were also very present in the home, placed high value on 'being there', and sharing in the life of the household including to some extent care work. Also included in this model was a subgroup of fathers who were also main breadwinners but who placed priority on relationships with their children as well as upon family life. With one exception, they were from the 1970s/80s generation. Third, there is the 'hands-on' father, all four cases from the current father generation. These fathers embraced an active caring identity and, with one exception, resisted a worker identity. While this model of fatherhood may be interpreted as being actively negotiated, it needs also to be understood in relation to historical and structural conditions.

Transmission across the families is not simple and progression linear from one type of father to another. In part the lack of transmission may be because we have only two strings of fathers and sons over three generations. On the other hand, there is much variation across two family generations – fathers and sons. Transmission within families can rather be observed in subtle ways in that one resource passed on by a father may be used in a different way by the son. As Michael Hurd suggests in a later chapter, his own family gave him the freedom to choose a different life from them. It is moreover in low skilled, working-class families where the changes in fatherhood are the most striking, exemplified in the Prentice fathers, where changes towards a new type of 'hands-on' fatherhood can be found taking place.

6
Intergenerational Transfers and Cultures of Transmission

In this chapter we examine transmission between family members at different life course phases, for example between great-grandparents and their children and grandchildren and between parents and adult children. We look at different kinds of resources which are transmitted between individuals from different family generations – both material resources and care, up and down the generations and the processes of reciprocity.

In looking at the patterns of resource transfers in families, we have borne in mind that the giving of resources and care by kin is not obligatory or mandatory, as the work of Finch and Mason (1993) suggests. Indeed, who transfers what to whom and in what circumstances are not matters of prescribed rules or obligation and are not made routinely to everyone or by everyone within a family. As discussed in Chapter 4, family responsibilities typically involve the negotiation of the ethic of care in relation to the needs of those needing care, the availability of others to offer care and so on. However similar needs do not generate a similar level of support (Qureshi, 1996). Chains of solidarity and gift giving occur in some families and not in others; some persons are 'legitimately excused' from care while others are targeted as carers in particular conditions and situations (Finch and Mason, 1993).

There is a further dimension of transfers that we consider. As well as looking at what transfers take place and in what directions, and the 'moments' at which such transfers become visible namely at particular life courses phases, we look at cultures of transmission: the kinds of rationalities which interviewees used to refer to intergenerational transfers or their absence. We will show how different cultures can develop in particular historical periods or across different generations in a family.

Culture, we suggest, does not so much determine transfers, these being the consequence of a variety of conditions and considerations, relating to meanings, justifications and rationalities concerning the processes of giving and receiving resources – or not doing so. Rather they provide an ideology of transfer to accompany the practice. We pose the question whether such cultures are familial in the sense of being transmitted within families and how far they are shaped by the historical context which also shapes the experiences of individuals and birth cohorts. Our methodological approach to the analysis drawn upon in this chapter is both to map the transfer of different resources and to examine the interpretations which interviewees gave to the transfers and the processes involved.

The evidence for intergenerational transfers

There is a growing body of European evidence which testifies to the extent of intergenerational transfers of resources even when considerable public support from welfare states is available (see Attias-Donfut and Arber, 2000; Bawins-Legros, 2002). Other studies suggest that intergenerational transfers, while they involve exchange and reciprocity between generations, are largely downward from older to younger generations. In particular, they point to the current grandparent cohort born in and around the post-war period being significant transmitters of resources. Studies in France and Germany, for example, show this middle generation giving the most with the younger and older generations being the main recipients. A French study of three-generation families shows high rates of material transfers from the middle generation (49 to 53 years old), with nearly two-thirds engaging in such transfers over a five-year period (Attias-Donfut, 1995). The French research suggests that if this generation gives to one generation it also tend to give to the other – that is the generations above and below. German research reports that 36 per cent of those between 40 and 55 years old who have at least one parent and one adult child gave transfers in the preceding year to their adult children (Kohli, 1999). The same study also shows a cascade to non-adjacent as well as adjacent generations (adult children and grandchildren).

While there is no comparable intergenerational research for the UK, similar findings would be unsurprising. The current grandparent generation, the children of the post-war 'golden age', might, from a historical perspective, deserve the title given to them by a French study: 'the generation of abundance' (Attias-Donfut, 1995). Increases in property ownership, property prices, earnings and savings are likely to be reflected in a growth in gift-giving during people's lifetimes as well as in legacies left to kin at death. Moreover, the upward occupational mobility experienced by many in the grandparent generation may have left them needing less material help from older generations, while the parent generation in Britain today increasingly requires material support from parents in order to achieve financial independence, notably with education, training and housing (Brannen *et al.*, 2002). There may, though, be some national differences. Intergenerational transfers of material resources could be lower in the UK than in a country like France since industrialisation took place earlier and more rapidly in the UK, with the consequence that ties with the countryside are weaker, and inheritance of land and rural property is less common.

There may also be some differences within countries. For example, material transfers from the grandparent generation are less likely among families on low incomes (e.g. Kempson and Whyley, 2000). More than a quarter of British households have no savings at all (HMSO, 2002). French and German studies confirm that the largest financial transfers are given by those with the largest assets (Kohli, 1999; Renaut, 2001).

In respect of care, cross-national studies have emphasised the major role that continues to be played in many affluent countries by informal carers, in particular relatives, both in the care of children and elderly people (EC Childcare Network, 1996; OECD, 2001). Jacobzone *et al.* (1998) estimate that up to 80 per cent of care for elderly people is provided informally. While many studies in the UK have shown that relatives, mostly grandparents, continue to be the main providers of childcare for working parents (most recently, see Woodland *et al.*, 2002), French research has found a similar pattern of childcare: 85 per cent of women and 75 per cent of men look after their grandchildren more or less regularly (without the presence of parents) either on a daily or weekly basis or during the school holidays (Attias-Donfut and Segalen, 2002). Emphasising the different directions in which care can flow, a study of employed or recently retired men and women aged between 50 and 64 living in two areas of England found that 41 per cent were providing care for disabled or elderly relatives, 17 per cent were providing childcare for at least one grandchild, with one in ten caring for both elderly relatives and children (Mooney and Statham, 2002).

The extent of care by family members may, however, vary between countries and over time. For example, in Denmark and Sweden today grandparents and other informal carers play a small part in regular childcare arrangements: the great majority of children attend formal services, which are now almost universally available in these Nordic welfare states (Moss and Cameron, 2002). At the same time in Sweden, increased targeting of formal services on more disabled elderly people may have led to some shift towards informal carers taking a greater share of eldercare in recent years; the same process has occurred in the UK (ibid.). It is possible, therefore, that there may be a gradual shift from informal care for children, as most countries increase formal services, whereas the situation in eldercare is less clear-cut.

Resources transferred and the direction of transfers

Crudely, resources may be typified as material or relating to the provision of care. In this study, material transfers included financial help, help with accommodation (including assistance in buying housing), and services related to improving the fabric of the home (DIY) and help with finding work. Care (already touched upon in Chapter 4) included childcare and eldercare. While care could also cover relational activities such as outings, babysitting and visiting, in our study the detail of such activities could not be captured within such long-time perspectives. Childcare included any sustained period of significant care, for example when adult children are working; less sustained or less significant help is therefore likely to be under reported. Eldercare consists in significant commitment as when an elderly person was cared for in a child's home. While less onerous eldercare was also mentioned, involving frequent or regular visiting and shopping, it too is likely to be under-reported.

Table 6.1 presents some of the main transfers which took place between generations in our study. It has only been possible to capture some of these intergenerational transfers; a comprehensive account would need research that focused on this issue alone. As already suggested, there are methodological difficulties in covering a long period of years in detail. Table 6.1 also concentrates mainly upon transfers between adjacent generations, between great-grandparents and grandparents, and grand-parents, and parents: in effect, between parents and children.

Thane (2000) concludes that at least since 1945 'families extremely rarely provided substantially for the material support of older people ... (not needing to do so) with the coming of universal pensions' (p. 434). This is apparent too in our families, most material resources travelling down the generations, that is, to children from parents – often jointly; distinctions between mothers and fathers are not usually made when talking about the transmission of money and accommodation. There is, by contrast, only a small amount of upward return of financial help, as when a son in our study sought to secure a pension for his father and

Table 6.1 Reported instances of intergenerational resource transfers in sample families

Direction of transfer	Financial support Down	Up	Housing help Down	Up	Household maintenance Down	Up	Childcare Down	Up	Eldercare Down	Up	Finding jobs Down	Up	Total
Brand	2	2	2		1		2			2	2		13
Ashton	2		1		1		1			1	1		7
Peters	2				1	1	2			2	2		10
Miller	1		2				2			2	2		9
Prentice	1		2				1	2		1	1		8
Samuels	1[a]	1[a]	1			1		1			1		6
Horton	2		1							2	2		7
Hurd	2	2	2	1						1			8
Kent	2		1				1			1	1		6
Smith	2	1	2		1	1	2			2			10
Masters	1		2			1	2			1	1		8
Hillyard	2		1				2			2		2	9
Total	20	6	17	1	4	4	15	3	0	17	12	2	101

[a] The reciprocity here was part of an explicit contract to repay material help given.

an employed daughter gave her parents financial help because they were 'struggling'. In the latter case this was represented (to the parents) as a reward for support with childcare which they had provided for a time while their daughter was working, even though this had now ceased.

Provision of accommodation was largely from parents to adult children with only one instance of help with housing going in the other direction. Help with house maintenance, however, flowed more equally in both directions: some great-grandfathers and grandfathers who were 'handy' helped their children and sometimes grandchildren, but 'handy' sons or sons-in-law also gave such help to parents or parents-in-law. (Help with house maintenance, recorded in only eight instances, is probably under-represented here since, in contrast to help given at the transition to adulthood or during parenthood and old age, we did not ask about it systematically.)

In a parallel way, help with finding a job was provided in some cases by parents to their children, either at first entry into the labour market or sometimes following a spell of unemployment. In most cases, parents spoke on behalf of *sons* rather than daughters. Help flowing up the generations was rare.

Thane also concludes that in the post-war years families have provided a great deal of services to older members and that 'this support was vital to the well being of very many old people' (ibid.) over this period. Older generations in families, however, far from being simply recipients of care are often major sources of care giving. Indeed, as Thane also points out, increased longevity has not brought a corresponding growth in dependency, as the health and fitness of older people and their independence have also increased. This points to flows of such resources both up and down the generations in some families, and this is confirmed in Table 6.1. The pattern of care provision is, unsurprisingly, contingent on who is being cared for: childcare flows down, especially from grandparents to grandchildren, while eldercare flows up, especially from the grandparent generation (but sometimes parents too) to great-grandparents.

While overall downward transfers outnumber upward ones, there is, as we shall see, extensive reciprocity within families. Moreover, the processes of transmission tend to repeat themselves over family generations. For instance, in contrast to cross-sectional studies which only examine concurrent or recent commitments, the life course perspective taken in our study indicates that those of the grandparent generation who have received, when they were parents of young children, childcare from older generations also tend to offer in their turn care to older generations. In general, therefore, as we shall see later in this chapter, one downward transfer is usually reciprocated by at least one upward transfer, as also found by Renaut (2001). In addition, those who receive tend to give but not necessarily to those who have given to them; they give to younger generations and the culture of giving is thereby transmitted.

Much of the research on care suggests gendered patterns of 'giving', and this is confirmed in our study. Women, usually grandmothers, provide childcare. In only one instance in the study did a grandfather provide significant regular childcare on his own (see Robert Kent, in Chapters 4 and 5). More often than not sons were involved closely in eldercare provided it was for their own parents but usually with the help of their partners (see Mooney and Statham, 2002 for a similar finding). Women tended to take sole responsibility for their own parents with men being 'excused' from too much responsibility. Similarly, other forms of transfer could be gendered. We have already, for example, referred to help with house maintenance being undertaken mainly by men. The Brand family, featured below in this chapter and in Chapter 7, and who record the highest level of intergenerational transfers among our 12 families, provide a clear example of how resources are transmitted down both male and female lineages – mostly material in the former case, mainly care in the latter.

Historical and life course 'moments' of transfer

The historical context within which transfers occur is significant and changing. The transmission of material and care resources by the grandparent generation in our study was taking place in particular demographic, economic and social conditions. As already noted, many of this generation – the generation of the post-war 'golden age' – have more material assets to transfer than other generations. Support from the current grandparent generation is moreover in particular demand since they are sandwiched between older and younger generations whose needs are increasing. The oldest generation (great-grandparents) is living longer, often into their eighties and nineties, often requiring care in late old age – though those with highest levels of dependency were most likely to have children somewhat older than the grandparents in our study. As the age of first childbirth increases, responsibility for elderly people with high care needs will increasingly fall on kin who are of working age (Thane, 2000).

The 1960s/70s generation is financially dependent for longer periods than formerly because of the extension of education and training. They are also having children later in the life course and at a time when it has become normative for both parents to continue working when they have young children, increasing the need for non-parental childcare. With today's parent generation having children at a later age, and the grandparent generation having become parents at a relatively young age, the grandparent generation in our study are relatively youthful grandparents.

Studies suggest that transfers of money, services and care occur in situations where there is deemed to be a 'need' for support, albeit 'need' is a term subject to social definition and processes of negotiation (Finch, 1989). Where a biographical approach is adopted some moments of 'need' are more privileged than others for capturing transmission processes (Pitrou, 1987; Guillaume, 2002). Examples of such moments include the transition to adulthood, becoming a parent, divorce or widowhood, and becoming frail in old age.

For the parent generation in our study, mostly born in the 1970s, the transition to adulthood had extended in duration and finished later in life, as a prolonged period in education had become more common. At the same time, state support has been increasingly curtailed. Periods of being in training or a student in higher or further education were times when financial help from parents was particularly significant. Middle-class members of the 1940s grandparent generation were better able to offer material help to their children at this stage than their working-class contemporaries: but they were also more able to provide financial help than their own parents, as several were at pains to note. Grandfather Michael Hurd relied on a state grant when he went to university in the 1960s, but as a new member of the professional class in the 1990s he gave financial help to his daughter Rachel when she decided to train as a teacher.

Marriage remains a transition when material support has been typically provided by parents, especially help with accommodation. Working-class families, particularly among the older generations, provided housing for their children when they started married life (see also Rosser and Harris, 1965). This was the case for five couples in the great-grandparent generation, three in the grandparent generation, and one in the parent generation. Some stayed with parents for a long time while others, in the great-grandparent generation, moved as soon as husbands returned from war. For working-class families in particular, the home and its setting is said to constitute

a defensive bastion, a protective resource not only in the material shelter offered by the house itself, but also in the accumulation of friendly social networks which can be used for economic exchange and finding jobs as well as *sociability* [our emphasis]. The house and its setting is an instrument of social integration, and a fortress against the many possible catastrophes which the family may suffer (Bertaux and Bertaux-Wiame, 1997).

This solidaristic pattern of living is evident in the Smith family, resident in the same neighbourhood in inner London for several generations. There was no upward mobility in the family generations who took part in the study. All of them worked locally in low skilled jobs. Many resources were transmitted: accommodation and a great deal of practical and emotional support, with particularly strong ties existing between mothers and daughters. The pattern of living with parents was repeated for the two first generations. Brenda, great-grandmother, described living with her mother in a tiny flat for 13 years following her marriage in 1945. When she, her husband and children finally got a council flat of their own around 1960, the experience of suddenly having so much space and so few people around was described by her as 'the most traumatic thing that happened to me'. When her daughter Pauline got pregnant and married soon afterwards, she and her husband Peter spent a brief period living with his parents. Then they went to live with Pauline's grandmother – regarded by the whole family as their 'real home' – before eventually getting a council flat in the same block of flats as Brenda. The current parent generation, Neil and Jane, did not live with parents but found a council flat with the help of Neil's father in the vicinity of both sets of parents. The whole family helped them with the move and with subsequent decoration and DIY work.

Housing was a significant and recurring theme in the interviews with members of this family. Great-grandmother Brenda reflected: 'I suppose housing's played a lot in my life. That's why I hate it when anyone's homeless.' However, the youngest generation – Neil and Jane – wanted to move away from the area. For them, family ties and support were increasingly outweighed by what they saw as a rising number of bad influences on the lives of their young children: drug problems, loss of community spirit, an influx of 'foreigners' and 'cosmopolitans'. The same theme was present also in Brenda's interview, the neighbourhood in her opinion 'going downhill' in recent years.

Provision of accommodation, especially by parents to help new couples with or without children to 'get by' until their own housing became available, was also described by grandparents who had grown up in working-class families but risen later into the middle classes.

Michael Hurd was occupationally upwardly mobile as was his wife Celia. In the 1960s, he returned home to the northwest of England with his wife following his time at university. They lived briefly with Michael's widowed mother while saving to buy a house (the family are discussed in more detail in Chapter 7). Also in the north of England, another grandfather, George Masters, a qualified industrial chemist, spent the first year of married life in the early 1960s living with his wife's parents until the new house they were buying was completed. Even the youngest generation of parents could still look to their parents – the grandparent generation – to provide a temporary roof over their heads. In the Hillyard family, Ben and Sarah, expecting their first child, lived with Sarah's parents rent-free while saving for a deposit on a house. While James and Juliet Kent were living with her parents for some months until their new house was ready for occupation.

Grandparents, especially in the middle class, might also help their children get established as homeowners. George Masters and his wife gave financial help to their son and his wife when they had young children and wanted to move out of their small flat into a house. They did so to compensate for the fact that, not living nearby, they were unable to help with childcare. While Juliet's father, a successful businessman, Robert Kent, not only gave money to each of his three daughters to buy a house, but had also bought a house in the country as a sort of family retreat: 'that's the house everyone uses at weekends...in fact I bought it in the children's names.'

When children are born, mothers (and very occasionally fathers) may give their daughters (in-law) help with childcare and other support. In the grandparent generation, mothers returned to part-time work, typically at that time when grandchildren started school often with help from their mothers. Some of the current generation of parents depended upon help from parents when they returned to work when their children were younger.

Young people and children were not generally expected to provide care in any of the generations, for example for siblings. Only in exceptional cases did they care for older generations. However, in one family – the Prentices – a number of major crises prompted daughters to take care of their younger siblings. The great-grandmother and grandmother, both eldest daughters in families of five, remembered having to step in to take care of their younger siblings when their mothers were ill for long periods. In the current parent generation, the daughter-in-law (from a different family) had a similar experience of having to take care of her sick mother during childhood and early teenage years. Such pressure to care as children was subsequently profoundly resented by the two older women while the young woman, Sheila Prentice (see Chapter 7), described having been very resentful at the time but had since endeavoured to come to terms with her disrupted childhood. In a few cases, too, a sister provided care for the interviewee's children for example, in the case of full-time employed mother Claire Ashton. Or an interviewee cared for nieces or nephews, for example great-grandmother Brenda Smith in earlier times (Table 6.1, being concerned with transfers between generations, does not include instances of resource transfer between members of the same generation).

Transitions such as the death of a partner were commonplace in the great-grandparent generation, but had not yet figured among the two younger adult generations. Such events might create moments when emotional support flowed upwards. Brenda Smith's first husband died when she was 48 leaving her with a 14-year-old child still at home. Pauline, Brenda's older married daughter, reported playing a major role in helping Brenda through this traumatic period: '[She was] absolutely shattered, I thought she was going to go off her head, ... she couldn't come to terms with it ... we moved in, had to abandon our home, for months'. Widowhood, in this case, provides a good example of the two-way flow of resources within some families. For, the death of Brenda's second husband released material resources, which she then transmitted to her adult children and grandchildren. Pauline's husband reported that Brenda had given £2000, a considerable sum in the 1970s, to each of her three children after being widowed a second time. Other events which might release material resources for transfer to younger generations include retirement and, in one instance in our study, the grandparents' divorce.

Our study sample largely excluded divorced family members. But this event and transition has become more common over time, especially among current grandparent and parent generations. It is said that this is likely to put an increased burden on matrilineal ties (Bengtson *et al.*, 2002; Brannen, 2003b; Trifiletti *et al.*, 2003). Divorce typically requires older generations to help younger divorcing generations, mainly through the maternal line (Attias-Donfut and Segalen, 2002; Bengtson *et al.*, 2002). An example of this in our study was grandmother Kate Miller who, as we saw in Chapter 4, was enabled to return to full-time employment because childcare was provided by her mother Jessie (albeit Kate had by then remarried). The reverse may also happen as when the grandparent generation divorces and requires practical or emotional support from the younger generation. (We have no examples of this since such cases were ruled out by the study's design.)

Cultures of transmission

So far we have focused upon what is transferred, by whom and at what moments of the life course transfers are more likely to take place. We now turn to consider the processes of transmission. The concept of transmission implies 'practices' (Morgan, 1999), which suggests not only actions but the beliefs and meanings people give to them. Over time, as over family generations, such social practices may constitute patterns of cohesion and association, on the one hand; or they may lead to fragmentation and difference. The degree to which actions and beliefs correspond may also vary. Finch and Mason (1993) argue that who gives what to whom in what circumstances is governed by a range of considerations which may or may not support what people express as their general, stated normative beliefs. Moreover, when one considers the broad processes of resource transmission in families over time, it is also necessary to pose theoretical questions about whose 'interests' govern transfers, especially where material transfers are concerned.

We have already referred, in Chapter 4, to the process of transmission being varied and complex. Kellerhals *et al.* (2002) argue that a number of different processes of transmission may be involved, including the influence of what they term 'normative reference marks', that is persons, groups and institutions with whom individuals identify or those from whom they distance themselves. Different historical generations may make their mark on whether and how transmission takes place and whether new beliefs are espoused. And cutting across historical generations, intergenerational transfers may also be shaped by particular family cultures. It is to these cultures of transmission we now turn.

Given the vast array and wide-ranging instances of resource transmission which will have taken place in our 12 study families over the time span covered by our three adult generations, it has not been possible for us or the study participants to be comprehensive in the review of transfers – both given and received. That would have required a different sort of study, focused exclusively on this subject. Nor has it been possible for us as interviewers to explore systematically the conditions and understandings that underpin each particular transaction. Apart from lack of time, the cultures that govern such acts of giving and receiving are *not* fully accessible to questions that assume some conscious project or calculation on the part of an individual. Indeed, whatever the way such cultures are reported, it is important to conceptualise the processes involved as *not* necessarily representing conscious projects or calculations by individuals and groups who are engaged in processes of reproduction and change. This idea is captured in the term 'family habitus' coined by Bourdieu (1990): this denotes a set of 'dispositions related to particular practices' which are not necessarily conscious or instrumental and which Bourdieu suggests may lead to regularities in patterns of transmission across family generations.

Thus, we can only expect to identify some of the general cultural meanings associated with resource transfers. In a biographical study such as ours, we hoped to find some facets of cultures of transmission in the language and form in which people gave their stories – for example the stress they placed on representing continuity or whether, as narrators, they individualised and placed emphasis on their own agency or whether they placed an emphasis upon fate and chance (Guillaume, 2002). But, it should be emphasised again, the way in which people justify giving and receiving resources may not be the full story.

How people describe intergenerational transmission is shaped both by life course phase and by historical generation. Most obviously, the kinds of relationships that people make may change. John Miller lacked what he refers to as a 'special relationship' with his grandparents in the 1940s and 1950s when he was a child. Now, in a different historical context (the late 1990s) and a different life course phase (grandfather-hood) he wanted to have a different kind of relationship with his grandchildren. Robert Kent was abroad a lot and very committed to his work when his own children were young, a practice that was common among many middle-class fathers in the 1970s. In the late 1990s and, as a grandfather, he wanted to compensate for his lack of involvement with his own children earlier in the life course in his relationship to his grandchildren. Joseph Ashton looked back on his relationship with his own children when he was very much a breadwinner and somewhat of an absentee father in the 1970s. As a grandfather, he was inspired by his son's example as a current father of two young children:

> I've often looked back and wish I had taken more time out to have been with them ... I've got a relationship with (grandson) that I didn't have with my own kids at that age. Because I was always out at work. I don't suppose the cuddles were there as much in the days with my kids. You see, like, I've seen my son bringing up his son and it's wonderful.

His wife, Shirley, made a similar point. As a grandmother, she wanted to spoil her grandchildren, while recognising that spoiling was not compatible with her role as a mother. Moreover, in relation to the current context in which her daughter-in-law was working full-time, she resisted the idea of caring for her grandchildren on a full-time basis despite her commitment to them: 'because then I would have to be stricter and I wouldn't be the fun grandmother anymore ... [if caring all the time] you've got to be a role model haven't you? ... I wouldn't enjoy it every single day ... (it would) make it more of a tie ... By choice probably would see more of them but wouldn't want to look after them.' Shirley Ashton thereby reinterprets grandmotherhood in relation to both the current social context and her own life course phase.

There are cultures of receiving as well as giving. Life course phase is likely to shape the reporting of care-giving and receiving. Great-grandparents are rather closer to the phase when they are likely to need care themselves, while grandparents are at a point in the life course when they are likely to be called upon to provide care (to older and younger generations). Current parents are, moreover, very much preoccupied with the care of young children and have the grandparent generation, their own parents, to buttress them against the care needs of the great-grandparent generation.

The following themes represent some of the ways in which across the generations families justify the giving and receiving of material and care resources. They are exemplified in relation to particular incidents and in particular family generations.

Duty, love, family mutuality: 'what goes round comes round'

The transmission of care and other resources may be characteristic of a particular family's culture that places an emphasis on hierarchy, duty and loyalty to the family group (Kellerhals *et al.*, 2002). All the great-grandparents grew up in an era when most people were not well off and when there was a minimal welfare state on which to fall back. Family members were forced to depend upon one another even if they did not want to. Brenda Smith (great-grandmother) commented explicitly on how, in her working-class close-knit family, giving to family members implied reciprocity in the longer if not the shorter term: 'you get it back ... what goes round comes round ... what you give you get back'. Great-grandmother Edna Ashton also refers to her family's solidaristic structure (large and close knit) as well as to a culture of looking after their own: 'We are ... from a big family ... we all know each other. We're very close-knit. Anybody in trouble – no problem. We would fall over backwards to help.' Her grandson, Luke, articulated the belief in the family's commitment to care for elderly members – 'That's what families are for if you ask me!' – but is uncertain that he personally would be able to do so.

In some families and in some situations care is mutual; it is reciprocated between specific individuals (Brannen *et al.*, 2003). We look in the next chapter in some detail at the pattern of solidaristic intergenerational relations typified by the Brand family, but here focus on the relationship between two members of the family. Great-grandmother Gwen Brand and her daughter Janice, as members of the 'pivot' generation talked about the help each had received from their own mothers when their children were young, how they felt that they had wanted to repay them in their old age, and the impetus this experience gave them to offer help in turn to their own children and grandchildren. Gwen reciprocated the help that her mother had given her by having her mother, when elderly and widowed, to live with her family for four years. Gwen had sisters available to care for their mother, but felt herself to be 'marked out' for the job, partly because of her position as eldest child and her life course phase (having grown-up children), but also because of her sense of 'specialness': 'I was always dad's favourite girl and always looked after mum.'

In turn, when her own daughters had young children, Gwen provided them with considerable help. On Janice's return to part-time work, for example, Gwen provided childcare, and then went on to look after her grandchildren after school. During the school holidays, her two sets of grandchildren came to her house. Gwen explained why she helped her daughters in terms of a commitment to caring for others and her status as a mother: 'I thought I was a mum, I should help them.' She was also concerned to 'make life better' for the next generation even though in material terms the next generation was in fact better off.

At the age of 54, Gwen's daughter Janice took early retirement despite having worked her way up into a 'good job'. She did this to have more time to visit and help her parents at a point when their health was beginning to deteriorate, and also to help with her grandchildren. Janice expressed no sense of loss or regret in having given up work. She was seen, she said, as the one to whom people in general turned for help; being helpful was described by her mother as an enduring aspect of Janice's personality. Gwen and Arthur, her husband, regarded Janice as somehow 'special', just as Gwen had earlier suggested that she was her own father's 'favourite'. Thus, in both cases, Gwen and Janice seemed to have singled themselves out from their siblings as being committed to the care of family. Janice saw herself as repaying her mother's help in the same currency, namely time: 'My mother has given me so much when I was young and needed a lot of help. And I felt I wasn't going to have my mum and dad for ever and I wanted to look after them . . . I can give them something...my time which is what I feel they gave me really as a child, especially my mum.'

Janice was repeating the pattern of family mutuality down the generations. As well as care for her parents, she was helping her own children: at the time of interview she was transporting one of her two grandchildren to and from school and caring for her after school. But Janice also contrasted the type of help she was able to offer her children with that which her own mother could provide. As well as care, she saw herself as able to provide an additional and different type of resource, illustrating how each generation in a family can put its own stamp upon the resources which are passed on (Bertaux and Bertaux-Wiame, 1997). In particular, Janice felt that she had been able to offer what might be viewed as a form of social capital, gained perhaps through her experience of employment: 'freedom, encouragement and confidence. I can give [daughter] more than my mother gave me, not that what she gave me, in her special way, wasn't just as important.' In part because of this, Janet, Janice's daughter-in-law, identified with Janice more than with her own mother, even though her mother looked after her daughter when Janet returned to work after maternity leave.

Janet, from the current parent generation, was also committed to a culture of family mutuality, helping her own parents financially because they were 'struggling', one of the few examples of financial support moving up through families. She said that, in the future, she would want to help her parents-in-law, Janice and Gordon, if and when they needed it: 'They've helped us out over the years, and, um, that wouldn't even be a consideration in my mind. I would do what I could.' Janet was consciously engaged in a struggle similar to Janice: both to repay and to repeat a pattern of caring for kin – yet at the same time seeking to break out of the mould set by her own mother in which care and family life had closely circumscribed her horizons. There is in Janet a tension between being a caring family member while also wanting her own children to 'get on' in the world and to do well for herself.

Even though we can see patterns of reciprocity between generations in these examples, and an awareness among family members of these reciprocities occurring, it is important to emphasise that the giving of resources in such cases was often unconditional, without calculation or expectation of return. Care and other resources were often explained as given out of love, any reference to exchange being couched in terms of loving relationships between generations. Great-grandmother Edna Ashton and her two sisters took care of their elderly grandmother when she (Edna) was at home with young children. (At the time her own mother was working, so for practical reasons was exempted by her kin from providing care except at weekends.) For Edna, the reason for doing so was obvious: 'It all boils down to love – the voluntary obligation to care for family members . . . she loved us and we loved her in return.' As we have seen, though, from Edna's earlier comment about coming from a close-knit family, in which members help each other, giving for love is not incompatible with giving out of a sense of family mutuality.

Receiving: staying independent, taking support for granted

Such cultures of family mutuality may not be expressed to the same extent when it comes to envisaging one's own care in old age. Most of those we interviewed preferred to think of themselves at this stage of their lives as continuing to be 'independent', rather than expecting care from other family members. Asked about their own care in old age, the obligation to care becomes weaker and a culture of independence stronger. The issue is most acute for the great-grandparent generation, which is most likely to require care in the short term and whose personal independence is consequently most immediately threatened.

Edna Ashton, who as we have just seen cared for her grandmother and who is strongly committed to family care, expresses only the 'hope' that her children will care for her and considers herself 'lucky' should help be forthcoming. The paternal great-grandfather in this family, Bill Ashton, talks about being independent and resisting the need to ask for any help. His wife Molly also wants to stay independent but puts her trust in their youngest daughter who is best off financially and to whom they are particularly close. Edna's daughter, Shirley, expressed similar hopes of help from family when she gets old and infirm but does not want to be 'a burden' to their children. Across all generations in the Ashton family, there is a pride in families being able to take care of their own elderly, which means not having to depend upon the state nor having to go into a home. However there is an underlying fear that they will not be able to manage in the event, and a reluctance to assume help from kin: help is to be hoped for, but it is not to be expected.

A culture of independence is similarly strong among young people. In giving their accounts of being the recipients of help from kin, young people often appeared to take parents' financial support for granted, as other studies have found (de Regt, 1997). This apparent lack of gratitude in relation to material transfers at the transition to adulthood reflects understandings of what parenthood means. Just as parents expect, and are expected, to provide for their dependent children, so their nearly adult children see the transition to adulthood as an extension of such responsibility.

This taken-for-grantedness was also apparent among some members of the grandmother generation. Diana Horton, grandmother, accepted her parents' material help when she got married as perfectly natural: 'a traditional thing anyway, that mothers do, don't they? ... You know, I mean I was, I wasn't deter ... I wasn't. I was grateful, but I mean I wasn't *overly* grateful. I think I just – it was just something that I expected them to do; after I always expected my father to sort out the problems.'

The generation providing help may not, however, view it that way, especially in retrospect. Maternal great-grandmother, Grace Horton, was annoyed that her daughter seemed to have taken for granted the help she and her husband gave on marriage:

> they had practically no money at all, so we had to help them quite a lot. And rather to my annoyance, Diana said to me quite recently – I'd just reminded them very gently that it would've been very difficult for them if they hadn't had some help. They could only have afforded one room, wet nappies hanging up, and I said, 'I don't think your marriage would've – ' 'Oh, yes, it would'. She said, 'Your help and Daddy's help was a great bonus'. 'Bonus?' I don't know what would've happened, quite honestly. I found a flat for them, and paid the premium on it ...

By contrast, an absence of parental help may not be a source of tension for the current parent generation in this family (or at least it was not mentioned in their interviews), even when financial help had been provided to the youngest brother. The current father concerned, Patrick Horton, accepted the parameters and conditions that resulted in his parents providing greater material resources for his younger sibling.

Independence from family: getting on in life

As we will discuss in Chapter 7, some families did not provide a great deal of support to one another. Intergenerational relations in such cases might be more specialised and differentiated, so that emotional support might be reciprocated but not services. Moreover, a culture of independence has a historical dimension. Members of the Second World War grandparent generation, now in their 50s, especially those who were upwardly mobile, were in a position where they could be less concerned with conserving the resources of the wider family. Growing up in a period of post-war reconstruction, welfare state expansion in which educational opportunities opened up, and strong economic growth, they could be concerned instead with individual progress and with their own *families of procreation* getting on in the world through education rather than through the transfer of family wealth. Their rationalities for giving were hence unsurprisingly framed less in terms of a commitment to family mutuality. In respect of material transfers, some were concerned with offspring doing well for themselves although this may change in the current context of collapsing pensions for the next generation.

Richard Samuels, grandfather, was the first generation in his family to go to university, benefiting from state support generous by today's standards, including payment of fees and grants for living costs. He described his career as both an 'investment' for his nuclear family, that is his wife and children, and as an individual project to make 'something of myself' and to get 'on the road to somewhere'. He and his wife sought to rise up occupational and housing ladders. In doing so, they received considerable help from the state: their own and their children's education, their public-sector jobs and so on. Not surprisingly perhaps, Richard was also very committed to state support. Family support, by contrast, was limited and highly conditional; when he had asked for money from his parents he had been expected to repay them, Richard's father by this time having retired on a small pension. Richard for his part helped one of his sons financially when this young man ran up debts at university – but on the strict understanding that the money would be repaid, an obligation which he felt his son had not honoured. Richard links his attitude towards his son to his own experience as a young man: 'I'm probably still thinking of the time when my parents didn't have enough money. My father was always very – I mean, he worked in a bank, anyway. He was always very tight.'

Richard also looked to the state as the ideal provider of care for the elderly, in preference to younger family members: 'We grew up expecting the state to do things, and I'm still very much in favour of that. I mean, I work for the local education authority ... and my wife works in the [public sector]. So we're still struggling to keep that going ... – I don't think I would want my children to feel that they had to look after me.' However he also linked his desire for independence to family culture, to his mother and grandmother who at 90 were still fiercely independent:

> That's very much what my mother thinks. So I've inherited that from her. Yeah, she did look after her own mother a bit, towards the end. I found a card at Christmas that was written by my grandmother,

who was ninety-something. Um, when just before she died, she actually had to go into a nursing home, because my mother needed to go away for a week, or something like that. It was my grandmother's documentation of how awful it was being in with all these ... elderly dependent people. Quite amazing ... I can see my mother really resisting that ... 'I don't want the family to look after me. I'll do it myself' ... I would like a very carefully tailored state system.

Richard's wife, Marjorie, was similar in her attitude to family obligations and considered that the state should help people to be independent. Having become adult in the 1960s, she had embraced the cultural changes of the times while, as a young mother, she lacked the freedom to enjoy them. She later thrived on the expanding educational and job opportunities for women in the 1970s and, as a mother of two young children, fought for financial independence and to make her way up the occupational ladder. The resources she drew upon were largely public – her own higher education to which she returned after becoming a mother, her children's state education, and her own employment in the expanding public sector. These resources gave both Marjorie and Richard a sense of 'independence', which in effect meant independence or *freedom from* family.

Marjorie was not caught between the roles of grandmother and daughter: her mother died the year Marjorie's first grandchild was born. But she was, in any case, not active in caring for either older or younger generations. Following her father's death, Marjorie's mother moved into sheltered accommodation with a nursing home attached, which Marjorie considered 'a perfect place for someone to grow old on their own in and become less able to look after themselves'. Although she had visited her mother regularly, Marjorie's intention had been to assist her in remaining 'independent' and to help her make her own 'choices' about care. Asked whether she felt any obligation to her mother, Marjorie exempted herself by making reference to the history of their relationship as never being 'close'. When Marjorie became a mother herself, significantly she rejected her mother's efforts to become closer. When her mother's health deteriorated, Marjorie never contemplated the possibility of her mother, who had remained in northern England, moving nearer to her, explaining that she had no ties in the south. She also justified this in terms of her own employment career.

In reflecting on her own care in the future, Marjorie was quite explicit. Her family would not be part of the solution: 'Whatever happens I would expect to manage it ... We might need some physical care which I would hope to be able to manage ourselves . . . I don't think (family care) works in this culture. I never want to be dependent.' Her vision of old age was to be on 'an equal footing' with those giving the care which, by implication, Marjorie saw as ruling out family. Such independence is rather different from what we term a culture of autonomy, which typifies the succeeding parent generation in this family and is considered next.

Individual autonomy: creating a life of my own

Young people today are said to be shaping their own biographies (Giddens, 1991; Beck and Beck-Gernsheim, 1996) according to their own personalised forms of normative reference marks (Kellerhals *et al.*, 2002). They focus, it is argued, upon personal identity construction, following a choice culture and adopting a relational orientation in which emphasis is placed upon self-realisation and the importance of self-fulfilment through one's relationships and plans (Giddens, 1991; Beck and Beck-Gernsheim, 1996). This culture is less about 'freedom from', which characterises the previous culture we identified: getting on and being independent of family. It is more about 'freedom to', that is, to create personal identities and lifestyles. Such identity politics is allied to a politics of diversity which gives individuals not only freedom of expression but the opportunity to give 'voice', through which individuals adopt and speak on behalf of particular lifestyles.

What is unclear is how far this arises from the fact that these members of the parent generation speak from a current as opposed to a past life course phase, and how far this is a manifestation of historical generation. In (historical) generational terms, it has been argued that a shift has occurred from the old idea of ethics as important for personality and identity, to one where aesthetics become the more important concern and where structural factors such as labour market uncertainty may compel young adults to prioritise consumption identities over worker identities (Bauman, 1998). Kellerhals *et al.* (2002) refer to this tangentially when they describe the current 1960s/70s generation as both 'utilitarian and humanist' at the same time.

The account given by Stephen, Richard and Marjorie's son, has elements that are suggestive of a culture of autonomy and identity creation. Like his father, Stephen went to university but, unlike his father, he did not follow a particular professional occupation or organisational career. He developed his long-term interest in music and 'drifted' into the music industry. After a while he set up his own business in music distribution. Stephen suggested that this was part of a 'family project' and a project for bringing up his children. In becoming his own boss, he was able to work from home and to choose where to live. In this and in their relocation to the countryside, Stephen believed that he and his wife Naomi were creating their own lifestyle: 'We're sort of trying to create...a life here that's sort of ideal in our mind's eye and we're somewhere close to it.'

Stephen's attitude to the education of his own children enabled the family to be similarly 'flexible'. He wanted to be more laid back than his own parents who sought to make their children independent. At the same time, here and elsewhere Stephen identified continuities with his family of origin. He said he espoused their middle-class values; he wanted to help his children 'get started' in life. He also wanted them to make their own choices however, considering that there was no 'right way' for them to go ('it's up to them'), and that they might have to change direction in their work careers as he had done. Yet he was also transmitting values to his children indirectly, ensuring that they had a broad exposure to music (his field of interest and employment) and encouraging them to be creative. As with other aspects of his life, Stephen traced this interest in music to his father.

Like his father, Stephen too stressed the importance of self-reliance defined in terms of not having to depend on family. But, unlike his father, he expected less of a role for the state while still being committed to free education and a free national health service. He was also not governed by ideas of what people 'ought' to do; there were no obligations, only a sense that people should take 'individual responsibility'. From this perspective, Stephen was more committed than his parents to a culture of family obligations and believed families should help with their elderly members.

His approach accorded very much with ideas of the 'enabling state', current in the UK at the time, expressed in terms of Third Way politics (Giddens, 1998). He did not believe that the state owed people a living but that it should be there for those unable to support themselves. Stephen's worldview was humanist. While endorsing a culture of autonomy and identity creation, he also placed limits upon personal responsibility and too much obsession with the self and thought that health and education should be provided free of charge:

> Another thing that's about me is [being] very self-reliant. I hate relying on other people. Other people let you down very often. And, er, so, in thinking about what I'm doing for my children, et cetera, it's – I've got to do it for them, I've got to provide for them, I've got to set

them up. And I'm not going to rely on the State or anybody else to help. Now, whether I think other people should, it's always a bonus if they do, and I don't kind of think anybody should do anything. It's – the individual should take more responsibility. If they can. Only if they can. Not – circumstances for people are really hard in some cases, and no matter how hard they try, no matter how much effort they put into it, it just doesn't work for them, and they do need help. And that I fully recognise. But to just expect it, to think that, um, the world owes you a living, it's not right. Not right. Um, in terms of caring, you know, looking out for other people, I'm not just inward looking, I'm not just saying, Yes, I'm very self-reliant, but at the same time, I do think it's important to look out for other people as well, people around you, to care for other people. Not to be totally self-obsessed. Um, so – you know, will help other people personally. Um, in terms of whether large organisations should – should have that feeling as well, I mean, yes, they definitely should, and this is what I'd vote for, free education and a free health service. But, um, somewhere along the line, a lot of personal responsibility as well.

Stephen's wife, Naomi, echoes some of Stephen's views. She is from a more traditional bourgeois family, where her mother was at home and family life was organised around her father, a member of one of the old professions. As the youngest of five daughters she was left to decide her future for herself. State support figured little in her biography, her education for example being private. She gave up her teaching post after her first child was born, but returned to supply teaching on a part-time basis. She had compromised in favour of her children. But she had sought to share some of the care with Stephen since he started working from home and for himself.

There are more tensions evident in Naomi's view than Stephen's. She was uncertain about the future despite their sense of autonomy in creating their present life. Moreover, Naomi suggested that while people should make provision for themselves, there should be limits to personal responsibility, noting that her generation may be becoming sceptical about their ability to make provision for themselves and their children. The example she cited was pensions, concerns about which had just entered public debate in the late 1990s:

Your old age is your responsibility if you're fortunate enough to be in a situation where, um, you can think about it and realise it. But the provision you make should be secure. I don't know what provision you should do, whether you should start putting money away every week. It is – it is your responsibility, if you can afford to put away a little bit towards it. But, um – that's a difficult one, because if you go and spend all your money and then you get old, you're still going to be provided for . . . And there has – I think our generation's getting a bit sceptical about it all, because money is – you know, people who think they've provided for their old age now find that they haven't.

Conclusion

Multi-generation families have the potential to pass on a variety of resources. In this chapter we have focused largely upon care, including childcare and eldercare, and a variety of material support: money, accommodation, financial help with housing, house maintenance and help with finding work. We have suggested that the Second World War grandparent generation is likely to have more material assets to pass on because of upward occupational mobility and growth in their assets, especially housing. This 'pivot' generation is likely to be in considerable demand to provide care to older and younger generations: for life course reasons because of grandparenthood; for demographic reasons because of increased longevity of older relatives (their parents when their health declines); and for social change reasons due to increased divorce and the growth in labour market participation of current mothers of young children.

From a biographical perspective, it is possible to identify across the life course of several generations a range of life course transitions during which help is particularly needed. But while these particular transitions repeat themselves, the context in which help may be sought or offered changes over time. Thus among the great-grandparent and grandparent generations, on marriage many couples looked to family to accommodate them, at least to start with. The current generation of parents required parental support during higher education, an increasingly common experience in this generation. For all generations the need for grand-mothers' help with childcare has been a persistent theme, albeit the nature and conditions of women's employment has changed.

As other studies have also found, transfers of different types of resources often go together. Moreover, transfers are more often passed down, rather than up, the generations. Almost all financial help was passed from older to younger generations, though care typically went in both directions. Most help was transferred by parents to children, although older generations might also help the younger non-adjacent generation, their grandchildren. Overall, therefore, transfers down were often accompanied by at least one transfer up the generations. The receipt of childcare from grandmothers, for example, might later be accompanied by the return of such help by their daughters when their mothers reached frail old age.

In the patterning of family relations and in the meanings that family members ascribe to their relations and transfers, we may identify different types of reciprocity. Elsewhere we have discussed reciprocities (Brannen *et al.*, 2003) including generalised reciprocity in which the giving of support to a younger generation, notably in the transition to adulthood, is reciprocated by support being supplied to a third party – the subsequent generation. Such a pattern is exemplified in this study in the way that parents repeat a pattern of giving support to children in the transition to adulthood down the generations; while specific reciprocities occur when a particular person is repaid for the care they have provided, in the same or different currency, for example between mothers (in-law) and daughters (in-law) notably in the exchange of childcare with eldercare (the Brand family discussed earlier). Reciprocity may be calculated, or it may be implicit and not recognised as an obligation to repay services rendered. Moreover, such a system of exchange involves processes of negotiation which are not binding; as we have demonstrated, a particular person is 'targeted' or targets themselves as the giver of care while others are exempt.

In this chapter we considered the ways in which family members of different generations justified giving (or not giving) to others and receiving resources from others. Such justifications we have suggested are cultures which are shaped by an interviewee's life course position – moments when interviewees are far from or near points of giving or receiving eldercare. They are shaped, too, by the historical periods at which transfer of resources occur.

A number of different cultural meanings which underpin processes of intergenerational transmission were identified. We have deliberately avoided the suggestion that these meanings define practices: indeed, a whole host of other considerations may come into play in determining who gives what to whom and when: for example, availability, affective closeness, need, and so on (Finch and Mason, 1993). However, these cultures are likely to say something about a particular family's strategies for reproducing different forms of capital. In some families, a culture of mutuality characterised a general pattern of solidaristic intergenerational transfers; while, in others, transfers were specific and not generalised. In some families, there was little reciprocity of material or care resources;

instead, a culture of independence prevailed that is of the household from the wider kin network. However this is not to say that other resources were not being transmitted within the multi-generation family, notably forms of cultural capital such as the desire for education. Particular cultures can be prominent in particular generations. The culture of family mutuality, for example, was strong in the great-grandparent generation who grew up in a period when social protection was minimal and who were forced to depend upon the resources of family. This does not preclude a culture, as an ideology if not as a practice, also appearing among younger generations. Indeed, a particular culture could permeate families across the generations, for example the culture of duty, love and family mutuality. In the case of the Brands it was particularly strong as it was separately maintained by both male and female lineages: through the culture of work – formal and informal among the men and through a culture of care among successive generations of women.

On the other hand, other cultures of transmission were more specific to a particular historical generation. Such a finding may be considered evidence of the importance of the historical milieu in which interviewees grew up and in which they learned a particular language to describe commitment: that is, whether families should provide for themselves or not. A culture of 'getting on' and 'independence from family' typified some members of the Second World War grandparent generation, both men and women (e.g. Richard and Marjorie Samuels), who, in the post-war period, took advantage of increased opportunities to advance in life and were able to depend upon the growing welfare state to support them (university grants). Such cultures as in the case of the Samuels was shared at couple and household level, buttressing them from influences from the wider family.

A rather different emphasis was evident in some members of the current generation of parents born in the 1960s/1970s (e.g. the Samuels' son Stephen), who grew up in a less economically stable period and who demonstrated a culture of autonomy and identity creation, expressed in the importance he attached to the exercise of personal responsibility for creating support, identity and lifestyle. We should, however, treat the expression of autonomy with some caution as indeed was evident in his wife's interview. As discussed elsewhere (Nilsen and Brannen, 2002; Brannen and Nilsen, 2002, 2003a,b), the language of agency and empowerment may be at odds with the structural context in which they are situated. Individual family members usually depend upon family resources in the context of state retrenchment in welfare and the deregulation of the labour market which no longer affords the employment protection enjoyed by their parents. Thus their 'independence' is premised upon individually negotiated solutions which may be highly precarious, for example a parent depending upon an employer to offer a discretionary benefit. This generation may stress their own efforts to be independent in a context of uncertainty, while remaining silent about support they receive to achieve it, whether from the state or family.

This last point indicates that being at the receiving end of resource transmission could produce rather different accounts from those of the givers of resources. The elderly and also the very elderly emphasised their own desire to be personally independent of others when they entered frail old age. Similarly, the current generation seeking to establish themselves in life stressed their own efforts in marshalling resources while playing down the support provided to them by their families in the process. Limits are placed on indebtedness as young people need and seek to demonstrate their individual and household 'independence' in the transition to adulthood and parenthood – to show they are able to stand on their own two feet and to support their children.

Intergenerational relations in families are patterned in different ways as we shall describe in Chapter 7. Cultural meanings, which individuals ascribe to resource transmission, may not neatly reflect those patterns but they are broadly complementary. We turn now to consider this patterning in the next chapter in which we develop a typology of intergenerational relations constructed using two structural dimensions: geographical and occupational mobility.

7
Towards a Typology of Intergenerational Relations: Processes of Reproduction and Innovation

The aim of this chapter is to examine intergenerational relations within each family and to look at each family *holistically* in relation to the social forces which push family members to carry on family patterns and those which pull them apart and lead them to strike out on their own. It poses the following questions: How far do multi-generation families pool resources across generations to support one another? How far does each generational unit differentiate itself from other generational units by being self-reliant or reliant on formal services? Further questions are framed in terms of ambivalences between generational members and household units which operate at different levels: at the structural level and in terms of social interaction, feelings and values.

In the chapter, we develop a typology of intergenerational relations. This suggests considerable variation, although we would not claim that the typology is in any sense exhaustive. To do this we plot each family in relation to two structural factors which we considered likely to shape intergenerational relations, through their influence on the resources which families have available to them and how they decide to deploy them: occupational mobility, particularly that of male family members; and the geographical mobility of generational household units.

Making sense of processes in multi-generational families

As discussed in Chapter 1, modernising influences upon family life have been long debated. Some sociologists have argued that families have become less solidaristic (Parsons, 1943), yet many empirical studies have shown the extended family to be alive and well, albeit in a modified form (see Morgan, 1975). In recent years, the debate has taken a new turn. Attention has changed to the conditions under which family members decide to provide support to one another. This has arisen out of a reconceptualisation of family responsibilities as subject to processes of negotiation rather than prescribed obligations (Finch, 1989) (see Chapter 4). Just as generalisations about how 'the nuclear family' operates failed to enlighten and have led to a more differentiated approach which takes account of gender, generation and other perspectives, so too we need to exercise restraint in studying multi-generation families and apply the process of differentiation to them.

It has been suggested that multi-generation families will constitute a valuable new resource for the support of individuals in the 21st century, particularly in the context of the weakening of household ties following divorce (Bengtson, 2001). However, while multi-generational families may offer personnel resources, namely several generations of kin, these may not be readily available. Moreover the ways in which family relations work vary: for family relations, including multi-generation families, are shaped by material and cultural resources, by beliefs and practices, by commitment to family obligation and by wealth, assets and life chances. Resources are utilised in different ways, at different times; they are required in differing amounts and for different needs and by and for different family members.

Within families, there is a creative tension between change and continuity, and between processes of reproduction and innovation. As described in earlier chapters, many resources, not only material and care resources but also values and practices, are transmitted between generations in families. Yet each generation may also develop, create or subscribe to its own: some parenting practices, for instance, are passed on while new practices are adopted in succeeding generations. Indeed, the passing on of one resource may lead to a change in another resource, in turn leading either to innovation or continuity. For example, parents may transmit educational aspirations to their children, a consequence of which may be that children move into different kinds of occupations from their parents and develop different social class affinities and lifestyles; or the provision of care by one generation for another may also open up wider employment opportunities with material consequences and different role models to transmit to the succeeding generation.

As we saw in Chapter 6, the transmission of resources is typically reciprocated but not necessarily in the same currency nor necessarily repaying the same family member who gave in the first place. However, as family members' life chances change across the generations, some may lack the resources to repay their parents or to provide similar resources to the next generation down. For example, employed grandmothers may not be able to provide care for their grandchildren in the way their mothers provided care for their (the now grandmothers') own children; but they may be in a position to offer financial help which may serve as some compensation (Dench and Ogg, 2002). Bertaux and Bertaux-Wiame (1997) describe such tension between continuity and change in the following way and suggest how one resource may be transformed into another and how the succeeding generation put its own imprint on resources:

> Because transmission of sameness reifies the heir [treats him as an object], it seems to carry the kiss of death. To become the subject of the heritage, the heir must act upon it by leaving his or her mark upon it . . . The new element involving both the rejection of the past and innovation, enables the heir to take possession of something that actually was passed on to him. The point is not simply that he must 'make something of what was made of him' as Sartre put it so aptly, but that he make something of what has been passed on to him (p. 93).

The tension between change and continuity typically generates *ambivalences*. Luscher (2000) identifies ambivalences in which different generations are caught up in a tension: between the reproduction of some aspects of their 'family systems' on the one hand, and innovation of other aspects on the other hand. Ambivalences have to be managed; they are *not* resolvable.

As Luscher (2000) and Luscher and Pillemer (1998) suggest, ambivalences take various forms. They may be apparent structurally, as demonstrated for instance in a change in occupational status across family generations, though this may *not* be interpreted by the participants concerned as having any particular significance, at least as divined at the point of a research interview. They may be present in family strategies, for instance when a household unit seeks to put geographical distance between itself and other households in the family. Or they may be expressed through feelings, in social interaction and interpersonal relations, and in values.

These different types of ambivalences may not, however, go together. Structural aspects of people's lives may pull in one direction, for example towards the reproduction of aspects of family relations while, to use Bourdieu's term, their habitus (Bourdieu, 1990) creates divergent life practices – individual and collective. Thus, over the generations, some families may reproduce the life chances of the older generation, as when wealth and educational capital are transmitted. However, younger generations, despite the transmission of assets and wealth which cushion their life chances, may, at the same time, seek divergence and differentiation from older generations, typically through values and life styles.

It is important in this discussion of ambivalences not to contrast in a simplistic either/or way structural factors against the agency of actors. The transmission of resources of different kinds is likely to involve processes in which much of what passes on, or is passed on, is taken for granted. For the cultural transmission of class and family cultures can be implicit as well as explicit (Bernstein, 1996). As Bourdieu (1990) suggests, habitus is not only calculative or intentional behaviour, it may involve 'reasonable or commonsense behaviour' – forms of 'spontaneity without consciousness'. In the sense that habitus involves 'produc[ing] history on the basis of history', the dispositions of individuals and groups are cumulative (p. 56).

A typology of intergenerational relations

In focusing upon the occupational mobility of men in the families and the geographical mobility of their constituent household units, we selected two *a fortiori* conditions which, on the basis of both theory and research evidence, we considered to be strong influences upon intergenerational family relations. In the former case, there is a wealth of evidence that men's occupational status shapes family resources and life chances. It seems likely, therefore, to affect the capacity of different generations to provide support, especially material support across the family generations, while inequalities in resources across family generations are likely to have an adverse effect on reciprocity. Changes in occupational status may also manifest themselves in changes in values and lifestyles, contributing to ambivalences.

With the historical separation of work from the household, geographical mobility increased (Grieco, 1987). Evidence that geographical mobility of households is associated with upward occupational mobility (Fielding, 1997) although still not clear cut. Nonetheless it seems likely to make the provision of certain kinds of support and services between family generations difficult to accomplish, at least on a daily or frequent basis. It may also disrupt social networks and sociability patterns among kin (Aldridge *et al.*, 2002). As studies have shown (Grundy *et al.*, 1999, for example), geographical proximity is a determining feature of frequency of contact between parents and children.

Occupational mobility

Over the 20th century until the late 1970s, there has been an absolute increase in occupational mobility for both men and women, by which we mean that the actual numbers of children in higher status occupations have been consistently higher than in their parents' generation. More space at the top was created for men and more in the middle for women (Goldthorpe and Mills, 2000; Aldridge, 2001). This is largely due to the expansion in employment opportunities in middle-class occupations, which have substantially grown in size relative to the working class (Heath and Payne, 2000). As we saw in Chapter 3, the picture from the 1970s is not clear cut, with evidence of gender differences in mobility, though overall, and if income mobility is factored in, social mobility appears to have at least faltered.

The analysis of occupational mobility in our twelve families has concentrated on men's jobs (Table 7.1), since women in the two older

Table 7.1   Men's occupational mobility over three generations (12 families)

Continuity of occupational status: low skilled (3)	Two families of unskilled/semi-skilled men One family of self-employed family builders
Continuity of occupational status: high skilled (2)	One family of senior managers/managing directors One family of electrical engineers (middle management level)
Downward mobility in occupational status from skilled to unskilled work (2)	One family with a great-grandfather in skilled work and a grandfather and father in semi-skilled work One family with a great-grandfather and grandfather in skilled work and a father (son-in-law) in unskilled work
Upward occupational mobility from skilled to professional/ managerial work (4)	Two families of great-grandfathers and grandfathers in skilled work and a father in a managerial occupation Two families of great-grandfathers in manual/clerical work and grandfathers and fathers in professional occupations
Upward and downward occupational status (1)	One family of a great-grandfather in skilled manual work/shopkeeper, one grandfather a professional worker, a father (son-in-law) in unskilled work

generations had intermittent employment careers following mother-hood. Moreover, these older generations of women typically worked part time. As already described in Chapter 3, women in the Second World War grandparent generation, married to middle-class husbands, who climbed their own occupational ladders did so at a later age, that is, *after* they had brought up their children. This *intra*-generational mobility on the part of women thereby matched the occupational progress made by their husbands *inter*-generationally. Some wives of manual workers also rose occupationally, entering non-manual clerical employment, and like their middle-class counterparts did so late in their work careers when their children were older. Their husbands, however, typically remained in manual work.

In five of the twelve families no change in occupational status took place between fathers and sons/sons-in-law over three generations; this pattern broadly reflects the national picture for cohorts of men born in 1910–19 and in 1940–48 (Heath and Payne, 2000). In four families, one or more generations of men were upwardly mobile occupationally, while in two families there was downward mobility. In one family there was both upward and downward mobility in occupational status across the three male generations. As nationally (ibid.), upward mobility across male generations is rarely long range: most has involved a move from skilled manual or clerical work in the older generation to professional or managerial occupations in the younger generation. No unskilled worker had a son or son-in-law who entered a professional or managerial occupation.

Geographical mobility

Historically, there has been much geographical movement in the British population. However, current evidence suggests that four in ten people nationally have stayed in the same local authority where they were born and only one in a hundred households has moved any great distance (Donovan and Rubenstein, 2002). According to Grundy *et al.* (1999), half of the people who have a father or mother or eldest child alive see them at least once a week, half of them living within a half hour's journey time.

The constituent households of half of our families have continued to live close to one another in the same town or same part of London, while in the remaining families at least one of the households in each family was living at a significant distance from the others. However, in all but two cases generational units were living in the same area of the country, broadly defined, as their kin; the exception was one upwardly mobile couple in which the grandfather had moved from northern

England to the southeast and a working-class household where the grand-parents had moved with their children from London to the southwest of England. On the other hand, reflecting the movement of the population in the early part of the century, some members of the great-grandparent generation in the 'stayer families' had been incomers to an area.

In this study, as is the case nationally, graduates were more likely to move than non-graduates (Donovan and Rubenstein, 2002). Most moves had rather less to do with jobs and rather more to do with life course phases or with improving the quality of life, notably with respect to housing. This is supported by recent national data, which also show that distant moves are more likely to be job related (ibid.). The case of the Prentice family, who moved from inner London to the southwest of England (see Chapter 5 and later in this chapter) exemplify moving in a search for improved quality of life, while Margaret Kent fleeing Nazi Germany in the 1930s (see Chapter 4) is an extreme example of a non-job related move where kin were an important support in the search for employment (as, for example, in the case of the Brand family with their family building firm, featured later in this chapter). Such kin support over jobs often reinforced the pattern of staying local, though this was not always the case in some middle-class families providing such support (as, for example, in the case of the Horton family where Bernard and Diana helped their son Adam find a job in television at some distance from their home, through talking to a friend).

Yet it is important to note that, despite the movement of half the families away from close kin, most maintained what Mason (1999) refers to as 'close ties at a distance' and were increasingly able to do so because of technological advance (Wellman and Berkowitz, 1988). On the other hand, it is significant that the two families who moved farthest away were those whose ties were affectively less close. In one case the 'movers' sought to put distance between them and their kin.

Four patterns of intergenerational relations

We plotted the 12 case-study families on a matrix in which male occupational status mobility is one parameter and household geographical mobility the other, allocating the case-study families to the matrix's four quadrants (Figure 7.1). Some families 'fit' the quadrant better than others; as the multi-direction arrows in Figure 7.1 suggest, this is not a hard and fast classification. Through an analysis of the life histories and life stories of these families, the cases in each of the quadrants were then explored to see how far each quadrant is suggestive of a particular

Occupation/occupational status

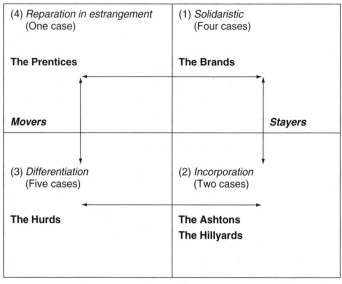

(4) *Reparation in estrangement* (One case) **The Prentices**	(1) *Solidaristic* (Four cases) **The Brands**
Movers	*Stayers*
(3) *Differentiation* (Five cases) **The Hurds**	(2) *Incorporation* (Two cases) **The Ashtons** **The Hillyards**

Innovation

Figure 7.1   Matrix of case-study families: occupational by geographical mobility.

pattern of intergenerational family relations with respect to the transmission of a range of resources. The range of resources covered includes: financial transfers and other material assets, the supply of services including care, sociability, emotional support, values and beliefs, and commitment to family obligations (Bengtson, 2001). Different forms of intergenerational transfers or 'capital' are often inextricably intertwined; for example the economic is bound up with the cultural and symbolic (Bourdieu, 1986; see also Allatt, 1993). Moreover one form of capital may be transformed into another. Thus, while occupational and geographical mobility may shape the conditions for the transmission of capital, they may also shape transformations from one form of capital to another.

Below we consider the quadrants in turn, illustrating each with the case of a particular family.

Solidaristic relations (quadrant 1)

The four families in this quadrant span the socio-economic spectrum. The occupations of the men in each family generation reproduced the occupational status of the older male generations, while geographically the different families remained close to each other. Three families are clearly within this quadrant while the fourth only fits on one dimension exactly since the youngest generation had moved away. The three generations in this family – the Peters – are however linked by several types of commitment, including: similar occupational interests and allegiance to a particular religious sect which is based in the town where the two older generations live. Moreover the youngest generation of parents was the recipient of frequent childcare support by the grandmother, Priscilla Peters, who acted in a very similar way to those who lived geographically close to their children, and had indeed recently given up employment to facilitate her provision of this support (Chapter 4).

Intergenerational relations in this quadrant are *solidaristic* (Luscher, 2000) in a traditional sense. There are of course many different kinds of solidarity in families (see Crow, 2002). In these families, habits and general dispositions lead family members to provide functional support of different kinds to one another – jobs, housing, childcare and eldercare – largely along *gendered lines*. In all four families, the grandmother generation is pivotal in the provision of care which involves what has been referred to as 'specific reciprocities' (Finch, 1989), that is, exchanges between the same set of persons so that a mother who receives childcare from her mother (the now grandmother) when her children are young repays her mother when she requires help in old age. This pattern of resource transfer is exemplified in the Brand family below, which overall most closely approximates to the solidaristic pattern, including showing the highest level of intergenerational resource transfers among our study families (see Table 6.1, Chapter 6).

The male lineage in the *Brand* family – Jimmy, Gordon and Sean – are directly related and all are breadwinners. Their wives – Mary, Janice and Janet – are and have been the main carers and household managers; Mary (great-grandmother) never worked after her marriage (apart from occasional fruit picking and cleaning), while Janice (grandmother) and Janet (mother) worked part time while their children were growing up. Janice increased her hours as her children grew older, but took early retirement aged 54 even though she had worked her way up into a responsible job in a local heath centre. Janet, her daughter-in-law and currently a mother of a young child, took maternity leave and resumed her occupation in the bank after the birth of her first child, but only part time. She was pregnant again at the time of interview, and was considering stopping working when her second child was born.

All three biologically related men are in the same occupation, working as self-employed builders, each eventually joining the family firm.

They are also united by an entrepreneurial spirit of running the business, upon which each generation has also sought to make its own mark. Over the generations, this business has played a central part in the 'family project', generating and transmitting material resources, not only capital but also housing and employment. Together with a large amount of informal help and care given by and received from female members of the family, the business provides for a great deal of family mutuality which in turn serves to reproduce a similar lifestyle and life chances across the generations.

Born in 1918, Jimmy Brand was 82 when interviewed. He had spent most of his life in the East Anglian town where the rest of the family lived. Having rejected his father's trade in corn and seed sales, which was not doing well at the time, Jimmy went into the building trade at 14, with the help of a word spoken on his behalf to the builder by his father. Later, returning home after serving in the army during the Second World War, Jimmy started a building business with his wife's relatives. At the age of 57, Jimmy retired and went to live abroad although he and Mary returned to their home in the family's home town each summer, maintaining close contact with younger members of the family.

Their son Gordon, born in 1946, left school at 15, like his father with no qualifications. He was apprenticed to another builder in the town, an occupation he felt was ingrained in him: 'it was just part of us really, the building trade. And . . . I'd always helped Dad . . . go on different jobs and that sort of thing . . . and . . . [it was] just natural progression really.' Aged 21 and his apprenticeship completed, his father asked Gordon if he would first do some contract work for the family firm. Later Gordon, aged 29 with a young family to support, set up a new firm with his brother thereby expanding the family business and building houses for the family to live in.

While the three men maintained the same occupational status, in the youngest generation Sean broke the educational mould by gaining qualifications. Born in 1969, he left school at 16 having gained a string of GCSEs. He described his childhood as 'a doing sort of childhood' and a 'close family sort of childhood'. He worked for his father in the school holidays – 'I loved it . . . I just liked working for my dad' – and spoke of the importance that his family attached to being 'good with your hands . . . the only way you got rewards were doing things'.

Despite this attachment to the family trade, he clearly felt the need to prove himself to his family since his skills were more non-manual than manual and not so highly rated by the older generations in the family. His chance to do so came later when the development of the family business required such skills: 'all of a sudden they'd got this guy who can cut it with a pen'. Through his subsequent training (resulting in a qualification in building management and a period working in contracts management in a large building firm), Sean was able to build up the family business – which had been until then a relatively small-scale operation – into something larger and more successful. This meant working even harder: 'To make the same margin, I work more personally. I think employers expect their employees to work more. More's expected out of the day's work, I feel squeezed, yeah. Where that will go I don't know.'

Now that Sean was running the business and it was doing well, his father felt he could retire and gain a pension from leaving his money invested in it. Significantly, Sean mentioned that he intended to make this happen for his father. When Gordon did retire, however, he planned to continue working for the family by doing up their respective houses.

Of the three men, the great-grandfather Jimmy had been the most geographically mobile, first through serving overseas during wartime and later by retiring abroad. But he retained strong links with the family's home town, not only keeping a house there to return to each year, but also through the ownership of other properties which provided funds for his retirement. By contrast, the two younger generations had lived in the town all their lives. The importance of 'place' is very clear in the accounts of family members. Gordon talked about the value he placed on bringing up his children where he spent his own childhood. For him, living 'near the water' (the estuary close to home) was important, a theme echoed in his mother's account of her life with Jimmy: 'I was on the water all the time. That is our life.' All three men – great-grandfather, grandfather and son – were boat builders in their spare time; sailing was moreover a *family* hobby involving wives and children. Gordon noted the continuity across the three generations: '[Sean's] just built a boat...it's something in our blood I think. You need the water...My father's the same and...my boy's the same. So, something about us.'

Similarly, 'place' figures in the accounts of the women in the family. While being 'close' also means ties of love and care, it also means belonging. One of the first things that Janet, Sean's wife, said in giving her life story in the interview was that she had lived in the 'same place' all her life. Talking about her new house, which Sean was rebuilding, she said: 'We both think we'd never probably move again.' Moreover, she described wanting to be like her parents-in-law, Gordon and Janice, by getting married in the same country church; the wedding had been 'very much a family time'. Janet drew out in her interview other family continuities, noting the similarity between her own parents' lifestyle and that of her mother-in-law's parents. She talked also about the ways in which both she and her father were conservative in their employment preferring to stay in the same job.

The solidaristic relations in this family generate considerable functional support, in particular through intergenerational transfers of care. We have already described, in the previous chapter, the reciprocities of caring between maternal great-grandmother Gwen, her daughter Janice and her daughter-in-law Janet, as well as how Gwen had been in a similar relationship with her mother. But both great-grandmothers, Mary as well as Gwen, provided childcare and other support to their daughters and daughters-in-law in the childrearing years, care which was being reciprocated now that Gwen and Mary needed help in old age. Similarly Janet was seeking to repay her parents for the childcare they had provided although it was also clear that they were continuing to help in other ways: at the time of interview the couple were living with Janet's parents while their new house was being totally refurbished through the business. There is an explicit language across generations of recognising help received during parenthood, and of the middle 'pivot' generation both wanting to repay parents in their old age and feeling impelled to offer help to their own children and grandchildren.

In addition to the range and scale of support provided by the close-knit kinship network, family relations emerge as paramount, dominating other kinds of relations and heavily gendered or, as Gordon put it, 'we keep to our own'. Reciprocities were strictly gendered. The women in the different generations relied on each other for sociality as well as for care, with a key role played by Janice in the pivot generation who provided both eldercare and childcare. All the men thought that the women were 'best' at caring for children, with Sean, the youngest adult generation, appealing to an essentialist rationale for his normative preference for mothers being the main carers – an important aspect of the solidaristic pattern: 'I mean nature gives it that . . . they are different.'

The parallel reciprocities which took place between the men involved transfers of material resources – employment, services and housing. The family business provided work for its male members and generated good returns. All three men had spent or were currently spending long hours at work, including weekends. The Brand men clearly demonstrate how continuities in men's occupations and continuities of 'place' play out through the family firm: providing not only employment but also housing and house maintenance to family members, so that the boundaries between work and family life were very permeable.

Yet despite strong pressures towards continuity within the Brand family, forces for innovation were also at work: solidaristic relations were accompanied by some ambivalence. Ambivalence emerged at the structural level: the father, Sean, had broken the educational mould by gaining qualifications. This was symptomatic of another type of ambivalence, a difference in values across the generations. Sean felt he had been 'held back' by his father from achieving more educationally, expressing ambivalent feelings about being prevented from taking the Eleven Plus and not going to grammar school. From the vantage point of the current period and his own status as a father, he saw qualifications as being crucial to 'getting on' in life.

Janet, his wife, also wanted more for her children than she felt she might have received as a child. Like her husband, she wanted their children to get on well at school and to escape from the rather narrow upbringing provided by her own (working-class) parents. For herself, she also harboured educational aspirations, 'something to fall back on when the children are older... I'd like to look back and say I've achieved this'. Jane, too, was torn between identification with the values of her own working-class family and those of her husband's more entrepreneurial family, seeking at one level to emulate the risk-taking spirit of the latter, while feeling rooted in the security and protection of her own family of origin.

These tensions were currently contained since Jane intended giving up work with her second child, while still hoping at a later date to pursue further education. For the time being the desire to 'keep close' to both families geographically, emotionally and socially – both in terms of sociability and the provision of support – was overriding. Any ambivalence relating to values, for instance, did not prevent her from choosing her own parents to look after her son while she continued to work part time following his birth.

There is evidence, too, of a similar ambivalence expressed by Janice. Contrasting the help which she gave her own children with that provided by her own mother, Gwen, Janice reflected upon the significance of her own employment. Having developed a career in employment, she felt that she could offer her own children something more by way of example, as described in Chapter 6 (p. 165): 'freedom, encouragement and confidence. I can give [daughter] more than my mother gave me.' However, Janice was careful not to draw too much attention to the generational disjuncture.

The remarks both of Janice and her son Sean and her daughter-in-law Janet show how, even though the family is highly solidaristic in its relations and the provision of support, each generation seeks to put its own stamp upon the resources which are passed on to them (Bertaux and Bertaux-Wiame, 1997). Janice's employment provided resources that contributed to her children's human and social capital, an aim that her daughter-in-law also harbours in a different way for her own children.

Quadrant 2: processes of incorporation

In the second quadrant, with two cases, the generations stayed geographically close but there was discontinuity in the men's occupational statuses. In the family which is first discussed here – the *Hillyards* – the father in the youngest generation was in low skilled work while the older generations of men were skilled workers; the great-grandfather (who was too ill to be interviewed) had been a self-employed nurseryman and his son, the grandfather, was a draughtsman, with both of them having run their own businesses at some point. However this structural fact made little impact on intergenerational relations within the family. The downwardly mobile male member (a son-in-law) was readily incorporated, the fact that he was a labourer considered unimportant by the family. Indeed, all the other family members interviewed commented emphatically and spontaneously upon the father's propensity for 'hard work'. This pattern we have termed the 'incorporation of difference'.

In many respects the two families in this quadrant resemble the families in the solidaristic quadrant. The family generations provided considerable support to one another, helping with money, housing, employment and so on, and were in addition emotionally close and saw a lot of one another socially (being geographically so close). The pivot generation grandmother in the Hillyard family, Thelma, provided help to both older and younger generations: her parents, parents-in-law and her nephews and nieces. Compared with the Brand family, however, their family practices were *less gendered*, with the women having an equally strong commitment to work as to family commitments. Thelma, for example, worked full time and had recently got a better job which had raised her awareness of missed employment possibilities: 'now that I have, you know, got a different job, I think I perhaps should've looked for something sooner and perhaps tried to have, you know, progress my career a bit more, and not just have been happy to just sit in the same old job all those years.' In her case, care commitments had not so far overtaken her strong commitment to paid work.

There was little expressed ambivalence in the Hillyard family. One reason for this might be that the youngest generation was about to enter parenthood (the baby's birth was imminent). Depending upon whether the mother in this family decided to stay in work after the birth, ambivalences may emerge between the father's strong commitment to paid work and the mother's to both care and paid work. Such tensions may play out *intra*-generationally, that is between the couple members, rather than inter-generationally. (The grandmother in this family had given up work when she became a mother. When she later resumed employment she worked very hard at both work and care, with some cost to herself.)

In the other family in this quadrant, the *Ashtons*, ambivalences emerged at the level of expressed values – between those of the great-grandparents and those of the two younger generations. Value differences reflected the structural difference in the men's occupational statuses. Bill, the great-grandfather, had been a highly skilled worker in the aviation industry, which he entered after wartime service and training in the RAF. He expressed considerable disappointment in his interview with his son's lack of application at school and his failure to learn a skilled trade in the way he had done. Joseph, the son, had given up an apprenticeship and taken a variety of semi- and unskilled manual jobs, while his own son Luke had followed his father's most recent line of work in window fitting.

An innovative pattern seems to be emerging in the youngest generation of the Ashton family which relates to changing *gender roles*. (This may also happen later in the Hillyard family when parenthood arrives for the youngest adult generation.) Earning low pay in less skilled jobs, Luke and Claire Ashton were sharing the breadwinning (both working full time) and the parenting of their young children. Indeed, Luke had changed his job and his hours to enable him to participate more fully in parenthood. The older family generations had readily accepted this new practice, which was supported by full-time childcare provided by Claire's sister, a non-employed lone parent.

Quadrant 3: processes of differentiation

The third quadrant contains five families, in which there had been significant upward mobility among the men: from skilled manual or clerical work to professional or managerial occupational status. This shift occurred in all but one case in the grandparent generation, grandfathers taking advantage of increased educational opportunities available after the War. The main occupations held by the wives also represented upward occupational mobility compared with their own mothers.

Moreover, the rise in occupational status of the grandfather generation was *followed* in three cases by a rise in their wives' occupational status, which occurred after having children. In these families, at least one of the households had moved away – in three families far from kin. In one case, the Samuels featured in Chapter 6, the move away was born out of a clear desire to be distant, reflecting differences in values but also a rejection of family 'closeness' and obligations.

This pattern is termed *differentiation* since, despite providing little everyday, functional support across the generations, family ties were maintained and were often affectively close. Intergenerational relations were more specialised compared with those in the solidaristic quadrant, with little care and service support provided (though this might increase in the future if elderly parents were to become frail), fewer opportunities for regular socialising and in some families clear differences in values and lifestyles. As support was more specialised and provided on a less regular basis, there appeared to be less of a concern for balancing reciprocity (for further examples and discussion of this, see Brannen *et al.*, 2003). More significantly, there was less of a commitment to gender norms in this quadrant, that is, that *women* should be the ones to provide care for grandchildren and for elderly parents. Instead a strong commitment was expressed in favour of *formal* sources of support including help from the state.

We illustrate this group of families by examining in some detail the *Hurds*. The members of the family who were interviewed were distributed fairly widely across southeast England: the maternal great-grandmother, Doreen, lived in East Anglia, her daughter Celia in the southern outskirts of London, and her daughter Rachel on the south coast. The wider family is even more far flung. The family of origin of Celia's husband, Michael, was in the northwest where he had lived as a child and then later with his wife and young children, before, aged 33, he found a job in London and the couple moved permanently to the southeast.

The story of this family of 'movers' is one of significant upward occupational mobility in the middle generation, facilitated as in other cases by the arrival of greater educational opportunity in the post-war period notably for the bright children of the working classes. Michael Hurd was born in a rural part of the northwest in 1937, the youngest of six children. His father trained as a fitter/turner and then set up a business in outdoor catering that he combined with running a sweet shop. He returned to his skilled trade during the Second World War, working in the local munitions factory, while wartime food rationing 'crippled' the sweet shop which eventually closed down. Michael's father became ill with heart trouble, leaving his family to eke out a precarious existence from disability benefit, taking in lodgers and growing tomatoes. Michael describes himself as a 'lonely' child and his health as 'a bit delicate', having had TB at the age of 9.

Despite absences from school, Michael took advantage of expanded post-war education. He passed the Eleven Plus, went to grammar school and from there in 1958, following a period of National Service, entered Oxbridge to study engineering. He enjoyed university where he indulged his love of jazz and met his wife-to-be, Celia, who came from the same university town and had trained as a nurse in one of its local hospitals. Coming from a similar poor working-class background, nursing represented significant intergenerational upward mobility in her own family. After graduation, Michael and Celia married, moved north and lived with Michael's recently widowed mother, another example of a working-class parent providing housing for a newly married child. Michael found work in a local chemical firm.

Having saved for a deposit on a house while living with Michael's mother, when he found a better job they moved and bought their first house. Still within the northwest, this was nevertheless, as Michael observed, 'a big move geographically'. In her account, Celia said that they waited to have children until they had moved out of her mother-in-law's home. After five years and with two young children and a wife to support, since Celia wished to be a full-time mother, Michael decided to move again because 'the job had got too repetitive'. This time they made 'the big move' south to London.

In the early 1970s, Michael was made redundant which came as an enormous shock to him: 'The idea that a job might ever come to an end in those days just didn't exist...I think it must have been old Harold Wilson who said...It's all right talking of the 6 per cent unemployed. But if you're one of the 6 per cent, then for you it's a 100 per cent.' The couple pooled their resources and Celia returned to nursing after a break of 10 years, though only for as long as Michael was unemployed. After 3 months and feeling greatly relieved, Michael found a new job with a public-owned utility, though the fear of unemployment haunted him. He described taking care ever after to have a fund of savings 'on fairly easy call' to cover such eventualities in the future. He stayed with the same employer for the rest of his career until the age of 58 when he was given early retirement at the time the company was privatised.

The couple had three daughters and the youngest, Rachel, the parent generation, married Graeme whose employment career consisted largely of unskilled work, his last main job being a hospital porter. After their first child was born, Graeme continued to work. But when Rachel decided to train as a teacher, Graeme gave up his job to look after the baby while they lived on social security and some help from parents on both sides of the family. After qualifying, Rachel assumed the main breadwinner role, thereby reversing the gendered pattern of work and care in her family of origin. With two children at the time of interview, Rachel was on maternity leave from her full-time job as a teacher while Graeme had been taking primary responsibility for childcare, which he combined with studying for a university degree.

Graeme had no difficulty in acknowledging Rachel as the sole bread-winner: 'I regarded my role as a father as more than what my father was, you know, the breadwinner.' Unlike his father-in-law Michael, he was unworried by the prospect of unemployment which he had experienced a number of times; he described being well used to signing on and to working for 'cash in hand' from work done 'on the side'. Again unlike his father-in-law, Graeme was not ambitious: 'I am not going to climb the greasy pole ... I'm going to get out of the rat race, and I'm going to do what I want to do.' While welcoming a second chance to study, Graeme did not expect to have a 'career' as such but thought he would change jobs every four years or so. Nor did he expect to work full time; his preference ideally would be for himself and Rachel to work part time, mainly though not entirely because of the children.

With Rachel as the main breadwinner, the socio-economic status of the household was determined more by her occupational status than by her partner's. In that sense the family was not downwardly mobile since downward mobility in the male line was counterbalanced by a reversal of gender roles in the current parent generation. Moreover, it is clear that Rachel saw herself as reacting against her own background. While she was growing up, her mother, Celia, was a full-time housewife and her father, Michael, was the sole breadwinner. Rachel described making a conscious decision not to be like her mother and is critical of what she sees as her mother's over-protection: 'I was very independent. I didn't really need somebody to be there to make me a drink ... when I got home [from school] when I was 14, but she seemed to think it was really necessary.'

Graeme also expressed regret about his own childhood, which he described as being spent in the shadow of his parents' disintegrating marriage and divorce. But, unlike Rachel, he talked about his mother not 'being there' because she worked nights. As a father, he wanted to 'be there' for his children in the way that his own parents were not and, as we have seen, wanted to avoid the 'rat race'. In both accounts there was a clear sense of both parents striving to create lives which are different from their own parents', but leading in very different directions: Rachel, the mother, to a strong work orientation, Graeme, the father, to a strong caring orientation. The complex interplay of gender and generation, employment and care is striking.

In this family, there are several forces for change: occupational status, geographical mobility and a departure from a gendered household employment pattern in the youngest generation. The 'differentiation', which we would argue characterises this family, originates in the middle generation, when Michael, having been through university and married a woman from the south, moved away from his northern kin to find better job opportunities.

His upward mobility from working-class roots into the professional middle class constitutes a major shift occupationally. It may, in addition, constitute a movement away from a close-knit solidaristic pattern of working-class life which, for survival purposes, means that kin must 'cleave to their own'. This, however, is less certain: Michael's family may never have fitted this pattern since, as he observes, his mother was a strong Methodist who involved Michael in the chapel. [There is some suggestion that Methodists in the northeast of England were more upwardly mobile than non-Methodists and it certainly seems to have opened up people's horizons (Moore, 1974).]

In Michael's interview, differentiation and its consequence of limited support, was suggested in his reference to the importance of 'self reliance'. Michael himself noted that the poverty in his own background had enabled him to develop 'a bit of an ethos of being self sufficient . . . that's stayed with me'. Moreover, he went on to suggest that this could have worked differently: 'I didn't feel forced to wear hand me downs that has been across the Hog's back three times. So I am damned if my kids are going to have to put up with that!' This theme resonated with his own Methodist upbringing which aimed, in his words, to make him a 'morally upright person'.

Moreover, this affirmation of the ethic of self-reliance was not a rejection of kin relationships, but rather foregrounded his commitment to coupledom – or, as Michael prefers to put it, 'We were a team' – and his support for and from formal institutions, both state and church. For Michael grew up in the protective embrace of the welfare state. Public provision played a very significant part in his life. There was the influence of his grammar school, which he had recently revisited, in particular the influence of the 'new headmaster' with 'new ideas' who had studied at Oxbridge and encouraged Michael to do the same. According to his daughter, Michael was a strong advocate of state education, unsurprising given his educational history. The public sector provided employment to Michael, as well as to his wife, two of his daughters and at least one of his sons-in-law. Looking to his own old age, Michael said he would look to 'professional help', rather than to family. Other sources of support mentioned by Michael also fell outside the family: the church in his youth, neighbours and 'medical help' such as the GP when bringing up children, his daughters' participation in the Brownies and the Guides.

The key part played by family in Michael's life is *not* in providing support (though he acknowledges that his parents sacrificed a great deal when he went to university), but in providing him with sufficient space to live his own life – that is, in *not* acting as a constraint. His gratitude to his parents is reserved for the 'freedom...they gave me just to do it...There was no pressure to follow a particular career, to go to a particular school, to go out with a particular girl, to read particular books'. (We can contrast this with the Brands where high levels of support combine with low educational expectations for the younger adult generations in the family.) This freedom granted to Michael may well have to do with the fact that he was the youngest in a large family. However, it gave him a similar sense of freedom not to direct his own children's lives, a view also strongly held by his wife. As he said, he had no desire 'to compensate for my own shortcomings and live my childhood again through my own children'. He wanted his children to lead their own lives: 'We encouraged [our own children] to make up their own minds and decide for themselves...By all means discuss it with parents but really it had to be their decision.'

Moreover, these strategies of divergence were accompanied by a good deal of reflection. Observing his daughter's marriage, Michael said, had led him to review his own assumptions about gender roles. He was supportive of Rachel's 'alternative way' of combining motherhood and employment and noted that 'one of the joys of my life' had been the way in which his daughters 'opened his eyes' – albeit that Celia seemed content to go on 'indulging' him by continuing to do all the housework! Once again we see the capacity of members of a particular generation to move beyond normative beliefs held about parenthood, to make ethical judgements about their adult children's practices. We have seen how such judgements are made in historical contexts and observed the actual results of these practices (see also Chapter 4).

In their relationship to their daughter and her new family, both Michael and Celia adopted a strategy of non-interference although they provided them with some financial support and continued to offer their services. They made a point of not visiting them at weekends and, when their daughter got in from work, they tried not 'to overlap too much': 'we shouldn't impose ourselves on them... It's their life, not ours'. Rachel's account supported this. She noted that she found out only recently that her parents disapproved of the fact that she and Graeme lived together before marriage; she said they would never be openly disapproving since they believed 'in freedom of choice'.

Nonetheless the ambivalences of intergenerational relations emerge, again, in the responses of the younger generation to the older generation's strategy of keeping their distance. Rachel was somewhat perplexed at what she saw as a slight 'standoffishness' in her parents. On the other hand, Rachel shared similar concerns about being independent agreeing that: 'in many ways [standoffishness is] a good thing because... I couldn't bear to have the kind of parents who... stuck their oar in.'

Quadrant 4: reparation under conditions of estrangement

The sole case in the fourth quadrant, the *Prentice* family, also represents change as well as continuity in intergenerational relations (Chapter 5). The occupational statuses of both men and women in this family were almost all unskilled. Remarkably, in this family, the grandparent and parent generations together made the break from inner-city London to the countryside a hundred miles away. Paul Prentice (grandfather) uprooted his wife and five children – including four teenage boys – in order, he said, to escape the influences of the inner city which he considered endangered his children. Paul and his wife Fiona kept the family together despite many housing and job difficulties including one return to London. Eventually they settled, with some surprisingly positive consequences. Yet the move away made little difference to them economically. They simply exchanged urban poverty for rural poverty, and were no longer able to draw upon help from family. In many respects until the move away, intergenerational relations in this family closely resembled those of a working-class family in the solidaristic quadrant, notably in the provision of accommodation (Paul and his family lived with Fiona's father for a while).

On the other hand, it is clear that family ties across the generations in this family had long been marked by strong feelings of ambivalence. In particular the women expressed considerable resentment about the lack of emotional support and childcare provided by their mothers at critical moments in the life course, especially when they had their children. It is significant that many of these tensions were expressed by the women in the family who were grandmothers and who were also mothers and daughters. In close-knit, working-class families, grandmothers have traditionally been the main source of intergenerational support often knitting families together (Chapter 2). This was very clear, as we have seen, among the other working-class families in this study. Strong grandmothers appeared to be able to counteract any lack of support from, or failure to provide by, the men in these families.

Through the move away from London, the youngest generation in the Prentice family – the young father, Andrew, and his wife, Sheila – were self-consciously remaking their lives. This transformation was not however economic, it had more to do with a change in practices, values and gender identities, in particular a commitment to care on the part of the youngest male generation (see Chapter 5 for a fuller discussion of Andrew and the men in this family). At a number of levels and in a number of domains, Andrew and Sheila were engaged in a process of reparation, hence our use of this term to describe this pattern of inter-generational relations: *reparation under conditions of estrangement*. The couple sought to break the cycle of transmission of negativity between the generations, which was particularly evident in the interviews of the two older female generations and especially in relation to childhood and the transition to motherhood. By contrast, Andrew and Sheila appeared to be making a conscious attempt to break with the patterns of their parents and grandparents, while at the same time remaining close in several senses to the grandparent generation who lived nearby in the countryside.

Andrew graphically described how his childhood and adolescence were affected when his parents had to keep moving on in search of new (short life) accommodation for their large family. Both he and Sheila wanted to create stability in their own children's lives by staying put; they had also developed a strong commitment to the countryside as a 'better place' to bring up children. In contrast to the parenting practices of their parents and grandparents, the young couple was committed to gender equality by sharing the bringing up of their two young children. Neither entered employment until the children were at school; instead they drew upon the resources of the state to support them. At an intra-psychic level, Andrew went through a process of coming to terms with the disruptions and disruptive relationships of his childhood and youth. He spoke of a journey of reflection which led to understanding himself and others: 'My own life, how I perceived that and, from look-ing at that, trying to see how I should bring up my own children. Watching other people and seeing how they do it.' However, he was silent in his interview about the enabling structural aspects which had supported him in being a hands-on father – namely the provision of state support (social security).

Conclusion

This analysis of intergenerational relations is schematic. The patterns we have identified of solidarity, incorporation, differentiation and reparation are only several among many possible patterns. Moreover a typology is of its nature static. To understand intergenerational family relations fully, it is crucial to take account of life course and historical time as we suggest in Chapters 1, 6 and 8. The typology refers only to broad processes of resource transmission and support which have taken place over time but which were elicited at a single point in time (at interview). While male occupational status and geographical household mobility do shape these patterns, it is also clear that transfers and reciprocation of resources which take place within families have their own dynamic.

In this analysis, two types of intergenerational relations stand out: the traditional solidaristic and the differentiated. These represent, in Durkheim's terms, two types of solidarity – mechanical and organic. In the case of the solidaristic (representing mechanical solidarity), there is less specialisation in the family's division of labour; these families provide and exchange a wide variety of resources intergenerationally. In the case of the differentiated, there is greater specialisation in the division of labour; the families transmit certain kinds of resources and support intergenerationally but have greater recourse to other, often *formal* sources of support. These patterns are generated by, but also serve to reproduce, occupational (dis)continuity and geographical (im)mobility.

The other two types of intergenerational relations represent cases in transit; they may lie on a continuum between the solidaristic and the differentiated. In the case of 'reparation in estrangement', the youngest (parent) generational unit seemed to be moving away from a pattern of traditional solidarity towards a process of differentiation – the repair and reconstruction of a different type of family (at the household level). Yet the current father in the Prentice family was silent about the means which enabled this to happen, namely their reliance upon the state to support sharing parenting. Indeed he seemed to be still remarkably committed to the idea of family support. The pattern of family incorporation in the other quadrant suggests that the Hillyard family is resisting forces of differentiation, notably the changes occurring in men's work – as indicated in the Hillyard father's lower status job and in the grandmother's determination to work equally hard at both paid work and informal care. The incorporation model, as exemplified in the Hillyard family, is currently closer to the solidaristic type of intergenerational relations than to the differentiated ideal type.

A key aspect of intergenerational resource transfers concerns gender. As the case analysis has indicated, in some families the transfer of resources is strongly gendered: women are the key providers and reciprocators of care, while men transfer other types of resources relating for example to self-maintenance and paid work. The 'solidaristic' families were characterised by such a strongly gendered division of labour, with the women members specialising in the provision of care and prioritising family obligations over their own employment. Mother–adult daughter relations were critical in reciprocating resources. The pattern was less gendered in the two 'incorporation of difference' families considered, namely in the youngest generation where the men and the women were sharing, or were about to share, care and employment.

In the 'differentiated' families, there was greater reliance upon and commitment to formal sources of support (and other kinds of social relations), namely those provided by the state, professionals and the community. Formal support frees women from having to take on so many caring responsibilities. Moreover, the youngest 'cross-class' generation in the family discussed in this quadrant (the Hurds) was reversing the conventional couple employment and care pattern, though with much less support provided by the family. Finally, in the 'reparation in estrangement' family, the force for renewal is vested in both men and women in the youngest generation, while the support for their non-gendered pattern of full-time care was state benefit. In contrast to the families with a differentiated pattern, they make no reference to this, Andrew especially emphasising his own agency and the impetus to come to terms with his past disrupted childhood.

Gendered patterns of work and care are breaking down *intra*-generationally among some couples in the youngest generation where, at least for a period of time, breadwinning and parenting are shared or where fathers become full-time parents and mothers breadwinners. It is notable that all of these cases occurred among the low skilled or in one case a cross-class family. It is hard to speculate what effects this may have upon intergenerational relations in the longer term. It is possible that a weaker mother–daughter tie, as is the case in some families in the differentiated and reparation in estrangement quadrants, may be an integral part of the process of intergenerational change and innovation. Thus while occupational and geographical mobility may be critical discriminants of intergenerational relations, the nature of relations between mothers and daughters may be also critical. Since the study did not set out to select family members from same sex lineages, it has not been possible to test this hypothesis.

In this chapter we have not unpacked the meanings underpinning intergenerational transfers; this is the focus of Chapter 6. Suffice it to note here that whatever the overall pattern of intergenerational transmission, families and family members may however view their relations as being characterised by solidarity, for example mutual trust, sense of belonging, and the transmission of at least some resources (Crow, 2002). Moreover, we should not assume that a sociological analysis necessarily matches the interpretations of those we study. This is why the study of different types of ambivalences is so important, showing as they do the limits upon resources people have available to them and the tensions people must contend with in living their lives.

In this book we have suggested that tensions arise and persist in families which manifest themselves in diverse ways through the materiality of life, through their unconscious dispositions and practices, through their ethical judgements, feelings, values and interpersonal relations. Such ambivalences exist even in families where the predominant pattern involves pulling together, indeed perhaps precisely because of such centripetal forces, as each generation and family member strikes out on its own. How far families as intergenerational relations manage those tensions is always a changing story.

8
Concluding Reflections

This book has examined employment and care in families with four surviving generations. Its lens has been generational relations: the transmission of these and other resources between family generations and generational cohorts. It has been about what it means to be a mother or a father in the workforce in different periods of the 20th century when very different mores governing gender roles and childrearing. It is also about care as it is provided and experienced in multi-generation families: being a child of one's parents, being a parent, a grandparent and a great-grandparent. Care is however only one resource among many which are transmitted intergenerationally and cannot be divorced from material resources and from social and cultural capital. Writing this book has therefore been a challenge because it encompasses so much of human life.

In our reflections in this final chapter we return to four central issues which cross cut the book. The first is the issue of change versus continuity and the nature of the changes which have taken place. The second is about the focus upon intergenerational relations. The third concerns the negotiation of change by family members. While the fourth concerns the way we study intergenerational relations and transmission and in particular the ways in which time is implicated. Our theoretical approach in thinking about these issues rests on the assumption that social action is the result of the interplay between structural forces and the agency exercised by individual family members in both time and space.

Change or continuity across the generations

Comparing our three generations as historical generations born in three distinctive periods, we may see an immense amount of change. For example, over the 20th century, the role of the state has expanded hugely and taken over many functions of families. Access to education and health has improved immensely, increasing opportunities and altering life courses. The growth of state education and health services have had an important impact on employment, providing growing job opportunities, many taken by women. Cash benefits – pensions, child benefits, unemployment and sickness pay – have been introduced and increased, reducing some of the financial demands on families and, in two cases of current parents, supporting radical changes in household gender relations. In particular areas, though, the British welfare state has been far less significant: in contrast to some other Northern European countries, in particular Nordic ones, British working parents, especially mothers, have been left with little option but to seek private solutions including part-time working hours and childcare from family members. In the 1980s and 1990s moreover government sought to reduce the role of the state and to make individuals and families bear a greater burden of risk.

Many of the changes observed in this book exemplify trends discernible in larger-scale studies and national statistics. However, what our study illustrates is that, when studied in finer detail, generational change is not linear, smooth or uniform. A trend is not the same as a transformation and it affects different groups to a lesser or greater extent. Moreover, continuities are often as striking as the discontinuities.

We saw in Chapter 2 that childhood is an experience where dramatic change has taken place. However, in some families the importance of grandmothers in holding families together is a persistent feature of children's childhood. Patterns in life course transitions also offer an uneven picture of change. As educational opportunities opened up for both women and men over the 20th century leading to a postponement of adulthood and parenthood, so many of the generation born in the 1960s/70s enjoyed an extended period in training and education; some saw this as a time to shape their own biographies, trying out a whole range of life modes (Brannen *et al.*, 2002). However, to assume that such a reordering of life course transitions – later entry into work and later parenthood – mirrors in a linear way trends in educational opportunity, fertility and family size is misleading. For the life course scheduling of transitions around parenthood was rather different among the middle generation born around the Second World War (Chapter 5). For this generation, marriage, entry into work and parenthood tended to coincide or occurred within a very few years – a pattern which stands in contrast to that which occurred among the younger and older generations either side of them, whose social transitions were staggered over a longer time period.

This lack of linear change in part reflects the *non-linear* pattern of labour market conditions which spanned our three generations – stability and high employment in the post-war period, enabling fathers to become parents without risk of unemployment, compared with greater uncertainty which obtained in the earlier interwar period and later in the 1980s and 1990s (Chapter 5). The scheduling of marriage in the life course also changed rather abruptly but only among the youngest generation – usually occurring after the birth of children if it happened at all.

The employment career of mothers is a story of both change and continuity. While motherhood, and the primary responsibility for childcare that went with it, defined women's lives in all three generations, there was still a good deal of employment, including the great-grandmother generation. It is true that, over the generations, women's employment careers were increasingly less fragmented, less marked by interruptions, and their work more skilled and more visible; but it is also the case that all three generations of mothers adopted a similar strategy of working part time. However, the conditions under which they engaged in paid employment were very different especially in the current parent generation. Many women in this generation had built up careers prior to motherhood, and most (though not all) were entitled to take maternity leave and to return to work after childbirth. Moreover the pressures to engage in paid work shifted abruptly in the 1990s for the youngest generation as government actively encouraged mothers' employment.

Fatherhood continues to be largely a story of continuity, with men as main breadwinners even if fewer are now sole breadwinners. However, as Mannheim suggested, generations are formed not only through collective exposure to the same historical events and experiences but also through sharing particular social locations (Mannheim, 1952), notably in respect of gender, social class and community. Some of the 1960/70s generation, notably the sons of low skilled workers who were main or sole breadwinners, used the decline in low skilled work as an opportunity to become more actively involved in the care of their children, and to enact new types of fatherhood identities.

Intergenerational relations in families

We have shown that multi-generation families, having a similar number of generations in common, are not all the same in terms of the resources they offer different generations. Patterns of intergenerational relations were shaped by occupational and geographical mobility. Some multi-generational families, being occupationally immobile and staying in the same geographical area, engaged in solidaristic relations: in their provision of support up and down the generations over time and, in reproducing the same kinds of family habitus, they showed the persistence of a culture of family mutuality. The Brand family in Chapter 7 was an example of a family in which successive generations of women provided care which was complemented by much material help from men in the family and the transmission of wealth and work through the family business.

On the other hand, patterns of generational relations and the cultures of transmission which go with these could be specific to a particular historical generation, which created a new type of habitus. A culture of 'getting on' and 'independence from family' typified some members of the grandparent generation, both men and women, who engaged in the differentiated type of intergenerational relations. They enjoyed improved life chances, having taken advantage of increased educational opportunities to advance in life in the post-war period, and they drew support from professionals, community organisations and the growing welfare state (e.g. university grants).

A rather different emphasis was evident in some members of the current generation of parents born in the 1960s/70s who grew up in a less economically stable period and a shift from the social to the advanced liberal state. Inscribed with the values of this new regime, they demonstrated a culture of autonomy and identity creation, expressed in the importance they attached to the exercise of personal responsibility for creating support, identity and lifestyle. Such 'independence' is premised upon individually negotiated solutions which may however prove highly precarious. However, as discussed below, it should be remembered that this generation was still mainly the receivers rather than providers of intergenerational support (e.g. from parents), which creates a tension in their stress on independence. Thus, unsurprisingly, they were often silent about the support they received, whether from the state or family, that is, about the structural context that facilitates and constrains their agency (see also Brannen and Nilsen, 2003b).

Before leaving the topic of change, there are some further points we wish to make about intergenerational relations.

The first is the importance of one particular generation as providers of resources. Much attention is currently being given to the burdens being placed upon the 'pivot generation' sandwiched between younger and older generation in a family who have needs which the 'pivot generation' itself currently lacks, for example in respect of settling down and frail old age. The jury is however still out as to whether mid-life family members are necessarily caught between the competing needs of the young and the old (Hillcoate-Nalletamby and Dharmalingam, 2001). However this middle generation has benefited from a particular historical location. While there is no other pivot generation with whom to compare them, this generation does occupy a rather privileged position: as sons and daughters of Hobsbawm's post-war 'golden age' they may warrant the description – a 'generation of abundance' (Attias-Donfut, 1995). Benefits available (to some more than others) include: better educational opportunities after the war; a growing public sector providing new sources of employment; rising living standards; better health and, later on, the growth of home ownership and rising house prices; changing gender roles and occupational pensions (see for example Bynner *et al.*, 2003; Wadsworth *et al.*, 2003). This adds up to a generation many of whose members were 'resource rich', providing help to both younger and older generations. Well placed materially, middle-class grandparents in particular were able to help younger generations. While with many women retired at a relatively early age or working part time, they can also provide care and other non-material resources.

The second issue is the gendering of intergenerational relations. Certainly solidaristic families in which the transmission of several resources took place seemed to be marked by gendered patterns, as when women gave care and men provided other kinds of services. However, it is important to stress that our study excluded multi-generation families where women predominated, although we saw hints of this in Chapter 2. Grandmothers were reported to be key figures who kept families together when men died or left the household. In some families, for example families marked by migration, mothers and grandmothers passed on personal resources to children giving them a sense of who they are (see also Delcroix, 2000).

A third issue, which both shapes intergenerational transmission and is shaped by it, concerns ambivalence or tensions which emerge between different family generations. They manifest themselves in different ways. Ambivalences occur as a result of strategic action, as when families decide to stay close together or move away. They may be interactional as when family relations are emotionally close or conflictual. Ambivalences emerge as a new generation adopts dispositions and habits which make them different from the older generation. Moreover, the transmission of one resource, for example educational aspirations, may lead to a disjuncture in the next generation as it develops different values. But people do not necessarily see their new values, dispositions and habits as being at odds with the old. An example of a change in norms concerned the (great)grandmothers who believed in mothers being at home (in accordance with their own memories of childhood and motherhood) but who negotiated different views with respect to the practices of their own (grand)daughters.

As illustrated, ambivalences occur even in solidaristic families, where the predominant pattern involves pulling together. In all families, succeeding generations will seek to some degree to strike out on their own and endeavour to make a mark upon resources passed on to them. How families consisting of intergenerational relations manage those tensions is of course a story which changes over time.

Ambivalences emerge depending upon whether we take the view of those transmitting resources or those in receipt of them. The very elderly emphasised their own personal independence often in the face of receiving much support. Members of the current parent generation underplayed their receipt of resources transmitted from older generations: in accordance with their project to 'be(come) themselves' they dwelt instead upon their own efforts.

This study focused upon a broad range of resources. It did not cover the transfer of inherited wealth, only material transfers which were *inter vivos*. Such transfers were made mainly on the basis of need in contrast to assets passed on at death which tend to follow the parity principle (Delcroix, 2000; Finch *et al.*, 1996).

This latter is an area of growing significance as people acquire larger assets in the context of home ownership and rising house prices. Where families transmit large amounts of material resources this seems likely to increase economic inequality and social exclusion, while lesser transfers of material resources may foster social cohesion – that is, they may help cement generational relations (Kohli, 1999). In the context of further welfare retrenchment in Britain, intergenerational transfers are likely to become more significant. This is already reflected in government policy through the Child Trust Fund, which is designed to encourage transmission and the saving habit among poor families through the state making a financial contribution to children's savings (H M Treasury, 2000a,b, 2001).

Negotiations in multi-generation families

As we have suggested, attitudes are changing among all three generations. Employment is seen as acceptable for today's mothers in the context of their increased educational qualifications, the advent of careers for women and the increased costs of parenthood. But general normative attitudes have to be negotiated in relation to real situations and their own biographies.

For many women in older generations, the importance of mothers 'being there' for children was interpreted in their own biographies as requiring women to find employment that 'fitted' around the family, meaning short hours and/or working only at certain times (e.g. evenings or school terms). This is still what many of today's mothers do, even if for shorter periods of the life course. But others renegotiate 'being there' as meaning 'quality time' with children, shifting the emphasis from quantity of physical presence to the process of active engagement with their children. Both courses of action may leave mothers feeling ambivalent: both those who limit their work or give up in the context of what may appear in retrospect as missed employment opportunities; or those who continue in paid work but consider that their mothering has not been up to standard.

All generations of women reconcile their own experiences of being mothered and their views and practices when they were mothers of young children with current mothering practices. In spite of their beliefs situated in their own experiences, grandmothers and great-grandmothers arrived at ethical judgements about the best course of action for their daughters to take. They recognised their daughters' need to work in contemporary conditions (especially for those who were well educated) and offered them considerable support (emotional if not practical).

Older generations of men might also negotiate normative beliefs. They too might have to question their own beliefs about fatherhood and fatherhood practices, in the light of the provocation provided by current generations of fathers assuming a more hands-on approach. Thus grandfatherhood emerges in some families as a vantage point for reflecting on and rethinking gender and care and, in one case, a redemptive opportunity to become more involved in care.

A disjuncture continues between the shifts occurring in mothers' employment careers and beliefs about what children 'need'. The importance of mothers 'being there' for children and suspicion of 'stranger care' run like threads across the generations, among women as well as men. For example, while the current father generation was more likely than their fathers and grandfathers to subscribe to the principle of gender equity in the labour market, some retained a gendered view about children's needs being best met by women. Through paying attention to the way some current fathers express their rationalities, we may see how they distance themselves from decisions about household employment – putting the choice on to mothers. In this way they can avoid at a manifest level contravening the general principles of gender equity which they adhere to. On the other hand, there were fathers in our study who were as participative as mothers in their children's care, namely those with limited labour market skills. There may be a time lag in attitudes coming into line with behaviour. It is possible, though, that the process of alignment is facilitated by social policies to support working parents which have until recently been absent in Britain but which have developed over the last 30 years or so in Nordic countries. In Denmark and Sweden, for example, where state policies have been particularly strong, including an entitlement to publicly supported childcare services for children from 12 months of age onwards, it is reported that most parents now regard children's attendance at such services as normative and desirable from the second year of life onwards (Jensen and Hansen, 2002; Lenz Taguchi and Munkammer, 2003). In Sweden, families expect 'a holistic pedagogy of health care, loving care and education throughout the pre-school age' (Lenz Taguchi and Munkammer, 2003, p. 31).

Not only has Britain lacked such policies. It has also lacked a language for talking about new forms of upbringing; a false dualism – 'home or childcare' – has been contested, rather than envisaging the possibility that young children could move between 'home and holistic pedagogy' and find both experiences complementary. In the absence of these conditions, the 1960s/70s generation of British mothers, like their own mothers and grandmothers, has sought to negotiate a relationship between employment and care which they can square with the prevailing beliefs of a still largely maternalist society.

Methodological reflections on intergenerational relations and transmission: attention to time

Generational relations and the transmission of resources across different generations involve different sexes, different households and different family generations who are located in different spaces and social milieux. Intergenerational relations and transfers also take place over time. Of necessity these involve retrospective accounts which are recounted in present time. Moreover the givers and the receivers of resources in these processes will have different perspectives upon the processes and upon that which is being transmitted. Thus time has to be conceptualised and brought more explicitly into our frame of analysis.

All this makes intergenerational relations difficult to research, creating challenges for research design and analysis. Time here has multiple meanings, at least three of which have been of particular importance to our enquiry. Different kinds of accounts are embedded in different time perspectives. First, there is time as in the *present*: the beliefs, practices, desires, demands of present family and work lives and also those which participants bring to bear in the immanent context of the research interview. Second, there is *life course* time: where participants are situated on the life course which, from a sociological perspective, is constituted by a series of career lines relating to a number of different spheres of life including work and care (Elder, 1985). Third, there is *generational* time: the 'generation units' in our study – great-grandparents, grandparents and parents – who represented three age cohorts who have lived through particular historical periods.

Time present

Interviews take place in the present and interview accounts are constructed in present time as interviewees switch between different speech modalities: from reports and narratives about the past to evaluations and argumentation made from present vantage points. The oldest generation in our study, who had experienced nearly a century of social change, recounted meta-narratives of progress in which they told stories of 'real struggle' of moral right over material degradation. It is important to understand that such accounts were given with reference to the current social context notably the achievement of higher standards of living.

Others who in time present found their pasts wanting included some whose childhoods had been marked by divorce or by their mothers working, again drawing upon the criteria of present day standards. A current mother might judge her childhood according to her current values relating to childhood rather than the values which governed her experience in childhood. Women and men in all generations viewed the lack of educational opportunities in the past in the context of increased educational opportunities and aspirations in the present. Conversely some, for example great-grandparents, viewed the past through rose-tinted spectacles. Seeing the 'good old days' as better than today again implies a present perspective (see also Samuel and Thompson, 1990). It is therefore important to be attentive to how the present shapes the telling of the past.

Life course phase

Time is also experienced in relation to the life course phase in which interviewees are currently situated, but also in relation to those asked about in the interview. Which phases people speak from will vary greatly in a study which spans the whole of a life. Two generations – great-grandparents and grandparents – were looking back at their lives from the vantage point of having brought up children and, in many cases, having completed their working lives which gave them access to a greater number of interpretative contexts (Nielsen and Rudberg, 2000). Great-grandparents were particularly distant from earlier life course phases. They were also distant from their great-grandchildren not only because of length of time and depth of lineage but also because the intervening generation, grandparents, assumed greater prominence in great-grandchildren's lives. Accounts of great-grandmotherhood were notably 'thinner' than accounts of grandmotherhood. Grandmothers, by contrast, had much more to say and also spoke both from their current position as the 'pivot generation' – as mothers of adult daughters, whom they witnessed trying to combine parenthood with employment, and as daughters of their (elderly) mothers.

In contrast, the current generation of parents (in their 20s and 30s) was in the midst of parenthood. Their accounts were in part shaped by the fact that they were currently engaged in caring for young children while at the same time being close to childhood. Consequently, they both viewed their own childhood from their relatively new status as parents as well as in terms of the remembered past. Thus it is not surprising that they put the parenting practices of their own parents under the microscope.

The individual's position in the generational hierarchy shapes generational relations. Thus the grandparent generation had relations with both older and younger generations for a considerable portion of their life course, as children and parents respectively, while the relations between the oldest and youngest generations in a four-generation family – were typically less intense and often relatively short lived.

Generational position in part determines who will be givers and receivers and also how they view giving and receiving. Being sandwiched between older and younger generations has placed the middle generation in an intercalary position. In other words, they look to the care needs of both older and younger generations at the same time, although they did not necessarily believe that they should be the main providers of care nor take on significant caring.

Because of the power involved in having and giving resources, for example care, those who give to younger generations may recall their gifts while those in receipt of such gifts may overlook them, as noted above. For receiving involves feelings of indebtedness as in the case of younger generations receiving help from older generations. In seeking to be independent at a life course phase when they must seek to provide for their children (as well as living in an age in which autonomy is much prized and dependency much criticised), they may wish to deny or play down that they need help and not wish to feel indebted.

An analyst of biographical accounts must take note also of the timing of a life course phase *for a given cohort or generation*. Thus we found that the grandparent generation who, on average, had children relatively young became grandparents rather earlier in the life course than the former generation. This had implications for their capacity and willingness to care for grandchildren, the longevity of their relationships with grandchildren, and possibly also for the way they spoke about their relations with grandchildren.

Generational time: pockets of history

In making sense of intergenerational relations and transmission, the past is construed as having some reality (Nielsen, 2003). In Chapter 2, for example, childhood constituted both socio-historical context but also, as Mannheim (1952) suggested, the context for shaping adult identities. Understanding accounts as resources of history is problematic, however, making it difficult to disentangle interviewees' narratives about the past from the way they have been shaped by current discourses, contexts and practices in present time (Nielsen, 2003).

The contextualisation of life stories is a theoretical as well as a methodological issue. Interviewees make very variable reference to the structural contexts and resources available to them (Nilsen and Brannen, 2002). Moreover even there interviewees refer to the structural conditions, as in the case of great-grandmothers describing childhood, the researcher may have to fill in much of what is unsaid: for example, to understand that most women of this generation lived through the economic uncertainty of the inter war years which was also a time when few opportunities existed for women either in education or employment.

But how much the researcher has to fill in will vary. It is significant that great-grandmothers from working-class origins in our study were more attentive to the socio-economic landscape than those from more advantaged backgrounds. Or it may vary by generation, with the parent generation least articulate about the impact of the socio-economic context and instead imputing agency to themselves. In this latter case this may be, as we have suggested, because the current generation is too close in life course terms to the situations they are witnessing. Or it may be because individualism and agency are highly valued in our society with its neoliberal politics, a rapidly changing economic climate and a reconfiguring welfare state. Or, again, it may vary because complex societies are not necessarily transparent to those living in them (Wengraf, 2004). It is perhaps easier to make sense of wider context with the lapse of time once change has occurred.

Moreover, the agency of our interviewees may be overplayed because of the concepts as well as the tools which social scientists apply to the study of the world. Concepts such as individualisation, it is argued, break the classical sociological link between structure and agency as two sides of the same coin and have a particular correspondence with current neoliberal political rhetoric. Individualisation may act as an ideological force which constrains us from making the connections between biography and society (Bauman, 2001; Nilsen and Brannen, 2002).

Looking to the future

What do we see as the implications of our study for the future? If welfare is to be provided from a combination of family, market and state, it is imperative to understand the role of families and their relationship to the other players. The importance of intergenerational relations both as a field of public policy and academic study is increasingly recognised, especially elsewhere in Europe. Further research is required in the UK. National or large-scale surveys are needed to complement work being done elsewhere to map patterns of intergenerational transfers at particular moments in time across different types of families. Qualitative work in particular families which examine intergenerational relations and how these change over time need to complement such large-scale snapshots. Our study excluded many significant groups; those with experiences of divorce and repartnering, and minority ethnic families. Attention should be paid also to the study of female lineages with strong ties between mothers and daughters and weak ties between male members. As we suggested in Chapter 1, there is a strong case for combining research traditions and approaches.

Turning to the future of intergenerational relations themselves, there are three areas of possible future change that we think particularly important. First, the future of fatherhood. We found evidence both of continuity and change. Men in the current parent generation have adopted a gender equality rhetoric in relation to employment. Many fathers are more involved in childcare, with some vivid examples of present day fathers assuming equal or primary responsibility for children. At the same time though, the intensification of employment for some fathers limits their availability: most current fathers in our study were 'work focused' and still only a minority 'hands-on'. But work-focused fathers also sought to develop strong relationships with their children, a rather different emphasis from the way their own fathers talked about fatherhood.

Which way will things go? In our study, the most participant fathers were working class: having few qualifications and little work experience or a history of low skilled employment. In two cases, their involvement was enabled (unwittingly) by the state, through social security payments, contravening the current policy aim of 'welfare to work'. Arguably, sharing parenting may be a more attractive proposition for this group than often unappealing employment opportunities. At the same time, this group is decreasing, as educational qualifications rise and all citizens of working age are encouraged to be in the labour market. Does the future hold out greater polarisation between fathers, or more of the middle way, the work-focused but child-oriented fathers of our typology?

A government committed to gender equality, including the care of children, might explore using public money to support parents reducing or leaving employment while caring for younger children. But, unlike current policies of extended maternity leave that are likely to increase the gendering of childcare, such policies should be aimed at men as much as women. Swedish-style, well-paid parental leave is one option, with the old idea of a 'citizen's salary' another (see for example Beck, 1998; Mouffe, 2000; Hardt and Negri, 2001).

But what, more broadly, of the future for parents and children? In particular, will a more comfortable alignment develop between ideas about parental employment and about what children need and 'are'? To achieve this will require a number of changes. These include a normative framework which makes children the responsibility of both fathers and mothers equally, premised on a new assumption that childcare can be undertaken by either parent with equal competence. It should require childcare for children which is widely available to a good standard. Children, whether or not their parents are employed, need to be seen as having an entitlement to such services because of their ability to enrich children's lives. Underpinning such a framework is the assumption that children are active participants in civic society and family life (Dahlberg *et al.*, 1999; Brannen *et al.*, 2000).

Second, what of the future role of the grandparent or pivot generation? As already noted, the current grandparent generation occupies a particularly important place in the intergenerational transfer of resources because of a historical coincidence of conditions creating a 'generation of abundance'. But these conditions may be ephemeral. Future grandparents may have less financial security and disposable material resources, not least because they will have had to pay more for their children's education and may have to concentrate on building up their own pensions. Demands for care from grandparents may continue high as more mothers work, and may also increase with respect to the very elderly (Thane, 2000). At the same time, future grandmothers, with higher levels of education, better jobs and more continuous employment records, may be less willing to leave employment in their 50s to take on increased care responsibilities. Indeed, with the growing pension *impasse*, more will have to work to an older age.

In short, therefore, the historical conditions which shape intergenerational relations are unstable and fluid. Grandparents are always likely to play a pivotal role in intergenerational relations and resource transfers, and there is no evidence of family members becoming more selfish and reluctant to pass on resources (see Gulbrandsen and Langsether, 1998). Still, the extent of that role may not remain constant, and could diminish from necessity rather than choice.

The third area of possible future change concerns the relationship and the division of responsibility between the state and the family. Changes in the state's role crucially affect demands on families. For example, state pensions have reduced the need for younger generations to financially support older generations. In other countries, for example Denmark and Sweden, universal provision of public childcare mean that grandparents and other relatives play little part today in the provision of regular childcare. A growing role for the state in such circumstances does not, though, necessarily lead to a substitution effect, in which the state does more and the family less. Rather, it may enhance the quality of family relationships by putting fewer demands upon them. Grandparents may take on occasional childcare, for example when children are ill. They are also people whom grandchildren said they liked to visit or stay with from choice.

But the state can also withdraw or target its efforts on fewer people, or refuse to accept new demands. Under advanced liberalism, the state expects its citizens to assume responsibility for a growing range of 'risks' faced by self and family, for example for funding longer and higher education for children, personal pensions and care in old age. The individual must also become an increasingly active subject, not only in managing all these risks, but by taking steps to become an employable worker, a good citizen and a better parent (see for example the *Every Child Matters*, Department for Education and Skills, 2003). In order to achieve these goals, more employment is being asked of people – longer hours and for a longer duration of the life course. There is an intrinsic tension here in the increase in responsibilities which is being required from individuals, families and family generations with respect to: employment, childcare and eldercare, and the provision of material resources.

How far such tensions can be soothed by talk of 'work–life balance' is debatable. For work–life balance assumes an opposition between work and the rest of life, has a one-dimensional view of time, focusing mainly upon time present, and assumes that time is a commodity which individually each of us can manage. As our book has demonstrated, lives are more complicated. Employment and the rest of life are not separate domains but are closely interwoven in people's lives over the life course and across generations. Time is more than a resource we measure in clock time; time is shaped in terms of life course commitments and commitments across family generations. While within a context of global neoliberal capitalism and increasingly powerful managerial technologies, the limits on the agency of the autonomous individual are certainly not reducing. With the increasing condensation of employment and child rearing in the middle years of a working life, as people enter the workforce later and have children at an older age, individual time-management skills (the cure-all of 'flexibility') may prove a weak solution without the accompanying growth of collective action that can shape more sympathetic structural conditions.

Bibliography

Abbott, A. (2001) *Time Matters on Theory and Method*. Chicago: Chicago University Press.

Aldridge, S. (2001) *Social Mobility: A Discussion Paper*. Cabinet Office: Performance and Innovation Unit.

Aldridge, S., Halpern, D. and Fitzpatrick, S. (2002) *Social Capital: A Discussion Paper*. April. London: Performance and Innovation Unit.

Allatt, P. (1993) Becoming privileged: the role of family processes. In I. Bates and G. Riseborough (eds) *Youth and Inequality*. Buckingham: Open University Press.

Aries, P. (1962) *Centuries of Childhood*. New York: Vintage.

Attias-Donfut, C. (1995) Le double circuit des transmissions. In C. Attias-Donfut (ed.) *Les Solidarites entre Generations: Viellesse, familles, Etat*. Paris: Nathan.

Attias-Donfut, C. and Arber, S. (2000) (eds) *The Myth of Generational Conflict: The Family and the State in Ageing Societies*. London: Routledge/ESA.

Attias-Donfut, C. and Segalen, M. (2002) The construction of grandparenthood. *Current Sociology*, 50(2): 281–294.

Attias-Donfut, C. and Wolff, F. (2000) The redistributive effects of generational transfers. In *The Myth of Generational Conflict: The Family and the State in Ageing Societies*. In S. Arber and C. Attias-Donfut (eds) ESA Studies in European Societies 2000. London: Routledge.

Bauman, Z. (1993) *Postmodern Ethics*. Oxford: Blackwell.

——. (1995) *Life in Fragments: Essays in Postmodern Morality*. Cambridge: Polity Press.

——. (1998) *Work, Consumerism and the New Poor*. Buckingham: Open University Press.

——. (2001) *The Individualised Society*. Cambridge: Polity Press.

Bawins-Legros, B. (2002) Introduction – filations and identity: towards a sociology of intergenerational relations. *Current Sociology*, 50(2): 175–183.

Beck, U. (1992) *Risk Society: Towards a New Modernity*. London: Sage.

——. (1994) The reinvention of politics: towards a theory of reflexive modernisation. In U. Beck, A. Giddens and S. Lash (eds) *Reflexive Modernization: Politics, Tradition and Aesthetics in the Modern Social Order*. Cambridge: Polity Press.

——. (1998) *Democracy without Enemies*. Cambridge: Polity Press.

Beck, U. and Beck-Gernsheim, E. (1995) *The Normal Chaos of Love*. Cambridge: Polity Press.

——. (1996) Individualization and precarious freedoms: perspectives and controversies of a subject-orientated sociology. In H. Paul, S. Lash and P. Morris (eds) *Derationalization: Critical Reflections on Authority and Identity*. Cambridge: Blackwell Publishers.

Belenky *et al.* (1986) *Women's Ways of Knowing*. New York: Basic Books.

Bengtson, V. L. (2001) Beyond the nuclear family: the increasing importance of multi-generational bonds. *Journal of Marriage and the Family*, 63: 1–16.

Bengtson, V. L., Biblarz, T. J. and Roberts, R. E. L. (2002) *How Families still Matter: A Longitudinal Study of Youth in Two Generations.* Cambridge: Cambridge University Press.

Benschop, Y. and Doorewaard, H. (1998) Covered by equality: the gender subtext of organizations. *Organization Studies,* 19(5): 787–805.

Bernard, J. (1972) *The Future of Marriage.* London: The Souvenir Press.

Bernstein, B. (1971) *Class, Codes and Control.* Vol. 1. London: Routledge and Kegan Paul.

——. (1996) *Pedagogy, Symbolic Control and Identity: Theory, Research, Critique.* London: Taylor and Francis.

——. (2000) *Pedagogy, Symbolic Control and Identity: Theory, Research, Critique.* Lanham, Maryland: Rowman and Littlefield.

Bertaux, D. (1981) From the life history approach to the transformation of sociological practice. In D. Bertaux (ed.) *Biography and Society: The Life History Approach in the Social Sciences.* London: Sage Publications.

Bertaux, D. and Bertaux-Wiame, J. (1997) Heritage and its lineage: a case history of transmission and social mobility over five generations. In B. Bertaux and P. Thompson (eds) *Pathways to Social Class: A Qualitative Approach to Social Mobility.* Oxford: Clarendon Press.

Berthoud, R. (2003) *Ethnic Minority Children and their Grandparents.* Conference paper on Kinship and Relationships beyond the Household. February. London: Royal Statistical Society.

Blanden, J., Goodman, A., Gregg, P. and Machin, S. (2002) *Changes in Intergenerational Mobility in Britain.* London: Centre for the Economics of Education, LSE.

Blumer, H. (1939) *Critiques of Research in the Social Sciences: I. An Appraisal of Thomas and Znaniecki's the Polish Peasant in Europe and America.* New York: Social Science Research Council.

Bourdieu, P. (1986) The forms of capital. In J. E. Richardson (ed.) *Handbook of Theory for Research in the Sociology of Education.* Westport, CT: Greenwood Press.

——. (1990) *The Logic of Practice.* Cambridge: Polity Press.

Bourdieu, P. and Wacquant, L. (1992) *An Invitation to Reflexive Sociology.* Cambridge: Polity Press.

Brannen, J. (ed.) (1992) *Mixing Methods: Qualitative and Quantitative Research.* Aldershot: Gower.

——. (2002) *Lives and Time: A Sociological Journey.* Professorial Lecture, Institute of Education, London, June.

——. (2003a) Towards a typology of intergenerational relations: continuities and change in families. *Sociological Research Online,* 8(2). http://www.socresonline.org.uk/8/2/brannen.html.

——. (2003b) The age of beanpole families. *Sociology Review,* 13(1): 6–9.

Brannen, J. and Moss, P. (1991) *Managing Mothers: Dual Earner Households after Maternity Leave.* London: Unwin Hyman.

——. (1998) The polarization and intensification of parental employment in Britain: consequences for children, families and the community. *Community, Work & Family,* 1(3): 229–247.

Brannen, J. and Nilsen, A. (2002) Young people's time perspectives: from youth to adulthood. *Sociology,* 36(3): 513–537.

——. (2003a) *Sociological Interpretations and Life Course Perspectives: A Case Study of Innovative Fatherhood*. Paper given at the British Sociological Association, York, April.

——. (2003b) Structure, agency and notions of choice. In A. Kollind and A. Peterson (eds) *Thoughts on Family, Gender, Generation and Class*. Goteborg: Department of Sociology, Goteborg University.

Brannen, J. and Pattman, R. (unpublished) *UK Case Study of Social Sciences: Gender, Parenthood and the Changing Workforce in Eight European Countries*. An EU Framework 5 Project.

Brannen, J., Heptinstall, E. and Bhopal, K. (2000) *Connecting Children: Care and Family Life in Later Childhood*. London: Falmer.

Brannen, J., Moss, P. and Mooney, A. (2003) Caregiving and independence in four generation families. In J. Brannen and P. Moss (eds) *Rethinking Children's Care*. Buckingham: Open University Press.

Brannen, J., Moss, P., Owen, C. and Wale, C. (1997) *Mothers, Fathers and Employment: Parents and the Labour Market in Britain 1984–1994*. London: Department for Education and Employment.

Brannen, J., Lewis, S., Nilsen, A. and Smithson, J. (2002) *Young Europeans: Work and Family Life; Futures in Transition*. London: Routledge.

Bryson, C., Budd, T., Lewis, J. and Elam, G. (1999) *Women's Attitudes to Combining Paid Work and Family Life*. London: Women's Unit, Cabinet Office.

Bynner, J., Ferri, E. and Wadsworth, M. (2003) Changing lives? In E. Ferri, J. Bynner and M. Wadworth (eds) *Changing Britain, Changing Lives: Three Generations at the Turn of the Century*. London: Institute of Education.

Cameron, C., Owen, C. and Moss, P. (2001) *Entry, Retention and Loss: A Study of Childcare Students and Workers*. (*DfEE Research Report*). London: Department for Education and Employment.

Chamberlayne, P. and King, A. (2000) *Cultures of Care: Biographies of Carers in the Two Germanies*. Bristol: The Policy Press.

——. (2001) *Cultures of Care: Biographies of Carers in Britain and the Two Germanies*. Bristol: Policy Press.

Cohen, B., Moss, P., Petrie, P. and Wallace, J. (2004) *A New Deal for Children? Reforming Education and Care in England, Scotland and Sweden*. Bristol: Policy Press.

Coleman, D. (2000) Population and family. In A. H. Halsey (ed.) with J. Webb *Twentieth Century British Social Trends*. Basingstoke: Macmillan Press.

Connell, R. W. (1990) The State, gender and sexual politics. *Theory and Society*, 19(5): 507–544.

Cornwell, J. (1984) *Hard-earned Lives: Accounts of Health and Illness from East London*. London: Unwin Hyman.

Corsaro, W. A. (1997) *The Sociology of Childhood*. London: Sage.

Crow, G. (2002) *Social Solidarities: Theories, Identities and Social Change*. Buckingham: Open University Press.

Dahlberg, G., Moss, P. and Pence, A. (1999) *Beyond Quality in Early Childhood Education and Care: Postmodern Perspectives*. London: Falmer Press.

Dally, A. (1982) *Inventing Motherhood: The Consequences of an Ideal*. London: Burnett.

De Regt, A. (1997) Inheritance and relationships between family members. In M. Gullestad and M. Segalen (eds) *Family and Kinship in Europe*. London and Washington: Pinter.

Delcroix, C. (2000) The transmission of life stories from ethnic minority fathers to their children. In C. Attias-Donfut and S. Arber (eds) *The Myth of Generational Conflict: The Family and the State in Ageing Societies*. London: Routledge/ESA.

Dench, G. and Ogg, J. (2002) *Grandparenting in Britain*. London: Institute of Community Studies.

Denzin, N. (1997) *Interpretive Ethnography: Ethnographic Practices for the 21st Century*. London: Sage Publications.

Department for Education and Employment (1998) *Meeting the Childcare Challenge*. DfEE: London.

Department for Education and Skills (2003) *Every Child Matters* (Cm. 5860). London: HMSO.

Department of Employment and Productivity (1971) *British Labour Statistics: Historical Abstract 1886–1969*. London: HMSO.

Deven, F. and Moss, P. (2002) Leave arrangements for parents: overview and future outlook. *Community, Work & Family*, 5(3): 237–255.

Donovan, P. T. and Rubenstein, T. (2002) *Geographic Mobility*. Performance and Innovation Unit. London: Cabinet Office.

Duncan, S. and Edwards, R. (1999) *Lone Mothers, Paid Work and Gendered Moral Rationalities*. Basingstoke: Macmillan.

Elder, G. H., Model, Jr, J. and Parke, R. E. (1993) *Children in Time and Place: Developmental and Historical Insights*. Cambridge UK: Cambridge University Press.

Elder, G. (1985) Perspectives on the life course. In G. Elder (ed.) *Life Course Dynamics: Trajectories and Transitions 1968–1980*. Ithaca and London: Cornell University Press.

Equal Opportunities Commission (2001) *Women and Men in Britain: At the Millenium*. Available at www.eoc.org.uk

Equal Opportunities Commission (2003) *Fathers: Balancing Work and Family*. Manchester: Equal Opportunities Commission.

Erben, M. (1998) *Biography and Education: A Reader*. London: Falmer Press.

Ermisch, J. and Francesoni, M. (2001) *The Effect of Parents' Employment on Children's Lives*. London: Family Policy Studies Centre with Joseph Rowntree Foundation.

Escobedo, A., Fernandez, E., Moreno, D. and Moss, P. (2002) *Care Work in Europe: Surveying Supply, Demand and Use of Care* (*Consolidated Report*). Available at www.ioe.ac.uk/tcru/carework.htm.

Esping-Andersen, G. (1990) *Three Worlds of Welfare Capitalism*. Cambridge: Polity Press.

——. (1999) *Social Foundations of Postindustrial Economies*. Oxford: Oxford University Press.

European Commission Childcare Network (1996) *Review of Services for Young Children in the European Union 1990–1995*. Brussels: European Commission DGV.

Fagnani, J. (2004) (with Geneviève Houriet-Ségard and Sébastien Bédouin) *Context Mapping, a Report for an EU framework 5 Project: Transitions: Gender, Parenthood and the Changing Workforce*.

Fielding, N. (2004) Getting the most from archived qualitative data: epistemological, practical and professional obstacles. *International Journal of Social Research Methodology: Theory and Practice*, 7(1): 97–105.

Fielding, T. (1997) Migration and poverty: a study of the relationship between migration and social mobility in England and Wales. *IDS Bulletin*, 28(2).

Finch, J. (1987) Family obligations and the life course. In A. Bryman, B. Bytheway, P. Allatt and T. Keil (eds) *Rethinking the Life Cycle*. Basingstoke: Macmillan Press.

——. (1989) *Family Obligations and Social Change*. Cambridge: Polity Press.

Finch, J. and Mason, J. (1993) *Negotiating Family Responsibilities*. London: Routledge.

Finch, J., Hayes, L., Mason, J., Masson, J. and Wallis, L. (1996) *Wills, Inheritance and Families*. Oxford: Clarendon press.

Firth, R., Hubert, J. and Forge, A. (1969) *Families and their Relatives*. London: Routledge and Kegan Paul.

Frønes, I. and Brusdal, R. (2000) *På sporet av den nye tid. Kulturelle varsler for en nær fremtid*. Bergen: Fagbokforlaget.

Furlong, A. and Cartmel, F. (1997). *Young People and Social Change: Individualisation and Risk in Late Modernity*. Buckingham: Open University Press.

Geertz, C. (1973) *The Interpretation of Culture*. London: Hutchinson.

Gershuny, J. (1993) Post-industrial career structures in Britain. In G. Esping-Andersen (ed.) *Changing Classes: Stratification and Mobility in Post-Industrial Societies*. London: Sage.

Giddens, A. (1991) *Modernity and Self-Identity: Self and Society in the Late Modern Age*. Cambridge: Polity Press.

——. (1994) Living in a post-traditional society. In U. Beck, A. Giddens and S. Lash (eds) *Reflexive Modernization: Politics, Tradition and Aesthetics in the Modern Social Order*. Cambridge: Polity Press.

——. (1998) *The Third Way: The Renewal of Social Democracy*. Cambridge: Polity Press.

Giele, J. Z. and Elder, G. H. (eds) (1998) *Methods of Life Course Research: Quantitative and Qualitative Approaches*. London: Sage.

Gillis, J. (2000) Marginalisation of fatherhood in western countries. *Childhood*, 17(2): 225–238.

Goldthorpe, J. and Mills, C. (2000) *Trends in Intergenerational Class Mobility in the Late Twentieth Century*. December (Working paper).

Goldthorpe, J., Lockwood, D., Bechhofer, F. and Platt, M. (1969) *The Affluent Worker in the Class Structure*. Cambridge: Cambridge University Press.

Gray, J. (2000) *False Dawn: The Delusions of Global Capitalim*. London: Granta Books.

Gregg, P. and Washbook, L. (2003) *The Effects of Early Maternal Employment on Child Development in the UK (CMPO Discussion Paper 70/03)*. Bristol: University of Bristol Centre for Market and Public Organisation.

Grieco, M. (1987) *Keeping it in the Family: Social Networks and Employment Chance*. London: Tavistock.

Grundy, E., Murphy, M. and Shelton, N. (1999) Looking beyond the household: intergenerational perspectives on living kin and contacts with kin in Great Britain. *Population Trends*, 97: 19–27. Autumn 1999.

Guillaume, J. (2002) Professional trajectory and family patrimony. *Current Sociology*, 50(2): 203–211.

Gulbrandsen, L. and Langsether, A. (1998) *The Elderly: Do They Continue to Save or Do They Spend Their Savings?* Seminar paper on Family Shifts and Intergenerational Dynamics, Liege.

——. (2001) *The Elderly: Asset Management, Generational Relations and Independence*. Paper presented to the European Sociological Association, Helsinki, August.

Gullestad, M. (1997) From 'being of use' to 'finding oneself': dilemmas of value transmission between the generations in Europe. In M. Gullestad and M. Segalen (eds) *Family and Kinship in Europe*. London: Pinter.

Hakim, C. (1995) Five feminist myths about women's employment. *British Journal of Sociology*, 46(3): 429–452.

Hallden, G. (1991) The child as project and the child as being: parents' ideas as frames of reference. *Children and Society*, 5(4): 334–346.

Halsey, A. H. (2000) Introduction: twentieth century Britain. In A. H. Halsey (ed.) *Twentieth Century British Social Trends*. Basingstoke: Macmillan.

Hammersley, M. (1989) *The Dilemma of Qualitative Method: Herbert Blumer and the Chicago Tradition*. London: Routledge.

——. (2004) Towards a usable post for qualitative research. *International Journal of Social Research Methodology: Theory and Practice*, 7(1): 19–29.

Hardt, M. and Negri, A. (2001) *Empire*. Cambridge, MA: Harvard University Press.

Hardyment, C. (1983) *Dream Babies*. London: Jonathan Cape.

Hareven, T. K. (1978) Family and historical time. In A. S. Rossi, J. Kagan and T. K. Hareven (eds) *The Family*. New York: Norton.

Harris, C. C. (1980) The changing relation between family and societal form in western society. In M. Anderson (ed.) *Sociology of the Family*. 2nd edition. Harmonsdworth: Penguin.

Harris, C. C. (1983) *The Family and Industrial Society*. London: George Allen and Unwin.

Heath, A. and Payne, C. (2000) Social mobility. In A. H. Halsey (ed.) with J. Webb *Twentieth Century British Social Trends*. London: Macmillan.

Hernes, H. M. (1987) *Welfare States and Woman Power*. Oslo: Norwegian University Press.

Hillcoate-Nalletamby, S. (2002) Solidarity across generations in New Zealand: factors influencing parental support for children in a three generational cohort, International Conference: Family Forms and the Young generation in Europe, Milan, September.

Hillcoate-Nalletamby, S. and Dharmalingam, A. (2001) *Solidarity across Generations in New Zealand: Factors Influencing Parental Support for Children within a Three-Generation Context*. Paper given at an international conference: Family forms and the young generation in Europe. University of Milano-Bicocca, Milan, September.

H M Treasury (2000a) *Helping People to Save: The Modernisation of Britain's Tax and Benefit System, Number 7*.

H M Treasury (2000b) *Saving and Assets for All: The Modernisation of Britain's Tax and Benefit System, Number 8*.

H M Treasury (2001) *Delivering Saving and Assets: The Modernisation of Britain's Tax and Benefit System, Number 9*.

HMSO (2002) *Social Trends*, No. 32. London: The Stationery Office.

Hobsbawm, E. (1994) *Age of Extremes: The Short Twentieth Century*. London: Michael Joseph.

Holtermann, S., Brannen, J., Moss, P. and Owen, C. (1999) *Lone Parents in the Labour Market*. Sheffield: Employment Services.

Inglis, F. (2000) *The Delicious History of the Holiday*. London: Routledge.

Irwin, S. (1995) *Rights of Passage: Social Change and the Transition from Youth to Adulthood*. London: UCL Press.

Jacobzone, S., Cambois, E., Chaplain, E. and Robine, J. M. (1998) *Long Term Care Services to Older People, a Perspective on Future Needs (OECD Working Paper 4.2)*. Paris: Organisation for Economic Cooperation and Development (OECD).

Jamieson, L. (1987) Theories of family development and the experience of being brought up. *Sociology*, 21(4): 591–607.

——. (2002) *Intimacy: Personal Relationships in Modern Society*. Cambridge: Polity Press.

Jensen, J. J. and Hansen, H. K. (2002) *Care Work in Europe, Surveying Supply, Demand and Use of Care*. Danish National Report at www.ioe.ac.uk/tcru/carework.htm.

Jones, G. and Wallace, C. (1992) *Youth, Family and Citizenship*. Buckingham: Open University Press.

Joshi, H. and Verropoulou, G. (2000) *Maternal Employment and Child Outcomes*. London: Smith Institute.

Kellerhals, J., Coenen-Huther, J. and et Modiak, M. (1988) *Figures de l'equité: Construction des norms de justice dans groupes*. Paris: PUF.

Kellerhals, J., Ferreira, C. and Perrenoud, D. (2002) Kinship cultures and identity transmissions. In B. Bawins-Legros (ed.) Filiation and identity: towards a sociology of intergenerational relations, *Current Sociology*, 50(2): Monograph 1, March.

Kempson, E. and Whyley, C. (2000) *Understanding Small Savers*. London: Pearl Insurance.

Kenway, J., Kelly, P. and Willis, S. (2001) In J. Demaine (ed.) *Sociology of Education Today*. Basingstoke: Palgrave.

Kessen, W. (1979) The American child and other cultural inventions. *American Psychologist*, 34: 815–820.

Kohli, M. (1999) Private and public transfers between generations: linking the family and the State. *European Societies*, 1(1): 81–104.

Krausz, E. and Miller, S. (1974) *Social Research Design*. London: Longman.

La Valle, I., Finch, S., Nove, A. and Lewin, C. (2000) *Parents' Demand for Childcare*. London: Department for Education and Employment.

Land, H. (1980) The family wage. *Feminist Review*, 6: 60.

Leira, A. (1992) *Welfare States and Working Mothers: The Scandinavian Experience*. Cambridge: Cambridge University Press.

Lenz Taguchi, H. and Munkammer, I. (2003) *Consolidating Governmental Early Childhood Education and Care Services under the Ministry of Education and Care: A Swedish Case Study (UNESCO Early Childhood and Family Policy Series No. 6)*, available at www.unesco.org.

Lewis, J. (1992) Gender and the development of welfare regimes. *Journal of European Social Policy*, 2(3): 159–173.

Lileström, R. (1981) The public child, the commercial child and our child. In F. S. Kessel and A. W. Siegel (eds) *The Child and Other Cultural Inventions*. New York: Praeger.

Lindsay, C. (2003) A century of labour market change: 1900 to 2000. *Labour Market Trends*. March. pp. 133–144.

Lowenthal, M. F., Thurnher, M. and Chiriboga, D. (1977) *Four Stages of Life*. San Francisco: Jossey Bass Publishers.

Luscher, K. (2000) Ambivalence: a key concept for the study of intergenerational relations. In S. Trnka (ed.) *Family Issues between Gender and Generations: Seminar Report*. Vienna: European Observatory on Family Matters.

Luscher, K. and Pillemer, K. (1998) Intergenerational ambivalence: a new approach to the study of parent–child relations in later life. *Journal of Marriage and the Family*, 60: 413–425.

Mannheim, K. (1952) *Essays on the Sociology of Knowledge*. London: Routledge and Kegan Paul.

Martin, J. and Roberts, C. (1984) *Women and Employment: A Lifetime Perspective*. London: Her Majesty's Stationery Office.

Mason, J. (1999) Living away from relatives: kinship and geographical reasoning. In S. McRae (ed.) *Changing Britain: Families and Households in the 1990s*. Oxford: Oxford University Press.

Mayall, B. (1994) *Children's Childhoods: Observed and Experienced*. London: Falmer Press.

McKee, L. (1987) Households during unemployment: the resourcefulness of the unemployed. In J. Brannen and G. Wilson (eds) *Give and Take in Families: Studies in Resource and Distribution*. London: Unwin-Hyman.

McKee, M. and O'Brien, L. (1982) *The Father Figure*. London: Tavistock.

McRae, S. (1999) Introduction. In S. McRae (ed.) *Changing Britain: Families and Households in the 1990s*. Oxford: Oxford University Press.

Miller, R. L. (2000) *Researching Life Stories and Family Histories*. London: Sage.

Mills, C. W. (1967) *Power, Politics and People: The Collected Essays of C. Wright Mills*. Oxford: Oxford University Press.

——. (1980) *The Sociological Imagination*. London: Penguin Books.

Mitterauer, M. (1992) *A History of Youth*. Oxford: Blackwell.

Mooney, A. and Munton, T. (1997) *Research and Policy in Early Childhood Services: Time for a New Agenda*. London: Institute of Education, University of London.

Mooney, A. and Statham, J. with Simon, A. (2002) *The Pivot Generation: Informal Care and Work over Fifty*. Bristol: The Policy Press.

Moore, R. (1974) *Pitman, Preachers and Politics*. Cambridge: Cambridge University Press.

Morgan, D. H. J. (1975) *Social Theory and the Family*. London: Routledge and Kegan Paul.

——. (1999) Risk and family practices: accounting for change and fluidity in family life. In E. B. Silva and C. Smart (eds) *The New Family*. London: Sage Publications.

Moss, P. (2003) Getting beyond childcare: reflections on recent policy and future possibilities. In J. Brannen and P. Moss (eds) *Rethinking Children's Care*. Buckingham: Open University Press.

Moss, P. and Cameron, C. (2002) Care Work and the Care Workforce: Report on Stage One and State of the Art Review, available from the Care Work in Europe website at www.ioe.ac.uk/tcru/carework.htm.

Mouffe, C. (2000) *The Democratic Paradox*. London: Verso.

Nielsen, H. (2003) Historical, cultural and emotional meanings: interviews with girls in three generations. *NORA Nordic Journal of Women's Studies*, 11(2): 14–26.

Nielsen, H. and Rudberg, M. (2000) Gender, love and education: The way out and up. *The European Journal of Women's Studies*, 7: 423–453.

Nilsen, A. (1996) Stories of life – Stories of living. Women's narratives and feminist biography. In *NORA Nordic Journal of Women's Studies*, 4(1): 16–30.

Nilsen, A. (2001) *On Life Course Transitions: Pathways into Adulthood*. Paper presented at the *ESA-conference*, Helsinki, August 2001.

Nilsen, A. and Brannen, J. (2002) Theorising the individual – structure dynamic. In J. Brannen, A. Nilsen, S. Lewis and J. Smithson (eds) *Young Europeans, Work and Family Life: Futures in Transition*. London: Routledge.

Nilsen, A., Brannen, J. and dos Dores, M. (2002) 'Most choices involve money': different pathways to adulthood. In J. Brannen, A. Nilsen, S. Lewis and J. Smithson (eds) *Young Europeans, Work and Family Life: Futures in Transition*. London: Routledge.

Oakley, A. (1986) Feminism, motherhood and medicine: who cares? In J. Mitchell and A. Oakley (eds) *What is Feminism?* Oxford: Blackwell.

O'Brien, M. and Shemilt, I. (2003) *Working Fathers: Earning and Caring*. Equal Opportunities Commission.

OECD (Organisation for Economic Cooperation and Development) (2001) *Starting Strong: Early Childhood Education and Care*. Paris: Organisation for Economic Cooperation and Development.

Office of National Statistics (2001) *Social Trends 31*. London: Stationery Office.

Office of National Statistics (2003) *Social Trends*, 2003 edition. London: Stationery Office.

Parsons, T. (1943) The kinship system of the contemporary United States. Reprinted in Parsons (1964) *Essays in Sociological Theory*. Revised edition. New York: Free Press.

Payne, G. and Roberts, J. (2002) Opening and closing the gates: recent developments in male social mobility in London. *Sociological Research Online*, 6: 4. http:www.socresonline.org.uk/6/4payne.html.

Pitrou, A. (1987) Interaction entre sphere du travail et speere de la vie familiale. *Sociologie et Societe*, XIX(2): 103–113.

Plummer, K. (2001) *Documents of Life 2: An Invitation to a Critical Humanism*. London: Sage.

Qureshi, H. (1996) Obligations and support within families. In A. Walker (ed.) *The New Generational Contract? Intergenerational Relations, Old Age and Welfare*. London: UCL Press.

Renaut, S. (2001) *Evaluating Family Support: An Analysis of Three Generations in France*. London: Institute of Family Studies.

Ricoeur, P. (1980) Narrative time. *Critical Enquiry*, 7(1): 160–180.

——. (1992) *Oneself as Another*. Chicago: Chicago University Press.

Riley, M. W. (ed.) (1988) *Social Structures and Human Lives*. Newbury Park: Sage Publications.

Roberts, E. (1986) Women's strategies, 1890–1940. In J. Lewis (ed.) *Labour and Love: Women's Experience of Home and Family 1850–1940*. Oxford: Basil Blackwell. pp. 223–248.

Roberts, R. E. L., Richards, L. N. and Bengtson, V. L. (1991) Intergenerational solidarity in families: untangling the ties that bind. In S. F. Pfeifer and M. B. Sussman (eds) *Marriage and Family Reviews*, 16(21). Families: intergenerational and generational connections, Part One: 11–46. Binghampton, NY: Haworth Press.

Rogers, R. S. (1997) The making and moulding of modern youth: a short history. *Youth in Society: Contemporary Theory, Policy and Practice*. London: Sage.

Rose, N. (1990) *Governing the Soul: The Shaping of the Private Self*. London: Routledge.

——. (1999) *Powers of Freedom: Reframing Political Thought*. Oxford: Oxford University Press.

Rosser, C. and Harris, C. (1965) *The Family and Social Change: A Study of Family and Kinship in a South Wales Town* (Abridged edition). London: Routledge and Kegan Paul.

Rossi, A. and Rossi, P. (1992) *Of Human Bonding: Parent–child Relations across the Life Course*. NY: Aldine Gruyter.

Samuel, R. and Thompson, P. (1990) *The Myths We Live by*. London: Routledge.

Scott, J. (1999) Family change: revolution or backlash in attitudes? In S. McRae (ed.) *Changing Britain: Families and Households in the 1990s*. Oxford: Oxford University Press.

Sennett, R. (1998) *The Corrosion of Character: The Personal Consequences of Work in the New Capitalism*. London: Norton.

Sevenhuijsen, S. (1999a) *Caring in the Third Way*. Leeds: Centre for Research on Family, Kinship and Childhood.

——. (1999b) *Citizenship and the Ethics of Care: Feminist Considerations on Justice*. London: Routledge.

Singer, E. (1993) Shared care for children. *Theory and Psychology*, 3(4): 429–449.

Skrede, K. and Tornes, K. (eds) (1983) *Studier i kvinners livsløp*. (*Studies in Women's Life Courses*). Oslo: Universitetsforlaget.

Social and Community Planning Research (1992) *British Social Attitudes Sourcebook: The First 6 Surveys*. Aldershot: Gower.

Social Community Planning Research (1995) *British Social Attitudes: The 12th Report*. Aldershot: Gower.

Thane, P. (2000) *Old Age in English History: Past Experiences, Present Issues*. Oxford: Oxford University Press.

Thomas, W. I. and Znaniecki, E. (1996) *The Polish Peasant in Europe and America*. In Eli Zaretsky (ed.). University of Illinois.

Thompson, P. (1977) *The Edwardians*. Hertford: Paladin.

——. (1997) Family myth, models and denials in shaping individual biographies. In D. Bertaux and P. Thompson (eds) *Pathways to Social Class: A Qualitative Approach to Social Mobility*. Oxford: Clarendon Press.

——. (2004) Researching family and social mobility with two eyes: some experiences of interaction between qualitative and quantitative data. *International Journal of Social Methodology: Theory and Practice*, 7(3): 237–259.

Trifiletti, R., Pratesie, A. and Simoni, S. (2003) *Care Arrangements in Double Front Carer Families*. Comparative Report. SOCCARE New Kinds of Families. New Kinds of Social Care: http://www.uta.fi/laitokset/sospol/soccare.

Tronto, J. (1993) *Moral Boundaries: A Political Argument for the Ethics of Care*. London: Routledge.

——. (2000) *Better Care: From the Managed Household to a Caring Society*. Paper delivered at the International conference. 'Work and family: Expanding the horizons', San Francisco.

Twomey, B. (2001) Women in the labour market: results from the Spring 2000 LFS. *Labour Market Trends*. February, pp. 93–106.

Urwin, C. (1985) Constructing motherhood: the persuasion of normal development. In C. Steedman, C. Urwin and V. Walkerdine (eds) *Language, Gender and Childhood*. London: Routledge and Kegan Paul.

Wadsworth, M. E. J. (1991) *The Imprint of Time*. Oxford: Oxford University Press.

Wadsworth, M., Ferri, E. and Bynner, J. (2003) Changing Britain. In E. Ferri, J. Bynner and M. Wadsworth (eds) *Changing Britain, Changing Lives: Three Generations at the Turn of the Century*. London: Institute of Education.

Wærness, K. (2000) *Hvem er hjemme? Essays om hverdagslivets sosiologi. (Anybody home? Essays in the sociology of everyday life)*. Bergen: Fagbokforlaget.

Warin, J., Solomon, Y., Lewis, C. and Langford, W. (1999) *Fathers, Work and Family Life*. London: Family Policy Studies Centre.

Wellman, B. and Berkowitz, S. (1988) Communities. In B. Wellman and S. Berkowitz (eds) *Social Structures: A Network Analysis*. Cambridge: Cambridge University Press.

Wengraf, T. (2001) *Qualitative Research Interviewing: Biographic Narrative and Semi-Structured Methods*. London: Sage.

Wengraf, T. (2004) Presentation at a Roundtable on Biographical Research. London: Institute of Education, 18 February.

What good are dads? In *Father Facts*, 1(1). Online, http//www.fathersdirect.com/files/pdf/ff1wgad.pdf.

Wilson, P. and Pahl, R. (1988) The changing sociological construct of the family. *Sociological Review*, 36(2): 232–272.

Woodland, S., Miller, M. and Tipping, S. (2002) *Repeat Study of Parents' Demand for Childcare (Research Report No. 348)*. London: HMSO.

Index